WINCHESTER VIRGINIA

ABSTRACTS OF WILLS

1794-1894

TRANSCRIBED BY

Dola S. Tylor

HERITAGE BOOKS
2020

HERITAGE BOOKS

AN IMPRINT OF HERITAGE BOOKS, INC.

Books, CDs, and more—Worldwide

For our listing of thousands of titles see our website
at
www.HeritageBooks.com

Published 2020 by
HERITAGE BOOKS, INC.
Publishing Division
5810 Ruatan Street
Berwyn Heights, Md. 20740

International Standard Book Number
Paperbound: 978-1-55613-415-9

C O N T E N T

INTRODUCTION

Winchester, Virginia, is unique in that it is an independent city and its records are separate and distinct from the county in which it lies. Many genealogical researchers come to the Frederick County Court House but are unaware of the wealth of information that is in City Hall. I have transcribed the oldest of births, deaths, marriages and wills to bring attention to this repository of vital statistics and to assist researchers in using the microfilm tapes of these records and/or in getting copies of items of their interest. Although many records were lost during the Civil War when, according to history, Winchester changed hands 72 times, wills begin in 1794, births and marriages in 1853, and deaths in 1871.

In this book are Abstracts of Wills that were recorded in City Hall, 1794-1894, as read from Virginia State Library Microfilm Tapes Nos. 47 and 48 of the original books of entry which now are stored in the State Capitol at Richmond. There are certifications by the Microfilm Camera Operators of missing pages 1 through 8 and 106 through 111 of Will Book No. 1. There are some instances of confusion in page numbering. Items chosen from Inventories and Estate Settlements are meant to give clues to occupation and financial/community status. These readings are from tapes of old, handwritten entries and are given in the best possible interpretation of the clerks' writing. Microfilm tapes of Winchester City Clerks Records are available to researchers in the Archives of The Handley Library, Braddock & Piccadilly Streets, Winchester, Virginia.

Dola S. Tylor
Transcriber

The beginning pages of this microfilm tape are very dark and only parts are legible. Following the certification that pages 1-8 are missing, are two pages with no visible page numbers. They seem to be the Bond for James WALL, executor for John WYNN, and the beginning of the will of Mary WOODS.

Pages 9?-15 Continues the will of Mary WOODS, signed 11 Feby 1794. Gives to Adam MINNEY? "my two-plate iron stove"; to James, Catherine and Sally BAILEY; to Peggy BAILEY, wife of Abraham: "one cotton bed gown and one cotton petticoat to her and her heirs forever"; to Elizabeth CASTLEMAN, youngest daughter of my brother David; to Elizabeth BAILEY, wife of John. Jno. BAILEY, executor. Wit: Mahlon SMITH, Conrad KREMER. Proved 6 Octr 1794. Bond acknowledged by James WALLS, George REED, Samuel COLVERT. Among estate items: Bond on John CONRAD, pewter mugs, plates, Saltsellers, pickel pot, 2 pots on stove, 2 candlesticks, one Bonnet, several petticots, 4 sheats. Appraisal recorded 1 Decr 1794; appraisers' names not found.

Pages 15-17: Appraisal of estate of George WILLIS, dec'd. Some items: 1 Hatters tearen, 1 Hatters iron, 1 hardning skin, 9 oz. Racoon fur, 13 oz. muskrat, 79 rabit skins. Appraisal to court, 6 April 1795. Appraisers' names not found.

Pages 17-20: Bond for Dorothy GLAZIER, Admr. of will of Christian GLAZIER, 6 April 1795. Some estate items: "The twining tools in full four Dutch frame saws, 6 plains, 6 augers, 7 Zenterbitts". Signed: Jacob SPERY, Jacob BOUCHER, Adam YOUNG. To court 31 Augt 1795.

Pages 20-21: Bond for the administration of Estate of Albert EAGER, dec'd. Elizabeth EAGER, Martin EREHART, George LYNN, Charles AULICK. To Hustings Court, 1 Febr 1796.

Pages 21-23: Bond for Conrad KREMER and Adam KIGER to administer will and make inventory & Appraisal of estate of Catharine HELPHENSTINE, dec'd. 6 June 1796.

Pages 23-24: Bond to administer estate of John DUFFIELD, dec'd. Mary DUFFIELD, Admr., James HOLLIDAY and Robert WELLS. 5 Sept 1796.

Pages 24-25: Bond to administer estate of Thos. JEFF, dec'd. James JEFFS, Admr., Peter LAUCK. 31 March 1797.

Pages 26-28: Appraisal by Jesse BUTTON, Daniel MILLER, John BOWMAN of estate of Albert EAGER, dec'd. Among items: 1 pair silver Shoe Buckles, 6 pairs Knee Buckles. Settlement, 2 June 1797.

Pages 29-31: Thomas McBRATNEY will: "All my property as followeth: All my property in Ireland to my father, Michael McBRATNEY." Mother, Ann. Brothers: William and Archebal. Friends: Joseph GAMBLE, and John KINGAN, executors, 15 ? 1800. Wit: Thos. BROOKS, Richd. NIORDAN, M. D. MAGSON. Proved 30 May 1800.

Page 32: Appraisal of estate of Thomas RAVENHILL, including slaves, 2 vols. of Moores Travels, 11 vols. of Smolletts England, 1 House Bible. Appraisal to Court, 3 April 1801. Signed: W. DAVISON, Nathan ANDERSON, Angus McDONALE, Apprs.

Pages 33-34: Bond for administration of estate of John HAYMAKER, dec'd. "That we, Mary HAYMAKER, Admr., and Daniel CLARKE, are held and firmly bound unto Lewis WOLFE, Joseph GAMBLE, Nathan ANDERSON, Charles BRENT." 20? Sept 1804.

Pages 34-37: Last will and testament of Dorothy GLAZIER. 23 Decr 1803. All property left after burial expenses to "my friend, Rebecca HAVILAND, wife of Samuel HAVILAND". Wit: Lemuel BENT, Benjamin ASHBY, Charles HUTCHERSON. Proved 30 Decr 1803. Signed: Edwd SLATER, Daniel CLARKE, Peter ELLIOTT.

Pages 37-47: Will of Lewis HOFF. "Principally and first of all I give and recommend my soul unto the hand of Almighty God that gave it. Nothing doubting but at the general resurrection I shall receive the same again." Wife, Catharine. Children: John, Lewis, Philip, Catharine, Elizabeth and Mary. Daughter Catharine's share "to remain in the executor's hands as long as her present husband lives". Executors: two sons, Lewis and John, and Henry Wm. BAKER. 16 Feby 1803. Wit: Jacob KIGER, Isaac BAKER, Jacob MYERS. Proved, 2 Septr 1803. Among items in estate appraisal: Eight-day clock and case, writing desk and bookcases, cloaths press, 2 big Wheels. Signed: George McCORD, Cornelius BALDWIN, John N. HEISKELL. 9 Mar 1805.

Pages 47-50: Will of Adam YOUNG. To wife Catharine all property as long as she stays single. If she marries, all divided to children. Charles AULICK and John MAY, executors. 20 March 1805. Wit: Edwd SLATER, John LYNN, George F. HAUGHMAN. Proved 29 March 1805.

Pages 50-54: Will of John KENESTER. All items pertaining to the distillery be sold for benefit of estate. All for use of wife and younger children "who I wish to live with her until they arrive of lawfull age or mary". Mentions "still house". Sons, John and George. Appoints Dr. Cornelius BALDWIN and George McCORD, executors. 24 Jany 1805.

Page 54: Inventory of estate of John JENKINS, dec'd. In part: lease for a lott and house at Yeast? Street, appraised at no more than the rent; 1 buroe, 2 tables, 1 box Quilts, 1 stack hay.

Pages 55 and 56 are missing.

Pages 57-60: Completes Inventory of Estate of John KENESTER (sometimes KENEASTER) and gives Estate Sales Account. Signed "By the Court", Thomas McKEWAN, CWCC. 3 Jany 1806. Unexplained name at bottom of page: Mrs. Sally ROBINSON, Piccadilly Street, Winchester, Va.

Pages 61-70: Will and Codicil of Henry BAKER. (Long Will, dark film) Has land in Winchester, Frederick County and Kentucky. Wife and seven children. Sons: Henry William, Isaac, Joseph, John, Abraham, Jacob; daughter: Elizabeth or Betty. To son, Abraham, a part of brick house on Water & Cameron Streets, property adjoining Mr. Phil BUSH. To son, Joseph, another part of brick house; to son, Jacob, remainder of brick house. To daughter, Betty, 200 pounds. Sons to get land "adjoining the great road leading from Winchester"; also plantation near Winchester. Jacob, Henry, John, Isaac & Abraham to give mother 240 pounds annually. 9 June 1806. Codicil to dispose of slaves. Wit: E. H.? HOLMES, Wm. HOLMES. Proved 29 May 1807.

Pages 70-78: Will of Samuel CALVERT. To son Samuel, of Lexington, Ky. Daughters: Mary and Milly CALVERT and Ann NORRIS. To wife Milly: "looms and implements in the shop and every other article of property now on said lot, including my riding chair and the harness thereto." Mentions apprentices, George SOMERVILLE and Redman NOAKS. Executors, Beaty CARSON and Obed WAITE. Wit: Adam KURTZ, James WALLS, John CROCKWELL, George M. FRYE. 1 May 1807. Proved 29 May 1807.

Pages 78-79: Appraisement of Estate of Adam YOUNG, dec'd, 5 April 1805. Among items: feather bed, chaff bed, 1 blue-edged bowl, 6 plates, 1 foot carpeting. John HEISKELL, John LEWIS, Edward SLATER. Completed 4 Sep 1807.

Pages-79-83: Henry BAKER Appraisement by Nathan ANDERSON, Daniel OVERAKER, John LINN. 17 June 1807. Among items: 1 Spinnett, $30, 1 Eight Day Clock, $60. Also 17 Windsor Chairs, iron Mortar & Pestal, 1 Parcle German Books, 1 Cloaths Press, 1 Mans Saddle. Appr. completed 29 Jany 1808.

Pages 83-85: Appraisement of Estate of Rachel WALKER, dec'd. Most expensive item was Clock & Case, appraised at $65 and purchased, at sale, for $65, by Frances KINGAN. Other items: Wooling bed Quilt, small blanket, half round Pine Table, Cow. Total appraisal: $171.95. Robert GRAY, H. BEATTY, Goldsmith CHANDLEE. Estate Sale, Octr 7, 1807. Administrators: Josh GAMBLE, Gilbert MEEM.

Pages 85-90: Will of Adam HAYMAKER. To son Michael "my mantion house". Mentions sons, Adam, Philip and Peter, and daughters, Elizabeth MARTIN, Mary HINES?, Catherine ANDERSON, and daughter-in-law, Christiana. Much about grandson, Adam HAYMAKER, "from his father, John HAYMAKER's estate". When grandson arrives at the age of twenty-one, he is to keep $20 for himself and pay one-seventh to each of his brothers and sisters (to wit: Elizabeth, John, Catherine, Philip and Margaret). Son, Michael, executor. 15 June 1806. Wit: John COPENHAVER, D. W. THOMAS, Michael COPENHAVER. Will proved by Daniel W. THOMAS and Michael COPENHAVER. HAYMAKER's bond, _____ day of April AD1808.

Pages 90-96: Will of James Gameel DOWDALL. To wife, Margaret, the dwelling house in Winchester "where I now live". Has lot purchased of Nathan CARTMELL & wife. To daughters, Jane & Rebecca, the tract of land or estate called Bellville, lying in Frederick County and purchased of R. & A. TURNBULL. To son, John, one hundred pounds. Tract called Cherrymeade to son Maxwell if "his conduct show a determination to return to the path of propriety and virtue". To Thomas KREMER in trust for daughters, Anne NOURSE, Jane DOWDALL, and Margaret RANSDALE, but never for benefit of husbands, Gabriel NOURSE and Stephen RANSDALE. Wife, Margaret, and friend, Arch'd. MAGILL, Execs. 3 Jany 1807. Wit: Wm. HILL, John IRWIN, Anthony KURTZ. Proved 4 Apr 1808.

Pages 97-99: Will of Tevault GILLNER. To Adam LITTLE, house and lot adjoining Daniel CLARK with all the locust posts on hand for making a fence. To James COCHRAN, bed and bedding and all other things including "one crock with cheese, one gammon?, and all cabages." To Edward SLATER, gray mare. 7 March 1808. Wit: Peter HAM, Samuel SLATER, Franowz? MURTIN. Proved 3 June 1808.

Pages 100-101: Appraisal of Estate of Adam HAYMAKER, dec'd. Includes walnut chest, sundry Bench Tools, Scales & Weights, Iron Vise, Chemical Still. 18 June 1808. J. N. DUNGING?, Michael COPENHAVER, John KIGER.

Pages 102-104: Distribution from Estate of John KEANESTER, dec'd. George McCORD, Executor. 1 July 1808. Cash payments, Nov 1805 to Jan 1808, to Hannah ANDERSON. Other expenses. Cash receipts from book accounts, notes, grain, rents.

Pages 104-105: Inventory and Appraisal of Estate of Samuel CALVERT, dec'd. Appraisers: James WALLS, Adam KURTZ, George M. FRYE. To appraise "in current money", slaves and personal estate. June 10, 1807. Much furniture, many blankets and linens, dishes and utensils, carpeting. (Appraisal not completed on page 105.)

Pages 106-111: Missing.

Pages 112-114: Inventory & Appraisal of Richard BOWEN, dec'd. 2 Oct 1808. Desk and Bookcase, much bedding and bedsteads, typer and all apparatus thereto, one ten-plate stove in the office. In Sales Account: 1 Table to David CASTLEMAN, 1 Gun to Lemuel BENT; rest of estate, including printing press, to John DARING. Appraisers: Lewis HOFF, Nathan ANDERSON, John BELL. Returned to court, 29 Septr 1809.

Pages 114-121: (Page numbering is not always clear. Page after 116 is 287? Pages 119 and 120 are missing.) Will of John BRADY who is "about to take a long and dangerous journey". To Peggy ALEXANDER, "child of about 5 years (daughter of my wife's sister) which now lives in my family". Wife, Elizabeth, and William CERFOOT and Joseph GAMBLE to execute will. "14 April one thousand eight hundred and hereunto have subscribed my name." Witnesses to will: Thos. PIERCE, Robert GRAY. At probate, Thos. PIERCE is living in Baltimore. Mentioned is 2nd day of Decr 1809 and in the 34th year of the Commonwealth, Edward JOHNSON, Mayor of Baltimore. Will recorded in court, 2 Feby 1810. Appraisal of Estate of John BRADY, 12 Dec 1809, by Elijah LITTLER, James RIELY, James D. VANCE. Among items: Waggon, four horses & Gears, 8 hogs, 3 fire grates, 2 milk cows. Recorded 2 Feby 1810.

Page 121: Thomas McKEWAN (McKEWING) appraisal. 31 July 1811, by Daniel OVERAKER, John SCHULTZ. Among items in small estate: 1 Negro & child, 1 cow, 1 Burow, Bed and Bedstead, 1 pair Gold Wts & Beam.

Pages 122-128: Will of Christian STREIT. To wife, Susanna, and at her death to be equally divided "among her children". To son, Jacob. "My wife" to execute will. 4 April 1808. Wit: Goldsmith CHANDLEE, Rev. Wm. HILL, Benezer POWELL. Proved 3rd day of April 1812. Bond made for Susanna STREIT, Edward SMITH, William HILL. Large inventory of personal estate and slaves made by Peter LAUCK, Lewis HOFF, Jn. BAKER. 1 May 1812.

Pages 128-139: Will of Charles AULICK. 14 March 1812. Among things to wife, Ann Mary: "my mansion house, my time piece, my tortoise shell snuff box, a tea chest made for her by son, Charles, my prayer ? brought from Germany". To son, Charles Andrew, Clothes and "my large cane marked C.A. and my white fur hat". To son, John Henry, "my cane with an an ivory head, my Dictionary and my Geography". To son, Frederic Albert, "my black fur hat, my blue coat and my cane with a silver head". To sons, George and William, the tools they now use as barbers. Gives to daughters, Catherine Elizabeth YOUNG, Susanna Christianna AULICK, Henryetta AULICK, Eliza Margaret AULICK. Requests sons, John, George and William to "follow the business they are now engaged in". Executors to be Archibald MAGILL, Lemual BENT, Cornelius GIBBONS. Witnesses: D. W. THOMAS, Peter HAM. Proved 1 May 1812. Archibald MAGILL and Samuel BENT, the other named executors, "refused the burthen" of executors. Ann Maria, the widow, declared she would not accept the provisions made for her in said will. Will proved by William THOMAS, the other witness. Appraisal of Estate made 5 May 1812, by Jo. BAKER, John LINN, Nathan ANDERSON.

Pages 139-140: Will of Elias RITTER, of Westmoreland County, Pennsylvania, "in low state of health but perfectly in my senses". Wife, Margaret, and nine children: Lestwick, Jacob, Elias, Margaret, Catherine, Susanna, John, Rosena and Mary. Date: _____ 1812. Wit: Nat. ANDERSON, Alex HOLLIDAY, James ANDERSON, Edward MARSH, John LINN. Proved 3 July 1812.

Pages 140-142: Will of John NULTON, 3 July 1812. To wife, Christianna, "my mantion house and Lott, for and during her widowhood". To son, John, "after he arrives to the age of twenty-one years". Daughter, Susanna. Sole executor: William HELVESTON. Wit: Conrad CONRAD?. Proved 31 July 1812.

Pages 142-144: Will of John WINDLE, "very sick and low in body". To wife, Eve, "house and lot in which I now live with all kitchen & household furniture and one spotted cow". "My dear children", unnamed. Brother, Samuel WINDLE and friend, Peter COONTZ to be executors. Wit: James SINGLETON, John MYERS, John DICK. Proved, 2 July 1813.

Pages 145-147: Estate of Thomas McKEWAN, Dr. George REED, Admr. Begins Decr 2, 1811 with cash from Mr. WHETZELL, Thos. TIDBALL; also from Mr. DAVISON for service at Poor House. Expenses begin 3 June 1811 with paying for digging grave, for flour, hay, doctor bills, etc. Total Ballance due the estate of Michael McKEWIN, $126.95. "The amount of the appraisal is not charged because the articles are all left in the hands of the widow." Recorded in court, 3 Septr 1813.

Pages 147-153: There is no name at the beginning of this will but it is signed by John LINN. Mentions when daughters, Elizabeth and Julian, "arrive to age eighteen". To these two daughters, stock in the Farmers Bank of Virginia. To wife, Catharine, "house and lott where Conrad CREAMER now lives". To Julian "house and lott wherein John COOK and his wife, Julian, lives". 6 May 1813. Wit: Edward MARSH, James & Nathan ANDERSON. Proved 3 Septr 1813. Appraisal and Inventory included Negro Prince, Cow, horse, waggon, farming tools, household items. Octr 23, 1813. Jo-- BAKER, Conrad K--?, Nathan ANDERSON.

Pages 153-157: Will of Jacob MICHAEL. Partly in German script. 18 May 1786. "I have concluded to undertake a jurney which might cause my death." "If I should die in the New Country." "Unto George LINN of this place and Daniel LOHR, of Fredericktown, all my property which I have behind in their hands." To Philip MICHAEL, my brother's son, born 6 April 1773. If he should die then all to brother's children. "When they should hear of my death so every thing shall lye quiet for two years." Winchester, "a paper purporting to be the last will and testament of Jacob MICHAEL, dec'd, in the German Language." Proved 14 March 1814. Wit: Lewis HOFF, Casper RINKER, Charles AULICK, Adrian ALBERT, Nicholas MESMER.

Pages 157-158: Appraisal of Personal Estate of Enoch MORRIS, dec'd. Among items in small appraisal: one Bed & Furnature, sugar Box, one large white dish, one Duch oven, one old book, $1 cash. Total estate appraisal: $24.26. Feby 14, 1814. Benj. LANGLEY, James HARRY, Thomas HUNSCIKER. Recorded in court, 1 Apr 1814.

Pages 158-161: Will of David OSBORN(E), "being of sound and disposing mind, memory and understanding". 22 Jany 1814. All of estate to wife, Margaret, and she to be sole executor. Wit: Daniel BIXLEY, Conrad CREBES, James HARRIS. Proved 29 April 1814. Mentions inventory presented by widow but not recorded.

Pages 162-164: Will of Isaac BURK(E), 1 Feby 1814. Wife, Sarah, to receive all real & personal estate to her and her heirs forever. Sarah to be sole executrix. Wit: Jacob KIGER, Stewart GRANT, Presley HANSBOROUGH. Bond for Sarah BURK, Executrix, and Nathan ANDERSON to administer will. Proved, 3 June 1814.

Pages 165-167: Will of Adam KURTZ, 1st May 1814. To "dearly beloved and faithful wife, Mary, all my estate". She to make use of or dispose of any part and not to have to account to any person. Directs no appraisement or sale of personal property. Single daughters to live with wife. Wit: James WALLS, Jesse BROWN, Leml. BENT. Proved 29 July 1814.

Pages 168-175 are missing.

Page 176: Begins "given under our hands & seals this 25th day of April 1814." George SIPS, Peter COONTZ, Conrad CREBS. At a Court of Hustings, 2 Decr 1814, the Appraisal of the Estate of Speak FLANAGAN, dec'd, was recorded.

Pages 176-178: Will of Mary LIPSCOMB. All worldly estate to son, Thomas, her sole heir. 24 Decr 1814. Wit: Abraham MILLER, Levi A. WICKHAM. Proved 3 Feby 1815. Bond for John PRICE to execute will.

Pages 179-180: Accounting for the estate of Jacob HOFFMAN with John DICK, one of the executors now deceased. Among items, paid Godfrey MILLER for crape for mourning, $9.75. 2 Feby 1815.

Pages 181-185: Will of Simon LAUCK, 21 Febry 1815. To wife, Catherine, lot on west side of Braddock. To son, John, brick house and lot at corner of Loudoun and Clifford. Sons: Jacob, William, Phillip, John, Simon. Daughter: Elizabeth. Mentions "when youngest son is of age". Brother, Peter, and Beatty CARSON to be executors. Wit: Lewis A. WICKHAM, John PRICE, Abraham LAUCK, Lemuel BENT. Proved 3 March 1815.

Pages 185-188: Will of William THORNBURG, 14 March 1815. To nephew, Robert THORNBURG, of Newberry, York County, Pa. son of brother, Jacob, the house and lot on Loudoun Street. To two children of nephew James THORNBURG (son of my brother, George) who died some years ago in Philadelphia. To nephew Daniel THORNBURG, of Frederick County, son of brother John. To friends, Beatty CARSON, Rev'd James WALLS, John PRICE. Beatty CARSON and John PRICE to execute will. Proved 31 March 1815.

Pages 189-193: Inventory and Appraisal of Estate of Simon LAUCK, dec'd. March 27, 1815. Among items: 1 tenplate stove, drum & pipe, 1 Bead and Beding and Bedsteat, several German books, gunstocks in the rough, 1 ladle skimmer & flesh fork. Signed: John CROCKWELL, Levi A. WICHAM, Thos. CURLET, Lem'l. BENT.

Pages 193-194: Appraisal of Estate of Robert McMUN, Senior, dec'd. All personal estate: 1 Lot of Books, Hoan & Razors, pair Scales & Weights, 1 hair trunk, silver watch, chest of carpenter's tools, 2 notes for $65 each and 1 note for $22.33. Appraisal of estate of Robert McMUM recorded in court, 2 June 1815.

Pages 194-195: Inventory of the Appraisal of Personal Estate of the late George HARDESTY. 5 June 1815. Made at the house of Cordenia HARDESTY. Mostly household items as window curtains, kettles, tub, flax wheel and smoothing iron. Produced in court, 4 Augt 1815. D. W. THOMAS, John KIGER.

Pages 195-196: Appraisal of the Estate of Francis DeSHIELDS, dec'd. Made 3 Augt 1815. Among items: Bead, beadstead, beading, kitchen wares. Appraisers: David RUSSELL, Joseph HARRY. Recorded: 4 Augt 1815.

Pages 196-198: Will of John LANTZ. 28 January 1815. Mentions his eleven children: Catherine, Elizabeth, Mary, Frederick, Maria, Margaret, Sarah, John, Sophia, Susanna and Rosanna. Gives to daughters Catherine and Elizabeth and to children of daughters, Susanna and Rosanna. If daughter Maria dies before receiving her legacy, it goes to benefit her son, John FLETCHER. Abraham LAUCK and Abraham MILLER, Execs. Wit: Edwd SLATER, Benjm. T. HAM, Peter HAM. Proved, 4 August 1815.

Pages 199-204: Income and Expenses of Estate of Charles AULICK, dec'd, with Cornelius GIBBONS, executor. Among items: cash of John BOWEMASTER, Jeremiah BOWLING, from large estate sale; paid expenses as coffin, $8, carrying funeral notice, 50¢, paid Jacob SECRIST for locust posts, J. WALL for water works, C. McCORMICK for tax. 2 August 1816.

Pages 205-206: Inventory & Appraisal of John HOPEWELL, dec'd. 9 Octr 1815. Among items: gold watch & chain, silver Epaulet, military Sash, military books, 3 cravats, cash in hands of Col. Gustine SMITH ($100). Appraisal made "at the tavern of Susanna STREIT." Edward SLATER, John CROCKWELL, D. W. THOMAS.

Pages 207-208: Will of Jacob KIGER. Wife, Mary. He had "interest in the store in company with Daniel OVERAKER and Stewart GRANT". Mentions brother Andrew KIGER's daughter, Mary. Wife, Mary, executriss and her brother Daniel OVERAKER, executor. 9 August 1816. Wit: Wm. M. HOLLIDAY, S. GRANTT, Samuel WINDLE. Proved, 2 May 1817.

Pages 209-210: Appraisal of Personal Estate of Nathaniel SHEPARD, dec'd. August 8th, 1817. Mentions Property in Richmond, $2,000. Notes & Bonds. Appraisers: Daniel HARTMAN, William BULL, John HOFF, Daniel OVERAKER.

Page 211: Inventory & Appraisal of Charles GRIM, dec'd. June 12, 1816. Among items: 1 parcel carpenters tools, 1 cross cut saw, only household utensils: 1 Pot & Skillet. Signed: William HELPHINSTINE, Andrew BAKER, Andrew KIGER, Conrad CRELPS. Produced in court, 3 Octr 1817.

Pages 212-217: Estate of John WINDLE, dec'd, in account with Peter COONTZ, executor. Among items: paid Sundry Witnesses attendance in the Count_ Court & clerks fees at the suit of COCKRAN, $28.44. Paid other court costs against COCKRAN. 30 Sept 1817. Estate account of John WINDLE, dec'd, with Samuel WINDLE, executor, produced in court 30 Sept 1817.

Pages 217-220: Will of Samuel WINDLE, Merchant. Wife, Ann. Children: Samuel Washington, Margaret Evelina, Sarah Matilda, & Richard, "and the one with which my wife is now pregnant". Mentions his aged mother. Has stock in the farmers Bank of Virginia. Daniel GOLD, and John IRWIN, to be executors and guardians of children. 26 January 1818. Wit: William HILL, Josh. GAMBLE, Thos. W. BLACKWOOD. Proved, 4 Sept 1818.

Pages 221-223: Will of Elizabeth HOFF. Gives to the President and Director of the American Bible Society of the city of New York, $500. Rest of estate, one share each, to sister Catherine, brother Philip, sister Mary TURNER and two children, brother Lewis and five children. Executors: Lewis HOFF (brother) and Wm. Henry BAKER. 11 October 1818. Will proven by witnesses: Daniel HARTMAN and Thomas HEITE, 30 Oct 1818.

Pages 223-224: Will of Martha HODGSON, advanced in years. To son, John, land, 900 acres purchased by Nicholas PURTLE, dec'd, "my brother", of Berkley Co, of Meshack LAXTON. All moveable & personal estate to son, John, and daughter, Jane CHRISMAN. Son, John HODGSON, sole exec. 20 March 1815. Wit: John KIGER, Adam BOWERS, Leml. BENT. Proved 29 Jan. 1819.

Pages 225-227: Appraisal of Estate of Samuel WINDLE, dec'd, 11 Sep 1818. Among items: slaves named Joe and Mary, Family Bible, pair mahogany card tables, dining & breakfast tables, 2 Vols. Village Sermons, 2 Vols. Dictionary Bible, Hymn Book. Signed: Josh. GAMBLE, John SPERRY, James RIELY.

Pages 228-229: Inventory of Personal Estate of John LANTZ, dec'd, Dec 9, 1818, by Peter HAM, Edward SLATER, Cornelius GIBBONS. Among items: Bed, Bolster, 2 pillows, Iron Mortor & Pestal, Steel yards, Scales, Lantran, Sow. Appraisal recorded 2 July 1819.

Page 229: Schedules and Appraisal of Personal Estate of Margaret DOWDALL, dec'd. Among items: cash found in desk in paper, $100.00 and Bushels Wheat in N. PARKINS Mill, $88.75. Signed: John BELL, John IRWIN, John MILLER. 30 April 1819.

Pages 230-236: Appraisal & Sale of Personal Estate of James G. DOWDALL, dec.d. 9 April 1819. Two old negro women, valued at $11, brought $4.50 at sale. Young negro man named Gilbert, valued at $700, brought $400 at sale. Negros were not sold till 6th of March 1821. Appraisers: John BELL, John IRWIN, John MILLER. Sale account recorded in court, 3 August 1821.

Pages 237-238: Appraisal of Property of Philip BOWERS, dec'd. Among items: "Cooper Stuff", saw, axe, planks, addzs, silver watch and trinkets. Signed: Jos. SLAGLE, John SLAGLE, (illegible). 29 Sept 1815.

Pages 238-239: Appraisal of property of Henry CANAFORD, dec'd. 3 Sep 1819. Among items: pine & walnut tables, 2 chairs, 2 Benches, 6 Saws, Tools, Glue Pot, small tick with feathers & "other small Trumpherrys." Total value: $60.62½. Signed: T. W. THOMAS, Edmund PENDLETON, Samuel H. LAUCK.

Pages 239-244: Appraisal and Sale of Property of Lewis F. MACHOLD, dec'd. 7 March 1815. Among items: a lot of German & English books with a variety of Music, 2 Shirts, 1 pr. Pantaloons, 1 pr. Silver templed Spectacles & steel case, 1 pr. Silver shoe Buckles. Appraisers: Wm. H. BAKER, Peter PRINTZ, David RUSSELL. In account with Elizabeth MACHOLD, Administration: articles in the hands of Henry Wm. BAKER "deposited in his hands by the deceased in his lifetime". After a "friendly case in court", Baker gave to the estate, $1,047. Sale of personal Property, March 11, 1815, and recorded in court 2 Feb 1821.

Pages 244-248: Will of Christian CRUM. All property to wife, Christiania CRUM. Daughter Rachel and two children, Mary Ann & Elizabeth, to live with mother. Also son John to live there as long as he remains single "unless they choose otherwise". No charges to be made against son Henry CRUM for one hundred dollars paid for a substitute for him in the last war. No charges against four sons, Christian, Lewis, Henery and John for horse, saddle and bridle given to each. Silver watch to grandson, Christian BOUTMAN. Appoints John CRUM and Philip STONE, executors. 30 April 1820. Wit: William Williams BLANCHARD, Geo. REED, Samuel SEBRIGHT. Proved 1 Sept 1820.

Pages 248-249: Appraisal of Estate of James SCOTT, dec'd. No date given. Among items: 1 pianoforte, pair card tables, 14 Benches, 24 Chairs, 1 Safe, 1 pair Globes. Signed: Jno. HEISKELL, Jno. BELL, Josh. GAMBLE. Recorded in court: 31 Jany 1823.

Pages 250-252: Appraisal of personal estate of Abm. M. SCHENK, "deceast", May 21, 1814. Several houses and horses, wagon, tent, 1 gin cage and contents, 50 gallons vinegar, 6 tight casks, and more. Signed: Geo. LEPS, William VANHORNE. Recorded 4 May 1821.

Pages 252-254: Estate account of Abm. SHANK, dec'd., with Mary BARTLETT, his Administration. Among payments made: to John DICK, Richard ADDAMS, James RUTTER, David MILBURN. At end shows balance due Mary SHANK. Recorded 4 May 1821. Signed: Abm. MILLER, Wm. VANHORNE.

Pages 255-274: Income and Expenses of the Estate of Samuel WINDLE, dec'd., and of "The Orphan Children of Samuel WINDLE." Daniel GOLD and John IRWIN, guardians. Many accounts receivable and payable for Mrs. Ann WINDLE and the children. Mentions buying clothing for Samuel and Evelina "about the time of their separation from the rest of the family". One item: cash "collection for the Reverend Wm. HILL -- Pew rent, $3.33". Period covered is Sept 1818 until recorded in court on July 19, 1821.

Pages 275-276: Will of Thomas CURLET, 18 Aug 1821. Wife, Susan to have all estate except books and manuscripts which are to be divided equally between sons William & Thomas. Mentions children: Comfort, William, Rachel, Francis, Margaret and Thomas. Executor to be son-in-law Jacob LAUCK and son William CURLET. Wit: Adam KURTZ, Wm. JOHNSON, William COCHRAN. Proved 3 Jany 1823.

Pages 277-280: Appraisal of Personal Estate of Elizabeth HOFF, 14 Dec 1818. Among items: Dimity curtains for 2 windows, 24 yards striped carpeting, 6 chairs, 2 large waiters, pictures in frames. Some purchasers at estate sale on 16 Dec 1818: John HOFF, Jno. G. MANSFIELD, Jeremiah DOTSON. Lewis HOFF, executor. Recorded in court 31 Jany 1823.

Pages 281-289: Will of Mary POWERS, 15 Sept 1818. Executor to sell house, lot and all personal estate. Wills to Mary SHOCK 100 pounds and a featherbed and its furniture; gives to Isaac & John HOFFMAN's eldest daughters, to Flora Ann HODGSON and Mary WARDEN. Appoints trusty friend John BAKER, sole executor. Wit: Abraham MILLER, John IRWIN. Proved 21 Jany 1823. Personal property appraisal dated Jany 4, 1823 contains, in part, one Lot Books, flower pots and curtains, and bonds/notes of Joseph SLAGLE, Charles FITZSIMMONS, Frederick ATTRICK?, Charles MAGILL. Mentions house and lot on Water Street valued at $500. Appraisers: Jacob BAKER, J. W. MILLER, John HOFF. Among purchasers at Estate Sale, 13 Feby 1823: Polly SCHROCK, Thos. GRIMSHAW, Philip WOLFE, Mary BAGLEY, Nelly HARPER. Recorded 28 Feby 1823.

Pages 289-306: "Memorandum of an Appraisal" made 7 April 1821, of the personal estate of the late Goldsmith CHANDLEE. Listed are many clock & watch parts, walnut cases and family Bible. Appraisers: Daniel GOLD, John HOFF, Henry BEATTY. Also includes Estate Sale. Recorded 31 Oct. 1823.

END OF WILL BOOK NO. 1

Pages 1-4: Appraisement of the Estate of Jonathan HARRY, dec'd. Among items: Notes of Hand signed by Daniel GOLD and Lewis HOFF, mahogany Burrow, 1 falling leave table, 2 Bibles. Signed: Conrad KREMER, L. H. WICKHAM, John LAUCK. Estate sale and appraisement recorded 2 April 1824.

Pages 5-7: The Orphans of Samuel WINDLE, dec'd. Accounting for income and expenses by guardians, Daniel GOLD and John IRWIN, from Jany 19, 1822 through March 1824. Example: cash to Mrs. Ann WINDLE for board and use of Sarah Matilda, Richard and Elizabeth Ann; cash to Michael and Mary COYLE in behalf of Samuel and Evelina. Recorded 2 July 1824.

Pages 8-9: Estate of Jonathan HARRY, dec'd. Among items are amounts due "to boarding of the deceased, 26 July 1821 - 5 Aug 1822, $70; due to washing and mending from 1 Apr 1819 until 5 Augt 1822, $50". James HARRY settled the estate account of Jonathan HARRY, 17 Aug 1824. Recorded 3 Sept 1824.

Pages 10-17: Estate of James G. DOWDALL, dec'd., including the Estate of Margaret DOWDALL, dec'd. Thomas KREMER, Admr. Income and Expenses beginning April 1819. Some items: cash to George KREPS for coffin, $15; cash for 5-1/8 yards Linsey for Esther; cash for support of family & negroes; load of clover hay from Stonymead. Balance due estate, Jany 1, 1821, $355.80. Estate settled and recorded 3 Sept 1824.

Pages 18-20: Sale Account of Personal Estate of Catharine HOFF, dec'd., 25 Octr 1823. Includes also list of purchasers and items purchased from the personal estate of Lewis HOFF, dec'd., which remained at the death of his wife, Catherine HOFF, who by his will was entitled to the use thereof during her lifetime. Some purchasers were Lewis and John HOFF, Benjamin CRUMBLEFOOT. Appraisers: Jno. GRAY?, Samuel REA, George REED. Lewis HOFF, executor. Recorded 3 Sept 1824.

Pages 21-23: Estate of Mary POWERS, dec'd., beginning Febr 18, 1823, with cash paid to John HODGSON for digging grave, $3; to E. HODGSON for attending court as a witness, $1.59; to Peter KREMER for crying sale, $1.75; to Joseph COOPER? a legacy left to his wife, eldest daughter of John HOFFMAN. John BAKER, executor. Recorded 9 Novr 1824.

Pages 23-27: Estate accounting, Goldsmith CHANDLEE, dec'd., beginning 10 Apr 1821, with cash from sale, cash found in desk and drawer and cash from many individuals. Total: $2,399.24½. Made payments including to Benjamin LANGLEY for crying sale, to Peter ADAMS for 1,000 shingles, to Richard MOORE for white washing, to Henry BEATTY, porder? of Eunice CHANDLEE. In court Decr 15, 1824, settled and adjusted the estate of Goldsmith CHANDLEE with the estate of Benjamin CHANDLEE, dec'd., his late administrator. Recorded 31 Decr 1824.

Pages 27-29: Estate of Henry BAKER, dec'd., in account with Henry W. and John BAKER, executors, beginning March 1807. Among receipts: cash from estate sale and from rents of Patrick SMITH and Beall BISHOP; cash from 966-3/4 acres of Military Land. Paid legatees: Elizabeth STOVER, Jacob, Isaac and Abraham BAKER, $122.78½ and $192.53 each. Recorded 31 Decr 1824.

Pages 30-32: Estate of Catharine HOFF, dec'd., with Lewis HOFF, Admr. Included, with dates 1803 to 1807, "delivered to Catherine HOFF, widow & relict of L. HOFF, dec'd, in conformity with his will". Income and expenses of estate. Balance due estate to be divided into five equal shares of $70.13 each. Recorded in court 31 Decr 1824.

Pages 33-34: Estate of Samuel CALVERT, dec'd., with Beaty CARSON and Obed WAITE, his executors. Long list of cash receipts and expenses, 1807-1810. Among items: paid Samuel CALVERT on account of a legacy, paid Obed WAITE for writing will, received cash for flour sold, paid Joshua NEWBRAUGH $9 for coffin, paid John ELSE for digging grave. Account continues to 1824 and is recorded in court, 4 Feby 1825.

Pages 35-36: Inventory of the Personal Estate of Edward SLATER, dec'd. Some items: cubbord, $2; mahogany table, $3; set of bed curtains, $2.50. Signed: Leml BENT, Jn. HEISKELL, John IRWIN. Recorded 5 Feby 1826.

Pages 36-42: The Estate of Mr. John DICK, dec'd. "In bedinence to an order of the Corperation Court of Winchester directed to us and after first being sworn whe the undersigners have prase the persenal astate of Mr. John Dick, deseast, as follows, Nover 22d, 1814." Among items: "half of one large harry, 1 load flags, rafters and joices, cart wheals, 3,000 spookes @ $15 per thousand, winser cheairs". Signed: Peter COONTZ, William HELPHENSTEIN, Simon LAUCK, Peter LAUCK. One purchase in estate sale: Isaac HOLLINGSWORTH, Tailors Goose, 35¢. Appraisal and Sale recorded 3 Feby 1826.

Pages 43-47: Appraisal of personal estate of Michael COPPENHAVER, dec'd. Court ordered, 28 Novr 1823. Many household items including Iron Tea Kittle, Touchoven, cridle, watter buckitts, stack of wheats, spining wheell, lot of old geers, Blacksmith tools. Signed: Michael HAMMAKER, Wm. LANGLEY, James HARRY. Income and Expenses of estate listed by Michael and Margaret COPEN-HAVER. One item: cash found in house of deceased, $363.50. Estate settled 5 March 1826.

Pages 47-49: Will of Andrew BAKER. To wife, Mary, all property during her natural life. Daughter, Mary Ann, to live with mother. Bequeaths to children: Henry, Samuel C., Mary Ann, and Rosanna BAKER and Margaret SINGHOUSE, wife of Samuel SINGHOUSE. Executor: son, Henry, and Samuel SINGHOUSE. 3 July 1826. Wit: John BELL, Samuel BROWN, Andrew KIGER. Proved 4 Augt 1826.

Pages 49-52: Will of Regina BUSH. Gives to niece, Regenah SHONBERGER, of Philadelphia, house and lot "I now occupy on Braddock Street", including red painted and blue painted chests and other furniture. Gives to Reginah BUSH, daughter of William BUSH, and to worthy friend, Rev. Abraham RICK. Appoints neighbor and friend, John W. MILLER, executor. 5 May 1826. Wit: Isaac HOFF, Geo. M. ADAMS, Daniel LINN. Made codicial, same date, re deed of trust from Stephen JENKINS. Proved 1 Sept 1826.

Pages 52-54: Orphans of Samuel WINDLE, dec'd., in account with Daniel GOLD and John IRWIN, Guardians. From July 1824 to July 1826. Long list of income and expenses for support of Sarah Matilda, Richard and Elizabeth Ann WINDLE by Joseph KENNY. Also to John and Michael COYLE for boarding and support of Samuel and Evelina WINDLE. Recorded 3 Novr 1826.

Pages 54-59: William S. CAMPBELL's Estate with George REED, Admr. From Jany 1816 to 1827. Income from selling many items including Jewelry and jewelry parts, watches and watch repair parts. Among expenses were cost of Board, Clothing and Scholing the Children. Recorded in court 3 March 1827.

Pages 60-61: Inventory of estate of Andrew BAKER, dec'd., taken on 30th day of January 1827. Includes "1 Lott on Loudon Street wheren Henry BAKER's house stands", six plate stove and pipe, smoothing iron, salt box, shovel. Henry BAKER, Admr. Recorded in court 3 March 1827. Apprs: J. SENSENEY, Saml BROWN, Andrew KIGER.

Pages 61-62: Inventory of Personal Estate of Samuel C. BAKER, dec'd., taken 30 January 1827. Household items and clothes. Henry BAKER, his Admr. To court and recorded 3 March 1827. Signed: J. SENSENEY, Samuel BROWN, Andrew KIGER.

Pages 62-64: Inventory and Appraisal of personal estate of Thomas LONG, dec'd., 10 Novr 1821?. Includes one horse sleigh, shot gun powder horn with pouch, two small spinning wheels, a hive of bees, two baskets. Signed: Abner HODGSON, Wm CAMPBELL, Robert HODGSON. Recorded 20 Mar 1827.

Mid-page 64: Joseph GAMBLE is sworn in as Commissioner of Revenue. Says he will "deligently and faithfully execute the duties of the said office with favour, affection, or partiality". 8 Sept 1824. Before: Daniel GOLD.

Pages 64-67: Continues the estate of Thomas LONG, dec'd. Made 13 Nov 1821?. Some items in Sale Account: a sasage bench choper, a box of soap fat, one small kegg, a pot without a bale, a woman's saddle. Robert LONG, Admr. Recorded 30 March 1827.

Page 68: Will of Margaret WINDLE, widow of Samuel. All property, real and personal, to daughter, Eve WINDLE. Wm. HELPHENSTINE, of the Borough of Winchester, appointed executor. 14 Decr 1818. Wit: Daniel GOLD, Mary BAKER, John IRWIN. Will was "provided" by the oaths of Daniel GOLD and John IRWIN, 2 Nov 1827.

Pages 69-72: Appraisal of Personal Estate of Regina BUSH, dec'd. made 2 Sept 1826(7?). Included old German Bible, clothing and apparel in the blue chest. Inventory by Sam'l. BROWN, Jos. SLAGLE, George BARNHART. The estate account, with John W. MILLER, executor, included cash to Henry W. BAKER & Sons for articles for funeral, cash paid Wm. DIXON for digging grave and attendance, paid BAKER & KERR for coffin & hearse. Received cash of John E. PAGE on John VON REISING Note. Appraisal and Estate Acct. recorded in court 2 May 1828.

Pages 72-74: Estate of Mary POWERS, dec'd., in account with John BAKER, Executor. Begins March 11, 1825 with cash paid Nelly HARPER, amount of Judgment obtained by her against the estate, $153.64. Received bond principle and interest from Joseph SLAGLE, Nicholas FITZSIMMONS, Jonathan ROBENSON; received interest on money loaned John W. MILLER, Jacob SENSENEY. Expenses to Feby 5, 1828. To court 2 May 1828.

Pages 74-81: George William and James Victor CAMPBELL in account with Thomas B. CAMPBELL, their guardian. Income and expenses beginning 1822. Example: To boarding, washing, lodging, making mending for Victor, one year, $65. In 1829, "By balance due J. Victor CAMPBELL, the surviving orphan" and 2 Aug 1829, guardianship account settled replacing William S. CAMPBELL, dec'd., with Thomas R. CAMPBELL, their guardian. (see page 83)

12

Pages 81-82: The Estate of Henry BAKER, dec'd. in account with Henry W. and John BAKER, executors. Dec 30, 1829. Balance due estate: $88.19½. Heirs: Henry W., John, Joseph, Jacob, Isaac BAKER's estate, Willim MORRIS & Elizabeth, his wife. Recorded in court 1 Jany 1830.

Page 83: James Victor CAMPBELL, orphan of William CAMPBELL, in account with Thos. B. CAMPBELL, his guardian. Beginning Jany 1829 with paying many bills such as for clothing, cyphering book, buttons for vest and pantaloons. Recorded 1 Jany 1830.

Pages 84-86: Estate of Mary POWERS, in account with John BAKER, exec. Paying expenses of estate such as: James M. MASON, attorney; Obed WAITE "for fee"; paid legacies to Flora Ann HODGSON, Joanna WILLS, Mary WARDEN. Recorded 23 Jany 1830.

Pages 87-89: Will of William D. BALDWIN, "sick & weak in body". Gives to brothers, Robert T. & Archibald S. BALDWIN "all my medical books and professional instruments, except my amputating instruments". Those to friend Dr. Henry See? HEISKELL. Gives to nephew Hite BALDWIN. Mentions wife Margaret and "dear little daughter Mary Julia". Margaret to have rest of estate and care of daughter. Brother, Archibald S., and father-in-law John C. SOWERS, to be executors. 17 Jany 1830. Wit: H. B. STREIT, John N. BELL. Proved 25 Feby 1830. Bond for John C. SOWERS, executor, to make inventory of estate.

Pages 90-92: Will of George TRESLER, "being about to take a journey and not knowing what may befall me." Wife and three oldest children not named. Wife to have all estate during her natural life. After her death, all property to be sold and divided equally among "my eight youngest children, viz: Jacob, George, Hannah, Joel, William, James, Mary Ann and Jane Eleanor. Had "heretofore paid to my three oldest children". Friend Beaty CARSON to be executor. 2 Oct 1822. Wit: Wm M. SPERRY, John CARTER, Adam D. KURTZ. Proved 2 April 1830.

Pages 92-96: James RIELY, Guardian of James P. RIELY, his son. Lists income & expenses beginning Augt 1819 with legacy bequeathed to him by James PEURVIS, dec'd., $500, and interest from that time to May 18, 1830. Also James RIELY, Guardian of Elizabeth Ann RIELY (now Elizabeth Ann WARD), Addison B. RIELY, and Cassandra M. RIELY, his children. Income & expenses beginning Oct 1820. Mentions receipts from Cassandra PURVIS estate and from CHAPPELEAR's executors. Guardian accounts settled 18 May 1830 and recorded in court 4 June 1830.

Page 97: Will of Nancy K. SLATER. All property to her three sisters, jointly, Betsy, Exalina and Susan. 2 April 1830. Wit: James P. RIELY, Chas. HULETT, Daniel GOLD. Proved 2 July 1830.

Pages 97-98: More on the Estate of Mary POWERS, dec'd., with John BAKER, executor. Among items: cash received from Alexander S. TIDBALL, $211.70. Total estate divided into 6 parts. Recorded in court: 5 March 1831.

Pages 99-101: Will of Frederick KURTZ. To daughter, Elizabeth KURTZ, house and lot in Winchester with restriction that daughter-in-law, Ann KURTZ is to live on said lot with said Elizabeth. Had made Deed of Trust on said lot to secure a debt of about $500 to the "Messers MILLERs for the payment of which it is expected they will wait". Mentions children of son Adam, dec'd., and daughter-in-law Ann: William, James, John, Frederick, Peter Kennerly KURTZ. John & Abraham MILLER to be executors. 24 March 1831. Wit: Obed WAITE, Solomon HEISTER. Proved 29 April 1831.

Pages 101-102: Will of Samuel CRISSWELL. Wife Elizabeth "all my estate, making any arrangements she thinks best". "My three children, viz: my son, Charles, my daughter, Isabella Jane, and my son, David Newton Riddle." Wife to be executor with no security required. July 12, 1831. Wit: John IRWIN, John R. McMULLIN, Jas. LITTLE. Proved 29 July 1831.

Pages 102-105: Estate of Regina BUSH, with John M. MILLER, Exec. Among income and expenses are Payments re Mary JENKINS Deed of Trust, paid Sheriff fee bill at suit of Jenkins, cash to Philip & Regina STINEBRIDGE (a legacy). Recorded 29 July 1831.

Pages 105-108: James Victor CAMPBELL in account with Thomas B. CAMPBELL, his guardian, beginning July 1830. Included "to cash spended in going to Staunton to bring Victor home, $28.50"; for shoes, penknife, pocket hand-kerchief, pair of skates, for making pantaloons, cloak, for purchase of hat". Recorded in court 2 Jany 1835.

Pages 108-109: Will of Adam LAUCK. To wife, Mary, whole of estate of all & every description after payment of debts and funeral expenses. After her death to children and grandchildren: Peter, one-fourth; children of Margaret, one-fourth; Catherine, one-fourth; Caroline, one-fourth. Friend and relation, John MILLER to be executor with no security required. 10 Jany 1835. Wit: Jas. P. RIELY, John FLETCHER, Thomas SPRINT. Proved 4 Apr 1835.

Pages 110-111: Estate of Speake FLANAGAN, dec'd., in account with Elizabeth FLANAGAN (Now Mrs. HELPHINSTINE, Admin.) Income & expenses beginning Feby 1814. Among items: paid Job S. HENDRICKS for coffin, $9; paid J. & A. MIL-LER for shroud, $4.50; paid Dr. BALDWIN payment for lot. Account goes thru June 1820. Recorded in court 1 Octr 1830.

Pages 111-112: Will of Elizabeth C. PEYTON. Sister, Louisa M. CLARK, to get all estate, real, personal and mixed. Mentions suit "now pending in the Court of Appeals in Virginia against the administration of Chas. MOORE, dec'd." $2,500 or the proportionate amount recovered of the sum to be paid to nephews, John & Henry CONRAD, the sons of dec'd. sister, Margaret R. CONRAD. Brother-in-law, William D. CLARK, Esq., to be sole executor. 11 Feby 1834. Wit: Obed WAITE, Daniel GOLD. Proved 2 May 1835.

Pages 112-114: Appraisal of Personal Estate of Abraham LAUCK, 9 April 1835, by Daniel GOLD, John IRWIN, Jos. SLAGLE. Among items: 28 shares Valley Bank stock, 3 books, german family bible, feather bed, under bed, bedstead & bedding with pillows & bolster, pair steel yards, sausage chopper & sifter. Total estate value, $2,950.75. Recorded 4 July 1835.

Pages 114-115: Estate of George TRISLER, dec'd., in account with Beatty CARSON, Executor, 1830-1834. In part: Cash paid George TRISLER's Note & interest; cash paid John HOPKINS for charge sent against RINKER. Estate balance, $182.56. Mrs TRISLER and her sons gave refunding bond to the executor and estate account was settled. Recorded 4 July 1835.

Pages 115-117: Estate of Samuel CRESWELL, dec'd., in account with David W. BARTON, Administrator. Begins Decr 1834 with items as paid cash for crying sale & ringing bell; paid John KERR for coffin for Mrs. CRESWELL; paid Moses MASSIE for digging grave; paid James WRIGHT for his accounts against Samuel and Mrs. CRESWELL; made several payments to banks & individuals "against notes". Received cash for "amount of debt due from David CRES-WELL, of Pennsylvania". NOTE: Mrs. Elizabeth CRESWELL, who was the executor of Samuel CRESWELL, dec'd., and also widow and devisee for life, leaving her own affairs to blended with those of the estate that it would have been difficult if not impracticable to separate them. Income and expenses of both estates are "annexed". Recorded 4 March 1837.

Pages 118-126: Inventory, Appraisal and Sale of Personal Estate of Samuel CRESWELL, dec'd., by David W. BARTON, his Administrator. Inventory and Appraisal, Decr 5, 1834, by John SENSENEY and Jacob COOPER. Some items: Clothes Press, some tobacco, long list of household items. Estate Sale, Decr 1834. Recorded in court 1 April 1837.

Pages 126-127: The Orphans of Samuel CRESSWELL in account with Abraham CRESWELL, their guardian. Examples, beginning Nov 1834: cash paid for expenses to Winchester; cash paid for removing children from town; one year's boarding. Income from rent of outlot and other rents. Through April 1837. Account settled 26 Apr 1837 and recorded 8 May 1837.

Pages 128-129: Will of Conrad KREMER, revoking all former wills. To daughter, Catharine FREDERICK, house and lot. At her decease, to her four children: Carline PARKER, Catharine SHERER, Julyann FREDERICK, and Elizabeth FREDERICK. Expressly mentions: to Catharine "my cow and silver Soup Ladle" and at her decease, cow and Ladle to Julyann FREDERICK, "said Julyann having been my principle nourse during my infirm state". Mentions granddaughter, Elizabeth FREDERICK. To grandson, Conrad KREMER, son of Peter, "my silver watch". To two sons, Peter and George KREMER, one silver dollar each. 30 March 1837. Wit: James HARRY, John HOOVER. Proved 3 June 1837.

Page 130: Appraisal of Personal Estate of Conrad KREMER, dec'd., as shown by George KREMER, Administrator. Among items: Silver Soup Ladle, mahogany Sideboard, 6 yellow Windsor Chairs, 1 Sow & Pigs, 1 Cow, 1 Kraut Tub. Charles H. CLARK, Lewis LINDSAY, Robert BRANNON. 7 Aug 1837.

Page 131: Will of James McCRACKEN. To Thomas & Charles RIELY, sons of James P. RIELY, house and lot "where I now live". Executors to sell personal estate for funds to buy tombstones "for my wife and myself". James P. RIELY, Alexander S. TIDBALL to be executors. 20 June 1836. Wit: Jas. H. CARSON, John CROCKWELL. Codicil, 21 June 1836, to authorize executors to sell house and lot in order to make equal division to devisees. Wit: Jas. H. CARSON, Michael HITE. Proved 2 June 1838.

Pages 132-133: Orphans of Samuel CRESWELL, dec'd., in account with Abraham CRESWELL, guardian. From April 1837 to April 1839. Among receipts and expenses: paid Adeline J. CROWLEY for tuition and articles of clothing; paid Luther WARREN for tuition and two years board. Account settled with "due the guardian from Gabella, Newton and Charles". Recorded 4 May 1839.

Pages 133-134: Will of Catharine HAAS. To brothers, sisters and niece: John HAAS, Mildred HAAS, Juliet COLLET and Marinda RUCKER, daughter of brother, John HAAS, "all my estate except my wearing apparel and silver spoons". Wearing Apparel to Marinda RUCKER and Spoons to niece, Catharine COLLET. Samuel BROWN to be executor. 14 July 1837. Wit: George SHARP, Richard R. BROWN, O. M. BROWN. Proved 4 Dec 1841.

Pages 134-135: Property Appraisal of Estate of A. WATSON, dec'd. May 9, 1840. Among short list of items: 19 yards carpeting, 2 pair bedsteds & 2 pillers, 1 Berush & Harness, 1 Horse. Signed: Philip SHEARER, George KREMER, Jr., J. KEENAN.

Pages 135-136: More on the accounts of Abraham CRESWELL, Guardian of Isabel, Charles and Newton CRESWELL, Orphans of Samuel CRESWELL, dec'd. 1839-1841.

Pages 137-138: Inventory and Appraisal of Personal Estate of Catharine HAAS, dec'd. Entire list: bureau, bedstead, 4 chairs, 2 tables, andirons/tongs/ broken shovel, tin tea kettle, broken skillet, 2 strips carpeting. Total value: $20.06. Plus 17 shares bank stock. Recorded 3 June 1843. Geo. W. SEEVERS, Jas. P. REILY, Wm. L. BENT, Apprs.

Pages 138-139: Appraisal of Estate of Mary RIELY, dec'd. Large inventory including mantle ornaments, 1 set German Silver Table Spoons, much used, and many quilts, one elegant. Jos. SLAGLE, Solomon HORN, Geo. BARNHART, Apprs. Recorded 2 Nov 1844.

Page 140: Will of Alfred WELLS, (a free man of colour). Bequeaths "unto my Betey WELL (a free woman of colour)". Was concerned that his children, Maria and Emily, should not be slaves after his decease. "I hereby emancipate, manu-mit and forever set free my said children, Maria now the wife of James WEBB, aged about eighteen years, and Emily, aged between twelve and thirteen." Appoints James KERN, executor. 7 Octr 1844. Wit: J. M. K. HOLLIDAY, James KERN, W. G. SINGLETON. Proved 2 Nov 1844.

Page 141: Will of Jacob HOFFMAN. 29 June 1845. "In consideration of much kindness shown and extended to me by John W. ARNOLD, in whose house I am now confined to a bed of sickness, I will all the right tittle? and interest possessed by me in a tract of Military land in the State of Mosoure." Wit: John AMIK, Geo. W. LEGG, L. P. COONTZ. Proved ____ Sept 1845.

Pages 141-147: Appraisal and Sale of Property in the Estate of Alfred WELLS. Appraisers: Peter KREMER, John FLETCHER, Robert REATHER. Among items: 49 Milk Pots, 13 bed quilts, Kitchen cubbord, Sider Barrel, Carioll. Sale in Nov 15, 1844, by James KERN, exec. Among items: Large Sausage Chopper bo't. by Zachariah KERNS for $4.35; Carryall purchased by James KERNS, $24.00; 5 Geese purchased by James W. JONES, $1.31. Page 147 partly covered by note saying "Estate of Alfred WELLS recorded 7 March 1846".

Pages 147-148: Estate of Abraham LAUCK, dec'd., in account with John and Peter MILLER, executors, with John MILLER, dec'd. Account begins Jan. 1835 with some items: paid Abraham GROVE for digging grave, paid note and interest to Margaret ORRICKS, paid John KERR for coffin and Hurse, sold 13 shares of Bank Stock. Recorded 7 March 1846.

Page 148: Appraisement of Estate of Eve WENDLE, dec'd., with appraisers: George W. GRIM, Hugh BARR, Edwd. HOFFMAN. Total estate: Bedstead, Bedding, one chest, 2 chairs, one note from Samuel SINGHAAS. Recorded 3 Oct 1846.

Pages 149-152: Will of Ann BROWN. "My great object" is to provide for my youngest daughter, Elizabeth H. BROWN, so she is not dependent on relatives or friends. Bulk of estate is plantation in the County of Fauquire, 500 acres, now rented and under lein to secure debts to two Banks. Due to Ann S. BROWN, $730, the price of a negro man who was sold. Execs. to sell plantation and, any remaining after debts and bequests, divide among three other daughters: Mary B. DAVIS, of Peoria, Illinois, Catharine S. ORWIN, of Missouri, and Sarah S. HOLLIS, of Winchester. Appoints friend and relative, Robert E. SCOTT, and Richard B. HORNER, of Fauquier, executors. 8 Jan. 1848. Wit: W. M. ATKINSON, Rev. B. T. LACY, William H. STRIET. Proved 4 March 1848. Inventory of all

Estate, real, personal or mixed, in Fauquier County, May 8, 1848, included 500 acres of Lands, 50 Barrels of Sound Corn, 4 Barrels of damaged corn, 35 Bu. Oats. Inventory in Frederick County included Bedstead & Featherbed, 6 Chairs, 1 Carpet, 1 Stanley Stove (everything very old). Signed: Rich'd B. HORNER, Exec. (Robert E. SCOTT refused being exec.) Recorded 3 Feby 1849.

2 pages numbered 152: Will of George REED, of sound mind but weak in body "believe it my duty to make this my last will and testamoney, Amen." Wife, Martha C., "shall enjoy all my real & Personal Estate during her natural life". After her death, to "my children". 9 May 1849. "This is my own handwriting." No witnesses. Proved 2 June 1849. Martha C. REED given letters of Administration with Robt. W. REED & George A. V. REED, her securities.

Second page 152-159: Many accounts of the Orphans of Samuel CRESWELL, 1841-1845, with Samuel CRESWELL and David PUGH, their guardians. Isabella, with Samuel CRESWELL, guardian, 1841-1845, paid for taxes, repairs, digging cellar, etc. and received rent from house & outlots. Due ward, Sept 1, 1845: $32.05. At a Winchester Court, 3 Feby 1849, "this guardianship account of Isabella CRESWELL, deceased" was recorded. Similar income and expenses recorded for Charles and Newton CRESWELL by their guardian, Samuel CRESWELL. Also an account for Newton CRESWELL with David PUGH, his guardian, which mentions payments to "former guardian". Accounts recorded in court 3 Feby 1849.

Pages 159-161: Will of William LANGLEY. Wife, Elizabeth to have all estate during her natural life "except she should marry again". Then entitled to "only her third". Mentions seven children (unnamed), 3 sons and 4 daughters. Wife to be executrix with no security. 17 May 1849. Wit: Daniel GOLD, Lewis LINDSEY, G. W. ANDERSON. Proved 4 Aug 1849.

Pages 161-162: Will of Emily WELLS. After payments of debts & expenses of funeral, rest & residue of all estate to Joseph W. LONG, in trust for sister, Maria, wife of James WEBB, "never for the use in any manner whatsoever of the said James WEBB". After decease of sister, to infant child, Alfred Burwell WEBB. Joseph W. LONG, sole executor, no security required. Jany 28, 1849. Wit: Peter KREMER, C. KREMER. Proved 4 Aug 1849.

Pages 163-164: Will of William C. LANGLEY. To wife, Hannah, all property "to be held and enjoyed all her natural life or so long as she remains my widow". At death of wife, "to my nine children". Friend and neighbor, Philip SHEARER, to be executor. 10 Aug 1850. Wit: J. Philip SMITH, Daniel GOLD, Alfred SEAL. Proved 7 Sept 1850.

Pages 164-165: Estate of Catharine HAAS, dec'd., in account with Samuel BROWN, Executor. Begins Dec 1841 with payments for postage, drayage; paid Lewis EICHELBORGER for printing and H. MILLER for attending court as witness. Leaving due the Estate in cash, $454.64. Distribution 11 May 1843.

Pages 165-167: Eliza Jane MERCER in account with James H. GRIFFITH, her guardian. Balance paid to present guardian, John D. CARPER. Mar 2, 1850. Also Margaret Elizabeth CARPER, late MERCER, in account with Hugh BARR. 4 Feby 1850. John D. CARPER, received balance of guardianship account "of my wife, Margaret Elizabeth CARPER, late MERCER" from Hugh BARR.

Pages 167-169: Will of Elijah NEFF. To sister, Ann HAYS, house and lot on Peyton Street "where I and my said sister now reside". Sister to get $50 annually. If estate provides more, excess to brother, Ezekiel NEFF. After death of sister, sell all estate, including stocks and securities and divide among brothers and children, including children of them that are dead and any, if there be, of Ann HAYS. Friend, W. G. SINGLETON, executor. 7 March 1851. Wit: John L. VON RIESEN, Isaac T. BAKER, Wm. DIFFENDERFFER. Proved 3 May 1851. Executor named in will "refused the burden" and Ann HAYS renounced her right to administer. George W. WARD appointed.

Pages 169-170: Will of Jacob ANDERSON. Executors to sell all estate. To son, Jacob. To Catharine & Marenda, daughters of dec'd. son, John C. AN-DERSON. To granddaughter, Ara Anna CAMPBELL, daughter of dec'd. son, James. To children of dec'd. son, Henry. Remaining portion equally divided between five surviving children, viz: Jacob, George W., Eliza Jane VAN HORN, William ANDERSON, Mary Ann DICK. Executors: two sons, Jacob & George W. 4 June 1844. Wit: David RUSSELL, N. SHIRER, J. S. CARSON. Codicil, Augt 14, 1851. Excluded Jacob from will because had otherwise provided for him. House and lot to George W. Proved 6 Septr 1851.

Pages 171-172: Lydia Ann COPENHAVER (late MERCER) in account with John A. BUSH, her guardian. On Octr 2, 1852, guardianship account settled and "accepted by John W. COPENHAVER, her guardian". Recorded 5 Mar 1854.

Pages 172-175: Appraisement of Elijah NEFF's property. Entire list: one house & lot (2 acres), 1 one-story house on Peyton Street, 1 two-story house and lot on Peyton Street, 1 clock, 1 tea kettle, 1 hair trunk. May 27, 1851. Signed: John T. VON RIESEN, Jacob MESSNER, Wm. DIFFENDERFER. Account receipts & expenses given. Account recorded Novr 1854.

2nd page 175-178: Estate of Ann BROWN, dec'd., in account with Richard R. HORNER, executor. In part, paid for support of Elizabeth H. BROWN, and received cash for rent of farm and many sales of corn. Cash received of James CARVER, rent for 1848, the same "being reduced to this to induce him to give up the farm". Recorded Jany 24, 1854.

2nd page 177: Will of Robert SMITH. Wife, Mary Ann, "all my real & personal property of every description for & during her natural life". At death of wife, all to Loudoun Street Presbyterian Church. Wife, sole executor. Wishes no appraisal or sale of any property she wishes to keep. 22 June 1854. Wit: J. R. TURNER, David RUSSELL. Proved 5 Augt 1854.

2nd page 178, pages 179-180: Will of Rachel LONG. House & lot on west side of Washington Street to two daughters, Caroline CLARK, wife of Alexander CLARK, and Harriet FOLK, widow of George FOULK. At death of surviving daughter, sell house and give 1 part to children of Caroline, 1 part to children of Harriet. Will written so son-in-law, Alexander CLARK, can't interfere with Caroline's enjoyment of her mother's estate. Will L. BENT, trustee to hold Caroline's share. Friend, William L. BENT, executor. 31 Jany 1853. Wit: T. A. TIDBALL, Joseph TIDBALL. Codicil, 28 May 1853, for sale of house & lot. Proved 5 Augt 1854.

Pages 180-183: Appraisal of Personal Property of Wm. H. HELPHENSTINE, dec'd. Some items: 2 looking glasses, 1 pair silver egg holders, 2 sets Winser chairs, demijohns & barrels. 15 June 1854. Dorsey WALTERS, Philip SHERER, John HOOVER, appraisers. Recorded Septr 2, 1854.

Pages 183-184: Will of Jacob CUNKLE, "being in verry feable health and not expecting long to live". To be buried in German Reformed burying ground.

All estate to wife, Martha, and two children, Mary Catherine and Alice Virginia. Wife, Martha A. KUNKLE, executor. 20 Decr 1854. Wit: Lewis T. MOORE, F. S. BOWEN, P. S. DAVIS. Proved 5 January 1855.

Pages 185-187: Estate of William LANGLEY, dec'd., beginning Septr 1850. Some items: cash paid on various accounts and on notes at Valley Bank; cash to John HOOVER "for vaulting grave"; receipts of Winc. Poto. Rail Ry. Account with Philip SHEARER, executor, settled Septr. 2, 1854.

Page 187: Will of Rebecca MILLER (undated, very short). That servant girl, Mary, become free upon arriving at age of twenty-one. Balance of property to be distributed according to law. John S. MILLER, executor. Wit: George F. MILLER, Lewis LINDSAY. Proved 7 April 1855.

Pages 188-190: Estate of Wm H. HELPHINSTINE in account with A. J. HELPHINSTINE, his admin. Income and expenses, including funeral expenses of Mrs. HELPHINSTINE. Amount remaining: $62.94. There being 8 heirs, this will give to each $7.86-3/4ths. Recorded Decr 6, 1856.

Pages 190-193: Appraisal of Real & Personal Estate of Rachel LONG, dec'd. House & lot, Washington Street, $600; some household items. Appraisers said above was all items shown them by Mrs. FOLK, daughter of the deceased. Appraisers: George K. KREMER, John S. MILLER, L. T. MOORE, Robt. B. WOLFE. Septr 6, 1854. House & lot sold as "directed in will" for $100 cash and balance in 3 installments for total of $775. Payments from P. S. CRABILL. Estate closed Jany 31, 1856.

Pages 194-198: Estate of Dewees BECK, dec'd., beginning June 1851. Some items: paid James MAGALIS, 3 months rent, $35; paid Mt. Hebron cemetary for ground and digging grave, $8. Long list of debts and interest payments against the estate. Debts larger than estate. "To pay which 72¢ in $100 of the principle of the several claims must be taken from the respective sums apportioned to each claimant." Abraham NULTON, Admr. (No formal ending or closing of account.)

Page 199: Will of James A. MARSTELLER. Wife, Harriet S. to "have entire use and control of my estate". Children: John W., Baker M., Roberta E., James C. 19 May 1857. Wit: Lewis BARLEY, A. C. MARSTELLER. Proved 1 Augt 1857. Wife to administer estate.

Pages 200-202: Will of George SMITH, a free negro. To Courtney LEONARD, the widow of Moses LEONARD, "my interest in house & lot in which I now live on Water Street, to be hers during her natural life only but rest of property in no wise liable for debts of said Courtney or of her late husband or future husband". After death of "my warm friend Courtney" house & lot to African Coloured Methodist Episcopal Church. To Henry WILLIAMS, hair trunks & sideboards; to Jim & Nelson WILLIAMS, one quilt each; to Sarah STRANGE, "one of my copper molds for baking cakes"; to Bob ROBINSON (the minister), my blue and my black frock coats. William R. DENNY, trustee, to "hold" for the church. 19 Jany 1858. Wit: Daniel BUSH, Isaac H. FAULKNER. Proved 6 Feby 1858.

Pages 202-204: Will of William SIGAFOOSE. To wife, Susan, house & lot on (blank) street, adjoining the property of Atwell SHULL & now occupied by Cornelius R. BARR. At wife's death, to daughter, Florinda. Charge daughter, Virginia KEPLER, with fifty dollars. Sell rest of estate and divide into 7 parts, for children: Virginia, Emily LANE, Virginia KEPLER, Georgianna, William, Martha Ellen, John Montgomery, Robert Baldwin. Parts for Georgianna, William, Martha Ellen, John Montgomery, Robert Baldwin to remain with trustees, Abraham NULTON and John W. BEEMER. Georgianna's part may be paid to husband if she marries. No bequest to daughter, Catherine and Milly Ann; already given to their husbands. 22 Jany 1858. Wit: illegible. Proved 6 March 1858.

Pages 204-210: Will of Lucy Ann LAYTON, a woman of colour. To William B. HARRISON, Esq., of Brandon, Prince George County; to son, William; to Alfred H. BYRD, $20, "to be expended by him in purchasing any little trinket he may select as a mamento of me". Wm. B. HARRISON to hold in trust for "my children, Mary or Mary Ann, Henry, Robert, Lucy and Willian LAYTON".
  William B. HARRISON & Richard E. BYRD, executors. 30 Octr 1856. Wit: John B. WILSON, John B. HIGGINS, L. N. HUCK. Codicil, 12 Jan 1858. Proved 1 May 1858.

Pages 211-212: Estate of Rachel LONG in account with Wm. L. BENT, her executor. Paid to Caroline CLARK and Harriet FOLK. Estate settled 3 July 1858.

Pages 212-215: Will of Nancy ALEXANDER. Gives to sister, Jemima ALEXANDER. Mentions several negroes, "if they should leave for a free state or Liberia". Property, after death of sister, to be sold and sent to Phil, Lucinda and her child, Alice. Share to be given to Sam "to enable him, when free, to seek a home out of Virginia". 21 May 1855. Wit: J. W. McG___?, G. J. MILLER, Robert B. WOLFE. Codicil mentions brother, John. Thomas T. FAUNT-LEROY, Admr. Proved 4 Sept 1858.

Pages 215-216: Appraisal of property of Nancy ALEXANDER, dec'd., recorded 2 Oct 1858. Appraisers: Jno. W. PAGE, Wm. L. BENT, L.T. MOORE. House & lot, jointly purchased by us (Gemima & Nancy ALEXANDER) and Jonathan STEINER valued at $700; some bonds including one of Catherine ALBERT; some household goods/furniture. Appraisal 17 Sept 1858.

Pages 217-219: 25 Decr 1858. "Instrument of Writing" by Ann E. SLOAT re deed made 14 May 1857 between John W. HAYMAKER and Sophia, his wife, and Joseph NEALE for house & lot northeast corner, Market & Cecil Streets, nearly opposite the city jail. Now in trust for sole use of Ann C. SLOAT, wife of Alexander SLOAT. Signed: Ann E. SLOAT. Wit: Geo. S. HAYNIE, W. P. LAUCK.

Pages 219-220: Will of Elizabeth TYLER. All to Rosannah HAYMAKER. Friend John Z. JENKINS to be executor. 13 April 1859. Wit: Alfred SEAL, W. G. SINGLETON. Proved 17 (or 27) May 1859.

Pages 221-223: Estate account of Ann LAYTON, dec'd., (col) (Lucy Ann LAYTON), William G. RUSSELL, Admr. Income and expenses as paid bills, taxes, doctors, attorney's fees. July 2, 1859, estate account of Ann STEPHENSON with Wm. G. RUSSELL, Admr., ordered to lie one month. Recorded 6 Augt 1859.

Pages 223-224: Will of George W. GRIM. 23 July 1859. All to wife, Catharine, and then to 3 children, Charles H., James W., and Martha Ellen FLEET. Directs that his body "be buried according to the rights and ceremonies of the Church and that funeral be conducted in a manner corresponding with my estate and situation in life." Wit: L. P. COONTZ, John A. BUSH, A. B. TANGUARY. Proved 7 Jany 1860.

Pages 224-235: Inventory, Appraisement and Sale Account, Estate of William SIGAFOOSE, dec'd. March 8, 1858. Long list of items including butcher's tools, 2 Stovers of beer, 2 Barrels of Vinegar. Dwelling house and lot purchased, at Sale, by M. BRANNON for $1,200.00. Appraisers: Alfred SEAL, Atwell SHALL,

Marcus COPENHAVER. Recorded 5 May 1860.

Page 236: Estate of Lucy Ann LAYTON, dec'd., in account with R. E. BYRD. Paid Patrick CUNNINGHAM, one of the legatees; paid William TAYLOR, his legacy. Recorded 2 June 1864.

Pages 237-238: Will of Mrs. Emily S. PAGE. "Under a marriage contract between my husband and myself, I have the right to dispose by will of my property, 3 bonds of Milton H. MOORE, now in possession of my brother, Philip SMITH, my trustee." Have a neat, iron railing put around the graves of my father, mother and sister Mary in the old Lutheran Burying Ground. Gives to nephew, Dr. J. P. SMITH, to sisters, Sydney BRUCE & Ariann HOLLIDAY, to nieces, Caroline MARKLAND and Elizabeth HALL, to Bishop MEADE, to Rev. Cornelius WALKER, to step-daughter, Mrs. Tom PAGE. Brother, Philip SMITH, executor. 16 Jany 1860. Wit: Charles CHASE, Bettie MYERS, Louisa BREEDIN. Proved 4 August 1860.

Pages 239-241: The Estate of William SIGAFOOSE, dec'd., in account with John W. BARNES & Abraham NULTON, executors. 4 Augt 1860. Cash received from Sale of Real Estate. Some expenses paid: Medical accounts; to Robert LONG for schooling; legacy to Susan SIGAFOOSE and paid Nichena? PARKER "who married one of the heirs". Other payments to Oscar BARR, Leonard E. SWARTZWELDER, Martha COPENHAVER.

Pages 241-243: Will of Elizabeth D. SMITH. Thomas T. FAUNTLEROY, Jr., executor. Sell everything to provide for support of daughter, Alfreda, as long as she remains unmarried. Mentions slaves, China and Dink and children and China's child, William. Slave Nancy to be held in trust for daughter, Josepha N. SWARTZWELDER. Mentions daughter, Ann MORGAN, wife of Wm. A. MORGAN, of Jefferson County, Va. Also daughter, Mary Ann SWARTZWELDER, wife of Dr. A. C. SWARTZWELDER. 19 Decr 1860. Wit: T. T. FAUNTLEROY, Jr., E. W. BERKELY. Proved 5 Jany 1861.

Pages 243-247: Will of Sawney BELL. Wife, Milly, and "my children by her: Lewis, Hubbard, Susan, Hector, and Ferguson and such others as may be born to me by her hereafter" and all property, real & personal & mixed, are bequeathed to Dr. Hugh H. McGUIRE and Hector BELL, Esqr., or survivor of them. Wife to enjoy property only during her widowhood. 20 June 1857. Codicil added, same day, to say "Milly and her children to be emancipated and set free forever". Proved 5 Nov 1859. Hugh H. McGUIRE and Hector BELL, executors.

Page 248: Will of Margaret PRITCHARD, 13 Jany 1857. All to five daughters, Elizabeth S., Mary A., Caroline V., Emily I., and Frances C. Executor: Elizabeth A. Wit: Matthias SHULTZ, Robert HAMILTON. Proved Feby 1862.

Pages 248-251: Will of Mary Ann SMITH. All to Harriet H. RUSSELL, sister. Mentions stocks and bonds. At death of Harriet H. RUSSELL, $1,000 to Rev. A. A. H. BOYD, Pastor of Loudoun Street Presbyterian Church or his successor. Servant girl, Celia WILSON, to be set free after death of sister, Harriet, if the laws of Virginia will permit. Nephew, James B. RUSSELL; dec'd. brother, Isaac RUSSELL; brother, W. G. RUSSELL; niece Mary Elizabeth GIBSON. Sister, Harriet, sole executor. 15 Novr 1861. Wit: D. W. BARTON, G. S. MILLER. Proved 5 April 1862. Last page has Inventory of Property of Mrs. M. A. SMITH, with no date, no appraisers named. Among items: Bonds on C. RINKER and Wm. D. BROWN.

Pages 251-252: Will of Sarah A. SPOTTS. Gives to brother, Marcus SPOTTS and wife; to "my mother"; to George and Ann SEVERS. Copy of Clark's Commentary on the Bible to Mr. Jacob SNYDER. "My handsome Bible" and $5 to Rev. Wm. C. EGGLESTON. Jany 10, 1862. Wit: Daniel CONRAD, R. E. SEVERS. Proved Jany 3, 1863.

Pages 253-254: Will of Georgeanna HAINES. Gives to uncle, William C. CLARK, to husband's mother, Evelina HAINES, to sister, Elexina, wife of N. W. SNYDER. Leaves money to educate nephew, Alexander Hamilton STEWART. Wishes gravestones for self and husband. John Ike BAKER, executor, and guardian of nephew A. H. STEWART. (no date) Wit: J. B. T. REED, J. W. CAMPBELL, John SAGAN. Proved Jany 3, 1863.

Page 255: Will of Maria HOFF. (very short) Septr 23, 1862. All to brother, Matthias SHULTZ and he to be executor. Wit: William S. MILLER, J. A. MILLER. Proved Feby term of court, 1863.

Pages 255-257: Will of Matthias SHULTZ. To Robert B. WOLF as trustee for my brother, Lewis O. SHULTZ; to sister, Elizabeth, and brother, William; to niece, D. WOLF; "for Milly"; to two graveyards, Lutheran and German Reformed. Forgiving George ANDERSON and Joseph RENNY their debts. Jany 29, 1863. Wit: J. A. MILLER, R. B. YEAKLEY. Proved 7 Feby 1863. William S. & George F. MILLER, executors.

Pages 257-259: White Hall, Hanover County, Va, April 19th, 1864. Will of Martha C. REED. Real Estate shall be sold but "not haistily or sacrifised". Son, John B. T. REED, to be executor and "manage my business". All that daughters, Anna J. REESE and Martha V. MILLER receive is to be free from control of husbands. Mentions grandson, Robert W. REED. Wit: Thos. & Jas. T. DOSWELL, T. A. LATHAM, W. JENKINS, Edward JONES. Codicil, Winchester, June 24, 1865: executor given power to let daughters have their portions should they be in needy circumstances. Proved 2 Sept 1865.

The following pages have faded writing and confused, repeated page numbers:

Pages 259-261: Will of William S. MAGRUDER, 7 Oct 1865. Evelina SEEBRIGHT to occupy "house and lot in which I now reside for during her natural life provided she takes care and raises in a proper manner my three youngest children and for caring for me in my sickness". Three youngest children: Mary Elizabeth, Henry Clay and Gatapie? MAGRUDER. Son, Charles, has paid no part of purchase of house. Wit: Illegible, W. CATHER, C. A. COONTZ, Irving G. SMITH. Proved 4 Nov 1865.

Pages 262-263: Appraisal of Property of William AKIN, dec'd., 9 Octr 1865. Items: tool chest and many notes, including those of Wm. CARPER and James H. WILLIAMS. Appraisers: William H. STREIT, John KERR, John Z. JENKINS.

Page 264: Appraisal of Estate of Evy M. BUSH recorded, 10 Feby 1864. Mentions note of Charles A. BUSH. Appraisers: P. HANSUCKER, George McCANN, P. SHERRARD.

Page 264: Appraisal of Estate of Evelina FENTON, dec'd. 5 Dec 1865. Appraisers: Robert STEELE, J. S. CARSON, John KERR.

Pages 264-267: Will of Dr. Hunter Holmes BOYD. To wife, Ellen F. BOYD, "on condition that she does not marry again" all my bond and property. To sons, E. Holmes, Philip William, and Andrew Hunter. To wife house

& lot adjoining garden of George SEEVERS, the 5 acre lot opposite the Accadamy buildings. Mentions servant, William PARKER, for whom wife is to care. To son, Philip William, "my gold watch"; to sons, Andrew Hunter and E. Holmes, $100 each to purchase a watch for themselves. Much about wife's bequests depending on her maritial status after his decease. Codicil appoints wife executrix, with brother-in-law, Philip WILLIMS. Will & codicil dated 1 June 1864. Proved 6 Jany 1866.

Pages 267 and 268, also numbered 258: Will of Brutus JOHNSON, a man of colour. 7 Dec 1857. Mentions wife, unnamed, and "my brother Shedrock JOHNSON, called Shack". All property to wife to use as she wishes. At her death, to brother who is to pay to each "of my brothers & sisters" $2.00. Wit: Darn RUSSELL, James KERN, Henry STRIDER. Proved Mar 3, 1866.

Pages 258-259, also numbered 268-269: Will of Newton W. SNYDER. Wife, Elexina, to be executor and guardian of "our dear children". She also to carry out last will & Testament of Georgianna HAINES, her sister. 19 March 1866. Wit: W. S. LORD, Dorsey WALTER. Proved 5 May 1866.

Pages 259, also numbered 269, and 260: Will of Washington G. SINGLETON. All to wife, Maria. "I have but a small estate, to subdivide the same among all my children it would be but a mite." Two eldest daughters, Mary OFFUTT & Virginia BROWN, have good & thrifty husbands. Two unmarried daughters, Georganna & Josephine, are not in good health and incapable of making a living. Sons, Obed W., Alexander C., and William A. "are harty men, they can do as I have done. Make their own way through the world". "I am heir at law of my deceased son, William Marcus, who is one of the devisees of his grandfather, the late Obed WAITE." June 11, 1862. No witnesses but will "being wholly in the handwriting of the testator" was proved by Tho. T. FAUNTLEROY & Edward HOFFMAN, 7 July 1866.

Pages 260-261: Will of Arabella B. LUCKETT, widow of R. T. LUCKETT. To Dr. Levin LUCKETT, brother of husband; to nephew, William M. ATKINSON or to niece, Juliet ATKINSON, or to sister, Betty J. ATKINSON and Juliet O. WHITE. Mentions "my mother". Sister, Betty J. ATKINSON, and W. William BENT to be executors. No witness. 29 June 1863. Handwriting proved by A. P. WHITE & Robt. B. WHITE, 4 Aug 1866.

Pages 261-269: NOTE at top of page 267: "This page is wrong number. The true 267 is 10 pages to the left." Appraisal of the Estate of Georgianna E. HAINES, with W. G. RUSSELL, John Ker, Edward HOFFMAN as appraisers of personal property. Brick house & premises, corner of Braddock & Cork Streets, appraised by John B. T. REED, G. W. ANDERSON, E. HOFFMAN. Recorded in court 8 Oct 1866.

Page 269: Will of John ENDERS. To wife, Mary Ann, all real and personal property, after payment of just debts. After her death, to be equally divided "between her children". Wife to be executor. 20 April 1867. Wit: W. G. RUSSELL, C. W. REED, G. L. MILLER. Proved 14 June 1867.

Pages 270-272: Estate Account of Mrs. Georgeanna E. HAINES with John J. H. BAKER, executor. Begins Jany 3, 1863 with cash received by Confederate Treasury Notes on hand at testator's death; paid debts; paid Mrs. Alysina SNYDER. Paid legacy to Eveline HAINES. Recorded, Oct Term of Court, 1866. Some purchasers at estate Sale: Geo. E. BUSHNELL, Sam NOAKES, Stephen HARRY, Mrs. J.W. CAMPBELL. Sale recorded 8 Oct 1866.

Pages 272-273: Estate of Eveline FENTON, dec'd., with Robert T. BARTON, her admr. Income & Expenses beginning Dec 1865 with cash received of Wm. S. BENT, administrator of Belinda FENTON, dec'd., for interest due on Bond in possession of Eveline FENTON. Paid taxes & fees. Estate account recorded at August Term of Court, 1867.

Pages 273-276: Estate Account of James ENDERS, dec'd., a Lunatic, in account with Lewis T. MOORE, Committee. Among payments beginning Aug 1865, paid John PARKER, express to Lunatic Asylum & Ambulance Service; paid John ENDERS for board; paid Servant Milly for wood; paid Dr. John R. CONRAD; paid Mt. Hebron Cemetery and for stone. Received cash for rents. Charles M. CONRAD administered estate. Recorded in Court, Aug term, 1867.

Page 277: Estate of Horace SMITH, dec'd., with John SMITH, Admr. Begins July 4, 1866 with credit for cash received of Rail Road. Paid legal fees; for coffin and digging grave. Wearing apparel of deceased appraised at $7.50, which administrator has not been able to sell. Recorded Nov Court, 1867.

2nd Page 277: Lewis N. HUCK, commissioner, in account with Lewis K. PRIT-CHARD, a Lunatic. Income & Expenses beginning Jany 6, 1866, with cash received of B. T. BARTON; paid atty fees; paid freight on package to Staunton; paid 5% commission. Balance in hands of committee, May 31, 1867: $218.04. Recorded Nov Term of Court, 1867.

Pages 278-280: Estate of Martha C. REED, dec'd., in Account with her executor, J. B. T. REED. Begins June 28, 1865 with paid Mrs. Martha V. MILLER; paid for digging grave; paid taxes and repairs to house; paid John FAGAN for tombstones. Received rent payments from many people, including Wm A. BRADFORD and Dr. FLINN. Recorded June Court, 1868.

Pages 281-282: Estate of Jacob GRIM, dec'd., in Account with John C. ANDER-SON, Admr. Begins Feby 25, 1868, with cash of Lydia N. HARRY for interest on Notes. Then to Oct 5, 1866 making payments as to Mt. Hebron for grave, $5; paid J. S. STACKHOUSE for coffin; paid H. BAETJER & Co account; paid 5% commission on cash receipts. Made distribution of $18.32¼ to each of these legatees: Joshua S. PEREGOY & Julia Aker, his wife; J. F. BLESSING & Emily Jane, his wife; Jacob LYDER & Lucinda, his wife; John W. GRIM; Cornelia GRIM; Chas. PEREGOY in right of wife, Elizabeth; John C. ANDER-SON and Mary E., his wife. Recorded Aug Term, 1869.

Pages 283-285: Estate Account of Martha C. Reed, dec'd. May 1869. Dwelling in Winchester sold for $3,500 to Christopher REED. Receiving rents from Dr. FLINN, Wm. BRADFORD, D. H. DEWS. Paid Anna B. J. REECE on legacy, $20; paid Martha V. MILLER on legacy, $25.58. Recorded Nov Term, 1869.

Page 286: Will of Sarah NULTON, wife of Abraham NULTON. Husband had conveyed deed to her on 24 June 1869. Should he survive her, he is to have use of this property for support of himself and "my daughter, George Anna". Three children: George A. NULTON, Harriet, wife of George E. HAINES, and Catharine HERBERT, wife of Joseph HERBERT. Decr ____ 1869. Wit: G. S. HAYNIE, illegible, S. P. HOLLIDAY. Proved Feby Court, 1870.

Page 287: Report of Sales made by L. T. F. GRIM, Admr. of W. H. REESE. Personal property so small that a public sale was inadvisable, so sold privately: a suit of clothes, $20; a Box of Tools, $15. This is all personal property except Bonds & Notes. Signed: Levi T. F. GRIM, Admr. Recorded in Court, 7 Feby 1871.

Pages 288-290: Inventory & Appraisal of the Personal Estate of Thomas D. McCAN, dec'd. 11 Feby 1871, Wm. S. CALOHAN, JP. One half of the stock of goods of the late firm of T. D. McCAN & Co. appraised in bulk at $7,000 is $3,500. In arriving at value of stock, used inventory taken immediately after death of T. D. McCAN by H. Clay KREB. Appraisers: Wm. H. STREIT, John N. BELL, J. P. HEIRONIMUS. Recorded in court 27 Feby 1871.

Pages 290-292: Will of Robt. B. WOLFE. Begins: "Before death, I desire to leave on record some expression of my wishes with regard to the desposition of what off property real and personal I die possessed". To daughter, Elizabeth Ann SCHULTZ, the farm on which she resides plus horses. To son Godfrey Miller WOLFE, tract of land east of Martinsburg Pike, near Joliffe Farm, given to daughter, Elizabeth. To daughters, Fannie R. and Catherine Otto, rest of estate including storehouse & dwelling on east side Loudoun Street, the homestead where I now reside, the lot adjoining occupied by Rev. G. L. LEYBURN. Date: "this March 1871". Wit: G. S. MILLER, W. S. MILLER. Proved Saturday April 1st 1871.

Pages 293-298: Appraisal & Inventory of the Estate of Washn. G. SINGLETON, dec'd. Frederick County, 21 Sept 1868. Among items: 1 refrigerator, mahogany Beaurow & Pair Dining Tables, 25 pieces Dinner Ware, corner Book Shelf & Books. Appraisers: George W. ANDERSON, Edwd HOFFMAN, Jas. STACKHOUSE. Some purchasers at Estate Sale: W. ROUTZHAHN, Randle MARTIN, Mrs. SINGLETON. Recorded, Frederick County Court, Jany term, 1869. A. M. GIBBENS, Clk. Recorded in City Court, 30 March 1872.

Pages 299-304: Will of A. J. HELPHINSTINE. All to wife, Ann Carr HELPHINSTINE, without any limitations or reservations. Wife to be executrix. 15 July 1871. Wit: L. N. HUCK, Frank G. WALTER, O. P. HELPHINSTINE. Proved April 6, 1872. Appraisal of Estate by: Edward HOFFMAN, Geo. E. JENKINS, Geo. W. KURTZ. Among items: 1 Piano & Stool, 1 parlor Cook Stove, carpeting, can bottom chairs, Bookcase & Lot of Books. Appraisal recorded 15 April 1872.

Pages 305-310: Estate of W. G. SINGLETON in Account with Mrs. Maria A. SINGLETON, Exec. Begins Dec 12, 1868 with cash payments to auctioneers, printers, for taxes, legal services. At settlement, May 4, 1872, not sufficient funds to pay debts so gives to each claimant 16½%.

Pages 311-316: Sale of Personal Property of A. J. HELPHINSTINE, dec'd., at public auction, May 3, 1872. Among items: 1 Piano & Stool, not sold. Some purchases by: A. C. HELPHINSTINE, Mrs. HELPHINSTINE, H. BESORE and W. DESHANN. Recorded 3 Sept 1872.

Pages 317-324: Martha C. REED, dec'd., Estate Executional Account & Settlement, Sept 23, 1872. J. B. T. REED, executor and trustee for two married legatees. Paid commission, Clark fee bill, C. W. GIBBENS fee bill; paid Judge PARKER for legal fees. House & Lot sold to Christopher W. REED for $3,500. Distribution of Estate to Martha V. MILLER, Anna J. REESE, and John B. T. REED. Recorded in court, Decr 7, 1872.

Pages 325-333: Will of John H. AULICK, a Commadore in the Navy of the United States, now in Washington City. "It is my will, intention and positive instructions." Mentions house & lots in Washington City as well as Brick House on 18th Street occupied by late son, Dr. Ralph O?. AULICK. Mentions having an interest in Cincinnati Gas Light & Coke Company. Bequeaths one-third to each: Son, J. Wiley AULICK; grandson, Richmond Ogston AULICK, the son and only heir at law of the late Richmond AULICK, of the US Navy; and grand-

daughters, Julia M. STOUT and Mary B. STOUT. Also gives to Alberta AULICK.
Executors to be J. Wyly AULICK & Samuel V. NILES, both of Washington, D. C.
14 Octr 1872. Wit: Chas D. MAXWELL, Wm. LEE, M. D., E. A. PROTORS. Most
of will done in D. C. but was recorded in Winchester Court, June 7, 1873.
Proved May 3, 1873.

Pages 334-335: Lewis K. PRITCHARD, Lunatic, in account with Lewis N. HUCK,
his Committee. Income & Expenses as cash received of R. T. BARTON, and paid
for clothing and clerk's fee. Settlement, Sept 5, 1873 with Funds of $242
due the Lunatic. Recorded Sept 6, 1873.

Pages 336-337: Will of Elizabeth CONRAD. Wills house on N. W. Corner, Kent
& Clifford, to son George W. CONRAD "if he does not rent the house or lot".
If son dies and leaves a "widdow", she shall have all rights & privileges
as long as she remains his widdow. Mentions "my children". Son-in-law,
James BELL to be executor. 29 April 1872. Wit: David BARRETT, Edward
JONES, J. W. HAYMAKER. Proved April 11, 1874.

Page 338: Will of Margaret BYRD. Residence and furniture to sister, Emily
FENESTER. Balance to sisters, Emily FENESTER and Ann WARD. 21 April 1874.
Wit: Fred. M. W. HOLLIDAY, Wm. BYRD. Proved May 18, 1874.

END OF WILL BOOK NO. 2

Page 1 is blank.

Pages 2-3: Appraisal of Personal Estate of Mrs Jane TURNER, dec'd., by
George KREMER, Jr., John HOOVER, John DIFFENDERFER, May 21, 1874. Small
inventory: household items totaling $46.80 and one Note of James S. WELCH
for $230. Recorded in court, 13 July 1874.

Pages 4-5: Will of Charles HARDY, 6 March 1874. Wife, Lucy, to get all
personal property including Rail Road or other stock. Also all real estate
with the request that she "appropriate a reasonable portion of her income
to support unmarried daughters, Martha and Harriet, so long as they remain
single". Friend, Henry KINZEL to be executor. Wit: George W. GRIM,
J. A. NULTON. Proved 20 July 1874.

Pages 6-7: Appraisal of personal estate of David BARTON, dec'd., by Stephen
STACKHOUSE, W. T. GILBERT, Sam'l. L. LAREW, 26 Sept 1874. Among items:
cash of $411.62; clothing and household items, rocking chair & 8 cane bot-
tom chairs; accounts due from E. PENDLETON, Stephen STACKHOUSE, W. L. DORSEY.

Pages 8-18: Appraisal of Personal Property of Richard SIDWELL, dec'd.,
30 Sept 1874. Some items: Walnut Side Table, Mahogany Lounge, Parlor Stove,
Linens, much carpeting; Stock in Shop & Yard: 121 sides, Dressed upper
leather, fine calfskins, cords of bark; long list of Bonds, Notes, and
Accounts due as that of Joel LUPTON, "doubtful". Has Shares of Capital Stock
in W&M Turnpike Co., and in "the Frederick County of the Valley of Va" which
is of doubtful value. Appraisal completed Octr 2, 1874, by John C. COE,
T. V. PURCELL, Wm. H. HARDY.

Page 19: Appraisal of Personal Estate of Benjamin ROBINS, dec'd. "No property found belonging to B. ROBINS." 14 Nov 1874. Appraisers: John G.
MILLER, B. NOONAN, Samuel EVANS.

Pages 20-21: Inventory & Appraisal of Estate of Margaret BYRD, dec'd.
July term of Court, 1874. Bond by J. R. RICHARDS, dated Mar 23, 1850;
Bonds of Geo. H. & Wm. BYRD. Total value of bonds and interest: over
$12,000. Household furniture devised to Mrs. E. FENESTER. Appraisers:
Wm. BYRD, Fred. W. M. HOLLIDAY, L. N. HUCK.

Page 22: Appraisal of Personal Estate of John ORRICK, dec'd., made by
court-appointed appraisers: Wm. M. ATKINSON, R. T. BARTON, E. Holmes
BOYD, April 10, 1875. Only item: 1 draft for $130.00. Due James FULLER-
TON, of Washington, D. C., as attorney, $32.50.

Pages 23-27: Will of Robert Y. CONRAD, Attorney at Law, "wholly written by
my own hand". To unmarried daughter, Catherine Brooke CONRAD, $500 annually.
Whole estate to be charged with said annuity until death or marriage of said
daughter. To son, Dr. Daniel Burr CONRAD, books and oil portraits of grandfather, Danil CONRAD, grandmother, Mrs. Powell, and "of myself". To son,
Holmes CONRAD, entire library of law books, 2 portraits of Govenor HOLMES &
other pictures as Kate and Sallie FAUNTLEROY may not choose. To son, Charles
Frederick, gold watch & shirt buttons plus $500; to son, Frances Edward,
razor, shaving, & toilet apparatus, ½ of wearing apparel plus $500; to son,
George Cuthbert Powell, encyclopaedia, dictionaries, books on languages &
other teaching books. House & lot to be chosen by any child. Sons, Daniel

Burr, Holmes and Charles Frederick to be executors. 19 Aug 1872. Codicil on real estate added 14 Sept 1874. Proved 17 May 1875.

Pages 28-29: Will of Lydia NEILL. All personal property and land in Frederick County to nephew, Lewis N. HUCK, with whom she has lived so many years. Land in Clarke County to Mrs. Catharine NEILL, wife of Dr. S. S. NEILL and at her death, to children "absolutely free from the debts of her husband, past, present and future". Lewis N. HUCK to be executor. 5 Feby 1875. Proved 21 June 1875.

Pages 29-32: Will of Evelina U. STREIT, Febry 20, 1874. "In consideration of the difficulties which may arise from not making a will, I have consented to dispose of my little property as follows." To niece, Elizabeth S. WALKER, personal property except small items to Fannie BRENT, Amie STREIT, Fannie, Emma and Nellie BROWN. Sell house and lot and divide to Susan BROWN, Potia BAKER, Emily C. BAKER, Amie STREIT. Proved 19 July 1875. Appraisal and Inventory of Estate of Evelina STREIT, dec'd., by John N. BELL, E. HOFFMAN, and George W. KURTZ. Misc. household and personal items, including 1 chamber set, consisting of W. stand, Ewer & Basin & Chamber Soap Stand. House and Lot sold for $1,150. Admitted to court, Augt 10, 1875.

Pages 33-42: Appraisal and Inventory of Estate of George KREMER, Jr., dec'd. 22 April 1875. Appraisers: Robt. T. KURTZ, Isaac H. FAULKNER, H. S. BAKER, C. B. HANCOCK. Inventory made according to rooms of the house, as "south room, upstairs; front room, east; garrett in front house". Much furniture. Venetians blinds; Piano, stool & coves; Bathing Tubs; 10 stoves rented out; much lumber and tools; many notes due. Margaret V. KREMER, Admin.

Pages 43-45: Will of Henry M. BRENT. "My father-in-law, Lewis HOFF, sister-in-law, Margaret Ann HOFF, died intestate. My lamented wife, Caroline Issabella, the mother of my three sons, inherited an interest in their real estates valued at $3,000, now $10,000." Mentions "large advances to and payments for my Charles Lewis BRENT". To each of my sons, Edwin Sours BRENT and Henry Moore BRENT, Jr., $3,500. "Feeling it equally incumbent on me to restore in money or kind whatever I received by or thru my lamented wife, Harriet Elizabeth, to her daughter and only child, Caroline Moore BRENT, I give and devise to my daughter, Caroline Moore, her mother's wardrobe plus spoons given to her mother by her father, Jacob BAKER." Sons, Edward S. & Henry M., Jr., in trust for wife and children of son, C. Lewis, not for his debts or control. Also a trust for daughter, Caroline Moore BRENT, in no manner subject to any future husband. Mentions codicil to will of Feby 7, 1859. Friend, William B. BAKER, and sons, Edwin S. & Henry M. BRENT to be executors. 22 April 1873. Proved Nov. 13, 1875.

Pages 46-48: Will of George W. LEYBURN. "George William LEYBURN, of Rockbridge County, now of Winchester." All property, real and personal, to wife, Elizabeth Winston LEYBURN. Mentions unmarried daughter, Isabella. Son, George L. LEYBURN, brother, John LEYBURN, and son-in-law, Thomas E. CONVERSE, to be execs. 10 March 1875. Wit: J. R. HOLT, J. H. HOLT. Proved 15 Nov. 1875. No mention was made of witnesses to will; handwriting of testator sworn to by J. B. RUSSELL and R. B. HOLLIDAY. Two of named executors, John LEYBURN and Thomas E. CONVERSE, refused executorship. The other named executor, as well as the widow of the decedent "having been proved non-residents of the US and in more than 30 days having expired since death of decedent and no distributee having applied for administration", E. Holmes BOYD was appointed administrator.

Pages 49-51:   Inventory & Appraisal of Estate of Rev. George L. LEYBURN, dec'd., 29 Novr 1875, by Wm. BOYD, E. P. DANDRIDGE, R. B. HOLLIDAY. Estate consisted of Certificates, City of Winchester Bonds, Virginia registered bonds, 20 shares stock of Union Bank of Winchester, bonds of unknown value of A. LEYBURN, Abijah THOMAS, W. T. & Thomas CAMPBELL, James T. JOHNSON, Robert MILLER.

Pages 52-57: Will of John KERR, 30 April 1870. To Eliza GLENHOMES, small house on northside of Cork Street, now occupied by Bennet HILLYARD. Also stock in Shenandoah Valley Bank and Nat'l. Bank of Staunton. To William BYRD, trustee, house and lot northeast corner, Water & Braddock Streets, plus $1,000 for benefit of children Cornelius KIGER has or may have. To William BYRD, trustee, stock in Winchester Gas Co. for benefit of children of Frederick H. ROSENBERGER by his present wife. To Geo. W. KURTZ and James P. KREMER, all tools, benches, utensils of trade used in and about my shop at a fair valuation and a sufficient amount of money to give to each a legacy of $1,000, and requests they see that grave shall be walled up and iron railing put around lot. (Written across this last bequest: THIS PART IS CANCELLED BY MR. JOHN KERR FOR BASE INGRATITUDE.) Set up trusteeship on his entire house on Loudoun & Water Streets to Market Square to be used for education of the poor, white children of Winchester. To longtime friend, Charles HARDY, $2,000. Lewis P. HARTMAN and Robert STEELE to be executors. 30 April 1870. Wit: John U. BELL, F. S. BOWEN. Changes made to will re Bennett HILLIARD, 10 Nov 1875. Wit: F. S. BOWEN, Robt STEELE. More changes, same day,to give to Stephen STACKHOUSE "all my ready made coffins & hardware, work benches, tools, hearse".

On page 55, there is another will with no mention of revoking a former will and/or codicils. It gives to Eliza GLENHOLMES, housekeeper; to Martha and Harriet HARDY, daughters of friend, Charles HARDY, dec'd.; to Theodore WINDLE, in trust for Emma KIGER, daughter of Cornelius KIGER; to John KIGER 92 acre farm in Frederick County; to Mrs. Mary ROSENBERGER, wife of Frederick H. ROSENBERGER, the three-story brick house corner of Loudoun & Water Sts. to be shared with her six children; Stephen STACKHOUSE bequest same as above. 10 Nov 1875. Wit: Wm. P. McGUIRE, Wm. A. BELL, G. T. MILLER, J. G. SMITH. Will was proved 20 Dec 1875, by John U. BELL, Jr., F. S. BOWEN & ROB'T STEELE. Codicils proved as executed on 12 Nov 1875 by Wm. P. McGUIRE, Wm. A. BELL, James G. SMITH.

Pages 58-64: Inventory and Appraisal of Estate of John KERR, dec'd., by James G. SMITH, S. P. STACKHOUSE, E. Holmes BOYD. Very large estate including such things as large Mirrors with gilt frames, much mahogany furniture, silk umbrella, rugs, coffins, lumber, hardware, stock in banks and railroad, Notes of Episcopal Female Institute and other notes. Appraisal returned to court, 22 Decr 1875.

Pages 65-68: Inventory and Appraisal of Estate of W. C. MEREDITH, dec'd. 4 Decr 1875. Appraisers: F. W. M. HOLLIDAY, Wm. L. CLARK, T. N. HUCK. Among items: mahogany & walnut furniture, marble top tables, refrigerator, baby's crib, molasses cruet, 4 safety lamps, many dishes, Theological and misc. library.

Pages 69-70: Inventory and Appraisal of Estate of Hugh H. McGUIRE, dec'd., Jany 26, 1876, with appraisers: Ed. M. TIDBALL, E. Holmes BOYD, Wm. M. ATKINSON. Total estate: 2 Bookcases, 1 old rocking chair, 3 old chairs, one settee frame, 1 lot of old Medical Books, mostly in French, 1 lot of old Bottles. A number of Book Accounts all of which are barred by Statute of Limitations & mostly worthless at all event. Appraisers thought not proper to value them at anything.

Pages 71-84: Inventory and Appraisal of Estate of Henry M. BRENT, dec'd.,
29 Jan 1876, with Lewis N. HUCK, Wm. B. BAKER, John G. MILLER, appraisers.
Large inventory beginning with cash in bank, $514.54; many Bonds, some
held as collateral security by E. S. BRENT & Shenandoah Valley Bank. Much
property in "Mansion House", including high post bedsteads, 5 Stoves, sheets,
pillow cases, parlor curtains, comforts, spring mattress, candle labras.
Additional inventory and appraisal in Shenandoah County, by E. T. HOLMES,
and Briscoe SHULL. Farm of 598 acres with house, household fixtures and
farm tools. Recorded in court Feby 12, 1876.

Pages 85-86: Estate of Jane TURNER, dec'd., in Account with R. B. YEAKLEY,
her admin. Begins June 2, 1874, with income received as that from Bond of
Nancy CLARK and Note of WELSH. Expenses included that for Coffin & tombstones, $16.00; digging grave, $2.50; appraisers & clerk's fees. Distribution was made to Mrs. Nancy F. CLARK and _____ McNABB. 19 June 1876.

Pages 87-93: Appraisal of Estate of Henry QUANTZ, dec'd. 19 June 1876.
Appraisers: John G. MILLER, Jas. H. BARNHART, Rob't. W. BRECKENRIDGE.
Among items: 1 large 4-horse Wagon, old wagon wheels, carts, axiels, one
new spring wagon, other wagons & parts, spokes, shavers, workbenches,
household items and blacksmith tools. Recorded 6 Sept 1876.   Sale of
personal Property of Henry QUANTZ, July 31, 1876. Among items sold: one
Lot of Wheels & Hubbs, Axels, Cart & bed, Tools, Anvill, Bellows, Rockaway.
Several purchases by Jon. VILWIG and S. F. LAYMAN. Household items purchased by Louise QUANTZ. Sale recorded 6 Sept 1876.

Pages 94-97: Will of Norval WILSON. To wife, Cornelia L. WILSON, house &
lot on Loudoun Street, all household & Personal property, all money, including "all monies of mine in my son Alpheus' hands". To wife also the
annuity due from Conference Funds, and gold watch. To son, Alpheus W.
WILSON, 3,000 acres land in Calhoun County, WVa. To T. H. HAVENNER and
"my daughter", Mary Cornelia HAVENNER, one half "my books". To daughter,
Augusta Virginia WILSON, bond for $3,000 by Edmund H. WILSON, now of New
York City. To son-in-law, Wm. G. GALLAGHER, 500 acres on Cheat River,
Preston County, WVa, and 100 shares Cumberland Turnpike stock. To son-
in-law, Wm. G. RUSSELL, Jr., 3 bonds on Thos. STRIDER and $420 due from
Corporation Court of Winchester. Wife, Cornelia T. WILSON and son, Alpheus
WILSON, to be executors. 18 June 1868. Wit: Jas. B. RUSSELL, Isaac W.
RUSSELL. Codicil, 14 Oct 1870: to Augusta V. WILSON, amount of bond due
from Ed. H. WILSON, $3953.14, less $1,000 to Alice, wife of Wm G. RUSSELL.
Codicil, 5 Apr 1873: to Augusta, house & lot on Loudoun Street, present
address. To daughter, Mrs. HAVENNER, return of "Wheeles chair furnished
to her mother". Among other bequeaths: "I leave my blessing with my
children. They have been a source of comfort to me." Wit: Jas. B. &
Isaac W. RUSSELL. Proved 18 Sept 1876. Cornelia L. WILSON is dead and
Alpheus W. WILSON, other named executor, refused the executorship.
Augusta Virginia WILSON to administer.

Page 98: Edmond ROBESON will. (very short will) To daughter, Mary S.
ROBESON, deed of trust on this house & lot to amount of $400. To wife,
Mary, all furniture and monies. Wit: Andrew HARKNESS, James KERN, John
HARDY. July 22, 1875. Proved 21 Sept 1876.

Pages 99-101: Estate of Mrs. Margaret BYRD, dec'd., in Account with Geo.
W. WARD, her admin. Begins Aug 1874, with income which is mostly from Bonds;
among expenses paid: to Casper NOONAN, hacks at funeral; paid taxes &
funeral expenses; paid balance to Miss Emily FENESTER & Mrs. Ann WARD,
wife of Geo. W. WARD, each $4,672.04. Geo. W. WARD, Admin., overpaid each

legatee by $227.96. Estate account recorded July 26, 1876.

Pages 102-103: Inventory and Appraisal of Estate of Hannah GRANT, dec'd. 20 Novr 1876, Samuel L. LAREW, Geo. W. ANDERSON, John H. NULTON, appraisers. Total estate: one bond on Isaac W. BROWN, col'd., dated Apr 29, 1872; Account of Savings Bank of Baltimore in favor of Hannah GRANT, col'd; one bed & bedding; one trunk & contents; 2 rocking chairs. Produced in court, 22 Novr 1876.

Pages 104-107: Inventory and Appraisal of Estate of Marion M. HITE, dec'd., 22 Novr 1876, with appraisers: C. B. MEREDITH, Chas. W. HENSELL, Philip W. BOYD, Frank G. WALKER, Henry BAETJER. Total personal estate: 20 shares stock in Union Bank of Winchester; 1 gold watch, Due Bill of Jno. W. CHAMBERLIN, dated Dec 11, 1869; deceased's interest in the firm of Hite & Wall, valued at $2,517.47. Mentions firm's Inventory of School Books & Circulating Library and shares of stock in schools as Valley Female College and Episcopal Female Institute. Much appraising went into calculating the deceased's share in the firm. T. T. WALL is the surviving partner. Produced in court 2 Decr 1876.

Pages 108-117: Sale Bill of Estate of Henry M. BRENT, dec'd., returned by R. T. BARTON, Admr. Begins with one eggbeater, 36¢. Long list of items including 50 Vols. "Enciclopedea" purchased by M. McCORMICK. Other items were: Parlor Furniture, Mirror, lamps, spring bed bottom, toilet cover, refrigerator, ice cream plates, 4-horse wagon. Purchasers: John HARMON, Geo. EAGLE, A. COLSTON, Chas. BOXWELL, Bush HAYTER, Dr. BROMBACK, and many others. Much bought by H. M. & E. S. BRENT. Featherbed, 56½ pounds, bought by John S. LUPTON. Bond of James STENSON "sued upon". Mentions claim vs estate of D. W. BARTON; Accounts due of Mrs. C. RIELY and Chas. J. BRENT (both are dec'd. and insolvent); Note of Jos. NEAL, insolvent.

Pages 118-119: Inventory and Appraisement of Estate of Norval WILSON, dec'd. 18 Sept 1876. Total inventory: one Lot Furniture, $100; one Lot Books, $30; 100 shares Cumberland Turnpike stock - worthless; Claim against Thos. STRIDER - worthless. Appraisers: W. G. RUSSELL, John H. MILLER, W. L. DORSEY. Augusta V. WILSON, Admr. Recorded 13 Decr 1876.

Pages 120-121: Guardianship account of Frederick W. QUANTZ in account with C. B. HANCOCK, his guardian. Begins June 1876 with cash received from Baltimore & Ohio Railroad Co. less fees of attorneys, clerks, commission. Balance due ward: $408.97. According to deposition of mother, ward was 21 years of age on 5 Sept 1876, so guardianship account is settled. Recorded Decr 18, 1876.

Pages 122-123: Inventory and Appraisal of Estate of Philip SHEARER, dec'd. with M. W. (later M. T.) ROYSTON, P. H. SHEARER, Alex. McCORMICK, appraisers. Small inventory, totaling $30.00. Parlor Stove, Ten plate Stove, Beaureau, 2 chares, 8-day Clock, 3 Dining Plates, 2 Goblets & 1 Tumbler. Produced in Court 13 Feby 1877.

Pages 124-125: Sale Bill of Personal Property of Marion M. HITE, dec'd. Dec 1876 - Jan 1877. Deceased had half interest in firm of Hite & Wall which was purchased by Thos. T. WALL, surviving partner, who assumed all debts of the firm. One gold Watch purchased by Mary A. HITE for $75; 20 shares Union Bank Stock purchased by Mary A. & Mary F. HITE. Produced in court 28 March 1877.

Page 126: Will of Manan H. AFFLICK, May 24, 1875. (Very short will.) All bonds and property to sister, Janet AFFLICK. She to be executrix. Wit: G. T. & W. L. MILLER. Proved 16 April 1877.

Pages 126-128: Will of Godfrey S. MILLER. All property and estate of every kind to three daughters, equally except in event of marriage. Two oldest daughters, Emma McConnel MILLER and Margaretta MILLER, to execute will and be guardian of younger daughter, Marianna. If any marries, that daughter gets one-fourth of the estate. Mentions 40 acres of land owned in Council Bluffs, Iowa and some lots in Marona County. 21 Decr 1876. Wit: C. W. REED, W. A. BELL. Proved 16 April 1877.

Page 129: Will of Abraham WASHINGTON. Appoints sister, Mary Jane PEYTON, executrix. To sister, house and lot on Baker Alley, Eastern Section of Town. To sister, all household items "together with my house, wagon and hogs". Acknowledges that deed of Brutus JOHNSON is right. 27 March 1871. His mark certified by James KERN, F. H. ROSENBERGER, Harry STRIKER. Proved 22 May 1877.

Page 130: Estate account of Philip SHERRER, dec'd. Philip HANSUCKER, complainant vs Philip SHERRER's Admr. et al - Defendants. Clerk of Circuit Court certified that the Accounts of Philip HANSUCKER, Admr. of Philip SHERRER, have been settled in above case. Recorded in court 5 July 1878.

Pages 131-133: Will of James STRIKER. All property to wife, Susan Catherine STRIKER. After her death, to son James H. STRIKER, 5-acre lot adjoining Kohlhousen & Baker. If he has no issue, this property to other children. To two sons, Vans (Vance?) W. and James H. STRIKER house & lot fronting on Market Street. After death of wife, lot on Cork Street plus money to daughter, Sidney HAMILTON, wife of David HAMILTON and her children by late husband, George CONRAD. Son, James H. STRIKER to pay $800 to daughter, Rebecca HAMILTON, wife of James HAMILTON. 3 May 1875. Wit: T. U. PURCELL, Chas. W. HOLLIS. Codicil 29 March 1877, to change amount of money to be paid to Sidney and Rebecca HAMILTON from $800 to $600. Proved 16 July 1877. James H. STRIKER, administrator.

Pages 134-135: Will of Elizabeth WALL. All property after payment of debts to two single daughters, Martha M. and Virginia A. WALL. Mentions "all my children and/or their descendants". Sons, Wm. W. WALL and T. T. WALL and son-in-law, James W. BARR, executors. ____ day of ____ 1877. Wit: P. O. FISHER, J. W. BARR. Proved 16 July 1877. Wm. W. and T. T. WALL refused executorship.

Page 136: Miss E. W. QUANTZ in Account with C. B. HANCOCK, her guardian. Begins June 1876 with amount received from B&O Railroad Co. and invested in bond. Payment made to magistrate. Guardianship account closed 17 Sept 1877.

Pages 137-142: Estate of H. M. BRENT, dec'd., in account with R. T. BARTON, Admr. Begins Novr 1875 with receipts from Shend. Valley Nat'l. Bank; paid John VILWIG and B. NOONAN in full for funeral expenses; many payments to Barton & Boyd, including "retainer fees in Suit in Chancery of M. B. BUSH Trust"; paid Jacob SENSENEY's estate and ROBERT's estate; paid E. M. BARR for walling grave of H. M. BRENT; mentions Suit of BRENT's Admrs. vs BRENT's heirs. Recorded in Court 17 Sept 1877.

Pages 142-145: Will of Elizabeth Ann SNYDER. To nephew, James Henry MARKELL, stone House and Lot on Braddock Street adjoining William T. GILBERT & others. House and Lot on Loudoun Street adjoining Shenandoah Valley National Bank to nephew, Arthur Senseney MARKELL and to his child, if he has any. To namesake and adopted niece, Elizabeth Baker BAILY, wife of Hezekiah B. BAILY, of Covington, Ky. Requests "neat & substantial tombstones for my beloved mother, my dear brother Henry and his two sons, John and Edward". Mentions David H. SNYDER, grandson of late husband Daniel SNYDER. Also gives to sister's friend, Mary P. GRIFFITH, wife of Aaron H. GRIFFITH. To nephew, Charles W. BAKER, son of brother Isaac BAKER, "my large gold Spectacles, formerly belonging to my father". Aaron H. GRIFFITH to be executor. Wit: Tilman SHUMATE, Nathan A. BRENT, Thos. G. MESMER. April 29, 1874. Codicil, 5 May 1877, appoints Isaac N. GRIFFITH executor instead of Aaron H. GRIFFITH, now deceased. Proved 17 Sept 1877.

Page 145: (very small will) Will of Hunter B. MARCH. Gives all property to Charles E. MARCH and he to be executor. Augt 17, 1877. Wit: Daniel BUSH, George E. JENKINS. Proved 17 Sept 1877.

Pages 146-147: Will of Ann H. RANDOLPH. All property to mother, Catharine HAMS?, of Brandow, Prince George County, Va. At mother's death, all to nephew, William Randolph SMITH, only son of "my deceased sister, Rose SMITH". 13 April 1874 Wit: William BYRD, Jennie BYRD. Proved 18 Sept 1877.

Page 147: Will of John LINN. To two sisters, Ann Elizabeth HOCKMAN and Catherine HOPEWELL, bond due from William EVANS for the Storehouse on Loudoun Street. Rest of estate to wife, Elizabeth LINN. 16 Novr 1876. Wit: Geo. F. GLAIZE, W. T. GILBERT. Proved 18 Sept 1877.

Page 148: Will of Nancy H. WHITE. (very short will) All to dear sister, Arabella B. LUCKETT. 1 Aug 1859. No witnesses. Proved 18 Sept 1877. Juliet A. McCAW subscribed that she was well acquainted with deceased's handwriting.

Pages 149-155: Estate of W. C. MEREDITH in Account with A. M. SMITH, his Admr. In 1876 and 1877, received cash from sale of books and household items. Paid expenses as stamps, rent of room to sell books, twine for packaging, and crying sale; paid Mt. Hebron for digging grave. Scheme of Distribution: distribute $961.16 among the $1,903.10 of indebtedness. Paid 50½% of bills owed to Dunlavy JONES, William T. GILBERT, Mrs. Hugh McGUIRE, Wm. H. STREIT and others. Account settled 15 Oct 1877. There were 4 pages of detailed accounts against Dr. W. C. MEREDITH.

Pages 156-158: Estate of Rev. G. W. LEYBURN, dec'd. Begins Nov 1875, with fees paid to Barton & Boyd for motion to qualify & proving will. Mentions suit in Bedford County of Baker vs Scruggs. Paid amounts to Mrs. E. W. LEYBURN, widow. In account with E. Holmes BOYD, Admr., receipts of division of bank stock, coupouns of Winchester bonds & railroad stock. Estate account closed 19 Nov 1877.

Pages 159-163: Will of Mary KOHLHOUSEN. To two step-sons, James H. MARSHELL and Arthur MARSHELL, each $600. They to receive "annual interest or profits from these amounts during their lifetime and principal to legal heirs after their deaths". 8 April 1876. Wit: Wm. BYRD, L. M. HUCH. Codicil, Octr 13, 1877. To The Trustees of The Diocesan Missionary Society of Virginia, $500. A note on F. W. KOHLHOUSEN for $300: at his death to Trustees of the Indian Mission. Note against "my brother Joseph PAINTER for five or six hundred dollars" to be assigned to John Rob't. PAINTER and Wm. Henry PAINTER, two deaf children, sons of Wm. Henry PAINTER. Requests suitable tombstones, in Mt. Hebron, for self and for Mrs. John MARSHELL to correspond with that of John MARSHELL. Gives to Trustees of Clinch Episcopal Church, Winchester, and to sister, Ann CARSON, Marion? County, Missouri. Mahogany bureau to Mary Virginia MARSHELL, daughter of Henry MARSHELL, and other bureau to Adeline SISCOE, Col'd. Friend, James B. RUSSELL, to be exec. 13 Octr 1877. Wit: Amanda E. HUFF, Harriet H. RUSSELL. Codicil, 14 Oct 1877, gives to James B. RUSSELL, amounts of any of above legacies that "become illegal or void". Wit: W. S. LOVE, F. W. KOHLHOUSEN. Proved 19 Novr 1877.

Pages 163-164: Will of John W. HAYMAKER. To wife, Sophia, all property of every kind. At her death, divide equally among children: to wit, George W., Edward D., Henry, Lewis, and John Isaac. 29 Jany 1872. Wit: John C. COE, John B. JENKINS, C. A. B. COFFROTH. Proved 17 Decr 1877.

Pages 165-166: Estate of Margaret BYRD, dec'd., in Account with George W. WARD, her Admr. Begins Decr 9, 1875, with amounts received from "Timberlake Claim, D. SOWER's Claim and D. FUNSTEN's Admr". Distribution to Miss Emily FUNSTEN, George W. WARD. Estate account closed 21 Jany 1878.

Pages 166-169: Estate of Evelina N. STREIT. Begins with cash paid for digging grave and hack hire; paid Mrs. SHIELDS and others for nursing board; paid state taxes for 1873-1875; made several payments to Wm. H. STREIT on house and lot with interest. Balance due estate: $165.08, $41.27 to each of Mrs. O. M. BROWN, Miss Potra BAKER, Mrs. Emily C. BAKER, Miss Annie STREIT. At court, 21 Jany 1878, settled the account of Samuel L. LAREW, Admr. of Evelina N. STREIT, dec'd.

Page 170: Appraisal & Inventory of Personal Property of Jno. W. HAYMAKER, dec'd. (Small inventory) Kitchen and bedroom furniture, Lounge, Sofa & Stools, 2 carpets, Bible, Picture Frames, "furniture upstairs". Total inventory: $141.00. 22 Dec 1877. Appraisers: Thomas LATHAM, Edwin G. JENKINS, C. W. ANDERSON.

Page 171: Will of Jacob McCORD. House and Lot "where I now reside" on northeast corner, Cork & Kent Streets to two daughters, Anny and Martha Virginia McCORD. Also all household and kitchen furniture. Daughter, Anny, to be executrix. 17 Novr 1874. Wit: Atwell SHULL, Chas. W. HOLLIS, David BARNETT. Proved 18 March 1878.

Pages 172-174: John Z. JENKINS will. Wife, Sarah, all property. After her death, to adopted son, Edwin G. GILES, including reasonable support of wife's sister, Rosannah HAYMAKER. Wife to be executrix. 29 Jany 1872. Wit: John W. HAYMAKER, John C. COE, C. A.B. COFFROTH. Proved June 2, 1873, in Frederick County Court. On 16 March 1878, James P. RIELY, Clerk of the County Court, certified that the foregoing is a true copy of John Z. JENKINS will as filed in Frederick County Will Book for year 1873. 18 March 1878, Frederick County presented authenticated copy of will to City of Winchester for recording as all property devised is in the city.

Pages 175-176: Will of Elizabeth WEAVER. To James WEAVER, of Luray, Page Co., portrait of his mother "now owned by me". Sell balance of property, including house and lot on west side of Loudoun Street and all contents. Apply to funeral expenses and just debts. Buy marble slabs for self and son, Lewis WEAVER, "who departed this life a few months since". Whatever remains to Rev. Samuel ROGERS, in trust for congregation of Braddock Street Methodist Episcopal Church South. Rev. Norval WILSON and Dorsey WALTER appointed executors. 10 July 1875. Wit: T. A. LATHAM, Margaret A. WILLIAMS. Proved 25 March 1878. 26 March 1878, Dorsey WALTER, the surviving executor named in the will, qualified.

Pages 177-178: Miss E. W. QUANTZ in Account with Charles B. HANCOCK, her Guardian. Begins June 15, 1877 with Interest received and payments made to Mrs. QUANTZ for ward. Feb 10, 1878, Charles B. HANCOCK settled Account in full with present guardian, John C. PFEIFFER. Recorded in Court 18 Mar 1878.

Pages 178-180: Will of Harriet A. MILLER. Silverware to granddaughter, Florence A. SHIELDS. To grandson, William MILLER, remainder of estate and he to be executor. 1 Augt 1870. Wit: Rob't. L. BAKER, Camillus S. BAKER, F. BAKER. On 8 May 1871 revokes clause giving to Florence A. SHIELDS and gives all to grandson, Willie MILLER. Proved 15 April 1878. At that time Rob't. L. BAKER is deceased. As no witnesses to codicil, Hays SHIELDS and Wm. B. BAKER verified handwriting.

Pages 181-189: Inventory and Appraisal of Personal Property of Mrs. Harriet A. MILLER with W. MILLER, executor. 1st and 2nd June 1878. Long inventory including: dozen parlor chairs, silk-covered sofa & two other sofas; large vases; candlabras; silk-faced window curtains; marble-top tables; damask linen tablecloths and napkins; 10 chamberpots; two silk chambers. Appraisers: H. S. BAKER, W. B. BAKER, Jno. J. WILLIAMS. Recorded in court 7 June 1878.

Pages 190-194: Inventory and Appraisal of Estate of Mary KOHLHOUSEN, dec'd. 19 Nov 1877, with W. L. DORSEY, John G. MILLER, B. NOONAN, Appraisers. Appraised household items as bequeathed to Henry MARSHELL, Adaline SISCOE, col'd., and to Wm. Henry PAINTER. Clothing, furs, wearing apparel to sister, Mrs. Ann CARSON, Palmyra, Mo. Included with balance of household items was cash in Union Bank of Winchester plus expected proceeds from claim vs. Joseph & J. A. McKAY and claim vs Arthur NULTON. Personal property sold and sale bill admitted to court, 10 July 1878.

Pages 194-195: Will of Betsy Ann HOLLIDAY. All property to Sally E. DAVISON, William D. GRAHAM, Richard J. GRAHAM. After their deaths, to Frederick W. M. HOLLIDAY who is appointed executor. 13 March 1872. Wit: Wm. L BENT, John H. NULTON. Proved 15 July 1878.

Pages 195-196: Will of Mrs. Sally E. DAVISON. All property to Betsy Ann HOLLIDAY, Wm. D. GRAHAM and Richard J. GRAHAM. After their deaths, to Frederick W. M. HOLLIDAY and he to be executor. 13 March 1872. Wit: Wm. L. BENT, John H. NULTON. Proved 15 July 1878.

Pages 196-197: Will of Richard J. GRAHAM. All property to Wm. D. GRAHAM, Sally E. DAVISON, Betsy Ann HOLLIDAY. After their deaths, to Frederick W. M. HOLLIDAY and he to be executor. 13 March 1872. Wit: Wm. L. BENT, John H. NULTON. Proved 15 July 1878.

Pages 197-199: Inventory and Appraisal of Personal Estate of George KREMER, Jr., dec'd., in the hands of C. S. W. BARNES, City Sargeant. All inventory is of Notes and Bills Due, most worthless. Among those are: Bond of James

GRAY to N. F. GIBSON, assigned to Geo. KREMER, dated Octr 30, 1838; Bond of Bennett CARLIN & J. N. STROTHER to Sam'l. R. ATWELL; Note on James H. GROVE, 1857; three Bonds of Ephraim KERN to James & Barnett LEWIS, 1856; Bond of Alfred T. & Mary D. MAGILL, 1857; Bond of Isaac & Mary C. BAKER to Houck & Leathers. Appraisers: R. Wm. WALTER, L. N. HUCK, C. B. HANCOCK. July 30, 1878.

Pages 200-202: Inventory and Appraisal of Personal Estate of Elizabeth A. SNYDER, dec'd. Among inventory: 30 shares SVNB stock; 4 shares WPRR stock; household furniture, carpeting, quilts, wine glasses, one "sick chair". Appraisers: Tilman SHUMATE, H. M. BRENT, H. Clay KREBS, Sam'l. L. LAREW. 27 Sept 1877. Recorded in court 26 Aug 1878.

Pages 203-204: Will of Margaret J. BARRETT. Body to be buried "in my Lot by the side of John McILWEE; neat, plain tombstone of marble". To Mrs. Catherine McILWEE, $150; To George McILWEE the amount of the note he owes. Gives to trustees of the Reformed Church towards payment of parsonage debt. To Pastor, Rev. Charles G. FISHER, the new Hymn Book plus what is owed on salary of pastor. To Mrs. Kate BELL, carpet on floor; to Alfred Hite, "my Bible". To executor, $10 for his time and attention. Any balance of estate to Alfred HITE and Margaret BLOCKLEY. Richard L. GRAY to be exec. 5 Aug 1878. Wit: H. B. STRIKER, Hannah HOLLIS, Martha J. PURCELL. Proved 16 Sept 1878.

Pages 204-206: Appraisal and Inventory of Estate of Elizabeth WEAVER, dec'd. 26 March 1878. Among items: Household furniture including two falling leaf tables, large Rocking Chair, Cashmere Shawl, Parasol, Stoves, Trunks. Total value: $69.90. Appraisers: C. FUNK, G. W. HILLYARD, T. A. LATHAM.

Pages 207-209: Sale Bill, Personal Property of Mrs. Elizabeth WEAVER, 29 March 1878. Among purchasers: Mrs. E. TAYLOR, N. J. MORGAN, R. W. WALTER, D. WALTER, A. HARDESTY. Recorded in court, 24 Sept 1878.

Pages 210-214: Appraisement and Inventory of Personal Estate of Evelyn BALL, dec'd. 18 July 1876. Among items: Walnut Breakfast Table; featherbed, quilts and blankets; 2 silk dresses and crape Shall; Shugar Box; 4 Bonnetts & Band Box; 2 lamps on Mantle Pease. Appraisers: Henry BESORE, James MANN, Charles C. BROWN (his mark). Estate of Evelyn BALL, in account with Wm. GORDON, her Admr. Begins July 1876 with payments for coffin, hacks at funeral, grave stones. Total disbursement: $421.39, leaving the estate balance of $285.38 which gave an amount of $57.07-3/8 each to: Mary PARKER, Peter DOCTER, Nancy JACKSON, Michael DOCTER, Betsy GORDON. As the distributees took many articles of personalty, there was no sale. Estate account closed 16 Dec 1878.

Pages 215-216: Estate of M. M. HITE with Dorsey WALTER, his Admr. Begins March 1877 with receipts of Sale, $2,831.09. Other receipts were funds from Accounts Due Hite & Wall, dividends on Bank stock. Payments made on debts of Hite & Wall and payments to many individuals; paid for grave stones, $100. Estate Account returned to court "to lie for exceptions" on 21 Octr 1878. Recorded in Court, 10 Decr 1878.

Page 217: John KERR's Executor Complaint against John KERR's Devisees, Defendants. From Clerk of Circuit Court of Frederick County to Clerk of Corporate Court of Winchester. The Accounts of Lewis P. HARTMAN and Rob't.

STEELE, Execs. of John KERR, dec'd., have "settled in the above entitled cause". Recorded by City Clerk, 13 Decr 1878.

Pages 218-219: Will of Mrs. Eliza J. CARSON, made 12 June 1876. (one paragraph only) Gives everything to daughter, Josephine W. CARSON who is appointed executrix and requests court to permit her to qualify without any bond or security. Wit: Edmund PENDLETON, Wm. L. CLARK. Proved 21 Jany 1879. On 30 Jany 1879, Josephine W. CARSON qualified for executrix but "executed a bond for Ten Thousand dollars without security".

Pages 219-220: Will of Ann E. McGUIRE. Leaves house she now lives in to daughters, Gettie and Annie McGUIRE, also all furniture therein. Son, Hunter, to be paid all money he has advanced on said house. March 16, 1876. April 12, 1876 addition to will: Should Annie "ever join the Romish? Church, she forfeits all interest in my property but Gettie to have during her life and sons at her death". "Gertrude to have some rememberance of her home, anything she wishes, also my sons." Will proved 21 Apr 1879. As there were no witnesses to will, Dr. Wm. P. McGUIRE swore to Testator's handwriting.

Pages 220-221: Will of Henrietta HODGES. House and Lot on east side of Cameron Street to daughter, Ann Virginia GRIFFITH. She to pay "my son, George W. SWHIER, $150 out of rent yearly and $150 paid to Jacob G. SWHIERS as they come of age. None of the money is to draw interest neather can this property be taken for eney debt of A. C. GRIFFITH." Gives to granddaughter, Henrietta GRIFFITH. Husband, W. V. HODGES, appointed executor. 8 March 1879. Wit: Charles H. GRIM, Charles D. SLOAT. Proved 21 Apr 1879.

Pages 222-244: Estate of Richard SIDWELL, dec'd., in Account with A. R. PENDLETON, his Admr. Begins Feby 1876. Long list of receipts and expenses. Most cash receipts are from "book accounts but some from notes". Some receipts from "leather sold". Some individual accounts due from Henry QUANTZ, Joseph BRUMBACK, Richard SIDWELL, Oyler & Co. Payments made "in suit of LEWIS" and to Barton & Boyd, Attorneys, "in CONWAY suit". Paid on many "distributive shares". Many credits and debits made "for errors". Mentions Mrs. R. J. (Thomasen) SIDWELL, widow. Account settled Apr 1879.

Pages 245-248: Will of Mary L. L. (or S. S.?) WILLIAMS, widow of Philip WILLIAMS, dec'd. To daughters, Lucy D. and Sarah Ellen WILLIAMS, the portion of Oak Spring Farm near Col. O. M. FUNSTER's, which belongs "to me independently". To daughters, Lucy D. and Sarah Ellen WILLIAMS and Mary T. D. AVIRETT, that portion of White Oak Tavern Farm "belonging to me independent of P. WILLIAMS". All other property to above 3 daughters and to sons, T. Clayton WILLIAMS and John James WILLIAMS. Appoints Holmes BOYD and John J. WILLIAMS as trustees to hold property in trust for daughters. Appoints John J. WILLIAMS executor. 9 June 1869. Wit: Mary M. TIDBALL, Susan W. TIDBALL. Codicils dated 11 March 1871 and 29 March 1879. Appoints son, John J. WILLIAMS as trustee and E. Holmes BOYD as executor. To Lucy Dunbar WILLIAMS and Sarah Ellen WILLIAMS that part of Oak Springs Farm "from my mother". Pay wages to servants, William and Nancy. Books in late husband's library to be divided between sons, John and Clayton and grandson, P. Williams FAUNTLEROY. Long codicil with many changes to original will. Another wit: Sally BALDWIN. Proved 19 May 1879.

Pages 249-251: Estate of P. C. L. BURWELL, dec'd., in Account with C. S. W. BARNES, Sergeant Committee Administrator. Begins Feby 4, 1879 with cash paid Clerks, R. WALTER, James B. BURGESS, Geo. GLAIS (Clarke Co.), J. P. RIELY. Paid property taxes. Apr 19, 1879, powers of C. S. W. BARNES, as Admr. are revoked and Mrs. Ann R. BURWELL qualifies as Admr. On 17 June 1879, C. S. W. BARNES ordered to pay funeral expenses of P. C. L. BURWELL from the $139.49 balance in Estate Account with residue to Mrs. Ann R. BURWELL.

Pages 252-263: Appraisement and Inventory of Estate of Mary L. L. (or S. S.) WILLIAMS, dec'd. 2 July 1879. C. S. BAKER, Stephen P. STACKHOUSE, Philip W. BOYD, Appraisers. (Long Inventory) Many rooms, as West Attic Room, SE Attic Room, Attic Hall, 2nd Story Hall, 2nd Story NE Room, Bathroom, Library, Dining Room, Parlor, 1st Floor Dressing Room, Ironing Room, Store Room, etc. Bedrooms had fire sets, wash bowls/pitchers, marble-top tables, chairs, plated candle stick, linen sheets, towels, tablecloths, napkins. Many books in library. Dining room had china & silverware and "several pairs candle lobbers". Much furniture in Parlor including "nest Japan Tables". Bathroom had Bath tub, Safe, Stove, Little fender, Shuvel Stand & Poker. Wash Room had washing machine and wringer.

Pages 264-267: Appraisement of Estate of Andrew HARKNESS, dec'd. Feby 20, 1878 with Appraisers: Meredith CAPPER, D. W. BROWN, John H. JENKINS. In inventory: many pieces of stone, marble, limestone, dressed footstones, chizels, drills spaid, mallets, cole stove, household items. Appraisal made of A. HARKNESS & Albun's Partnership, giving footage of stones & tools; then one-half to Harkness. Inspected & approved Augt 29, 1879.

Pages 268-272: Estate of David BARTON, dec'd., in Account with A. R. PENDLE-TON, his Admr. Begins Sept 11, 1874 with expenses such as paid Appraisers; paid Dr. G. L. MILLER's Account; paid for iron railing for burial lot; paid Attorney's and witnesses fees, and "fee for recovering from Stackhouse"; paid Jacob S. & Anna R. LAUCK "on share". In receipts: "funds from Stack-house". Admr. Account to Court 21 July 1879 to lie for exceptions. Record-ed in Court 15 Sept 1879.

Page following 269 is numbered 272.

Pages 273-275: Will of Addison B. RIELY, of Baltimore, Maryland. Estate to wife, Ann R. RIELY, for support of herself and children. Wife appointed executrix and guardian of children. 10 Sept 1852. Will proved in Baltimore City, 27 Sept 1852. True copy of will, 19 Jany 1877, by Chief Judge of the Orphans Court of Baltimore City, recorded in Winchester Court House, 23 Octr 1879. On motion: Ann R. BURWELL, formerly Ann R. RIELY, took oath as required by law to be executrix.

Pages 276-278: Will of Henry D. GRIM. All property to wife, Elizabeth, as long as she remains "my widow". If wife, Elizabeth, dies or remarries, house on Market Street, adjoining property of Mr. JOHNSON, goes to children, Hunter B. & Frank GRIM. Testator and son, Charles H. GRIM, own jointly a house and lot. If Elizabeth dies or remarries, testator's half interest in that house and lot goes to Charles H. GRIM with the charges that he pay $150 to each of the following children: Fanny BARR, Kate V. BEAN, Cammillus GRIM. Daughters' money to be "free, quit and clear of husbands' control". Makes bequests to children: Washington, Lizzie, Fanny BARR, Kate V. BEAN, Charles H. GRIM. Had already given to sons, Stewart & Wesley. Daughter, Lizzie, married "against my will and consent". Appoints son, Charles H. GRIM, executor. Wit: Wm. V. HODGES, James M. FRYE. 2 May 1879. Proved 15 Decr 1879.

Pages 279-282: Will of James MARSHALL. "It having become proper for me to make a will principally to provide for my sister-in-law, the widow of my brother, John." Divides estate into four parts: to brothers, Robert and Henry, sister, Susan and children of brother, John. Gives $800 a year to Rebecca MARSHALL, widow of brother, John. Brother, Henry, and brother-in-law, Dr. R. C. AMBLER, appointed executors. 4 Jany 1856. Codicil, 9 Jany 1856 requests no security be required for executors. Codicil, Decem 3, 1856, re Bonds of nephew, James MARSHALL, of Warren. Codicil, April 20, 1862, Books show how he handled the Account as Guardian of the children of his brother, John. 14 Feby 1870, He had lost much in the Civil War so changes the annuity for widow of his brother, John, to $400 a year. Brother, Robert, has died so now devises to his children and to the two children of his deceased son, Thomas. Codicil, Octr 20, 1872, re small tract of land in Clarke County, owned jointly with brother, Henry. All to Henry. Will proved 15 March 1880. R. C. AMBLER, one of the named executors, is dead and Henry MARSHALL, the other named executor, refuses. Holmes CONRAD is appointed to administer.

Pages 282-287: Will of Ann H. TALBOT, dec'd. In Circuit Court of Polk Co., Iowa, Aug 16, 1879. Ann H., wife of H. Marshall TALBOT. Mentions Deed made Apr 6, 1853, in Winchester, Va., to Oliver M. BROWN. Wishes this property to be sold and proceeds to go as follows:

1. To Tillman SHUMATE; 2. To Xenophon WHEELER, of Chattanooga, Tenn.; 3. To Rebecca Jane SIDWELL, "payment for board"; 4. To Caroline HARDER, of Saylorville, Polk County, Iowa, "for her faithfulness to me in health and sickness; 5. To Catherine Maria ADAMS, of Des Moines, Iowa, "daughter of our sister, Maria SMITH, dec'd"; 6. Remainder to my husband, H. Marshall TALBOT, of Polk County, Iowa. Tilman SHUMATE appointed executor. 22 May 1879. Wit: Wm. G. BAGG, Sophia G. WATROUS. Codicil, 2 June 1879, Husband is now deceased so his part to niece, Catherine M. ADAMS, of Polk Co., Iowa and $200 to Elizabeth M. MATTHEWS, of Baltimore, Md. Proved Sept 13, 1879. Authenticated copy received in Winchester Court, 15 March 1880. Tilman SHUMATE refused executorship. E. P. DANDRIDGE appointed Administrator.

Pages 288-289: Will of Mary PINE. "I, Mary PINE, of great age and sound mind." Appoints grandson, James Stewart GRANT, executor. All estate to daughter, Elizabeth A. GRANT, widow of Charles GRANT. Wit: Charles M. GRIM, George W. HENRY, John B. T. REED. Feb 13, 1880. Proved 15 March 1880.

Pages 290-295: Guardianship Accounts of Earnest MARSHALL and Emma MARSHALL in Account with S. A. AFFLICK, their guardian. From March 1876 through Aug 1879. Cash received from interest on Bonds of Taylor MILTON and C. DINKLES and from P. AFFLECK Estate. Payments were mostly to Mrs. A. E. Afflick for board. Accounts recorded in Court, 18 March 1880.

Pages 296-313: Estate of Richard SIDWELL, dec'd., in Account with A. R. PENDLETON, his Admr. Begins Oct 1874 with Cash Recpts. from many sales of leather and from payments on many accounts, the largest of which is "F. H. GRUPY & Co. on leather sold". Long list of expenses paid, as cost of Sale, extra hands for work, freight costs, postage on letters to debtors. Many payments to "Dandridge & Pendleton for settling accounts & suits thereto". Note Payable of Richard SIDWELL in Shenandoah Nat'l. Bank. Note of N. T. CONWAY, given by Richard SIDWELL for $500, dated

June 1, 1871, payable 1 day after date. Admr. rejected this note because of statute of limitations. "Conway was a lunatic before the bar of statute of limitations applied and continues to be so." Richard SIDWELL was executor of Estate of Hugh SIDWELL, dec'd. Administrator's report accepted by Court, 19 April 1880.

Page 314: Will of Fanny DAVIS. (very short) All to son Robert DAVIS and he to be executor. (no date) Wit: R. T. BARTON, H. M. BAKER. Proved 17 May 1880.

Pages 315-323: Will of Miles WHITE, of Baltimore, Md. To wife, Margaret H. WHITE, all household & kitchen furniture, horses, carriages and harness. Also house & lot where now living: 36 South Sharp Street. Also gives her "for her natural lifetime and no longer, ground rents producing $3,000 per annum". To Mary BERRY and Martha CHAPPEL, $200 each, per annum. To children of nephew, Jason TRUEBLOOD, dec'd., 160 acres of land plus $500. To nephew, Mike W. TRUEBLOOD, "if living at time of my death", 160 acres of land in Aley? County, Iowa. To nieces, Mary & Minarva TRUEBLOOD, $3,000 of Secured Mortgage Bonds of Manelta? & Cincinnati Rail Road; To grandson, Miles WHITE, son of "my son, Frances WHITE", all lands between Aisquith & walls of Greenmount Cemetery, & other lands. To Sarah Elizabeth WHITE, daughter of son Francis WHITE, land including 2,000 acres in Iowa. To grandson, Francis A. WHITE, son of son Francis WHITE, land in Baltimore; To grandson, Richard J. WHITE, son of son Francis WHITE, land including 2,000 acres in Iowa. Son, Francis WHITE, is authorized to sell any land during the minority of the grandchildren. To each of WHITE grandchildren mentioned above: 200 shares of stock in B&O Railroad and $500 plus $3,200 of 2nd Mortgage Bonds of Manelta & Cincinnati Railroad. To Miles White NEWBY, son of niece, Martha NEWBY, 160 acres of land in Iowa. To Miles WHITE Beneficial Society of Baltimore, $100,000. Also gives to sister, Rebecca WHITE, of Raysville, Indiana and her grandchildren. Son, Francis WHITE, to be sole executor. Wit: W. Tazewell FOX, James McNEAL, Jr., J. Swan FRICK. Francis WHITE died 12 March 1876. Will proven 16 March 1876, Baltimore City. Presented in Winchester Court, 17 May 1880. Francis WHITE qualified as executor.

Pages 323-324: Will of Julia A. KURTZ. Nephew, Robert D. DODD, has been supporting her. He is to receive all her property including her house on Main Street. There is a Lien on her house held by Lewis A. MILLER. Nephew, George W. KURTZ, to be executor. May 12, 1877. Wit: P. T. KURTZ, Jas. P. RIELY. Proved 19 May 1880.

Pages 325-326: Inventory and Appraisement of the Property of Mrs. Ann H. TALBOT, dec'd. Total inventory: Brick House at corner of Braddock and Amherst Streets, partly occupied by B. NOONAN; brick and frame house "just south of this": the open space and the house and lot adjoining Barnhart; 3 US Bonds; some cash. Appraisers: Jas. H. BARNHART, Frank G. WALTER, N. A. BENT. Admitted to record 22 June 1880. Realized from the sale of property: $3,552.00.

Page 327: Will of R. J. McK. HOLLIDAY, dec'd. Proved 22 July 1880. No subscribing witnesses; S. N. HUCK & S. T. MOORE verified handwriting. Will followed: To wife, Mary C. HOLLIDAY, all property with below proviso: Son, Frederick, has been "for some years paying off my debts but for which I would be ruined". To him, deed for property on Market Street. Son, Frederick W. M. HOLLIDAY, and Sam'l. T. HOLLIDAY, executors. 2 Septem 1857.

Pages 328-331:   Will of Susan BRENT. To son, Nathan A. BRENT, house and lot on Braddock Street "where I now live".   Said house and lot to pay for other bequests: To daughter, Sallie A. METZGAR, $50 (to be held in trust by son, Nathan) free from any control of her husband, Frank METZGAR. To daughter, Ann SHEPHERD, and to son, Wm. Theodore BRENT, $50 each. To her three children, Sallie A., Ann and William Theodore, Bond of Lloyd Logan for $1,000. To grandchildren, Henry M. B. BOWEN and George A. BOWEN, children of daughter Elizabeth, all rights to land in Shenandoah County in name of Mary WOLF & Others. Henry M. BRENT to be executor. _____ day of Jany 1876. Wit: B. NOONAN, Jas. P. RIELY. Codicil 24 Jany 1876: Personal property left to children, Nathan A. BRENT, Sallie A. METZGAR, Ann SHEPHERD, and Wm. Theodore BRENT. Second codicil, 27 Feby 1879 changes bequest of Lloyd LOGAN bond to daughter-in-law, Susan Hill BRENT, wife of son, Nathan A. BRENT, as "some compensation for her great care during my prolonged sickness". Proved 18 Oct 1880. H. M. BRENT, executor named in will, is non-resident of state but is allowed to administer will.

Pages 331-332: Estate of Thomasin SIDWELL, dec'd., in Account with J. Ed WALKER, her Admr. Begins April 1880 paying expenses as funeral costs, Dr. Love's medical Account, for tombstone. Received amount from A. R. PENDLETON, Admr. of Richard SIDWELL, dec'd., less expenses. Remainder of estate is distributed, $83.00 to each: Martha S. & Ann M. SIDWELL, E. J. PHILLIPS, Cornelius H. WALKER, Mary F. SIDWELL. Estate Account recorded 20 Decr 1880.

Pages 333-335: Mrs. Emma V. Baker in Account with Wm. H. Baker, her guardian. Begins Decr 1878 with proceeds from selling many bushels of corn; rents from Heist, Denny & Seibert, house in Maryland; amount from H. CONRAD, executor. Made payments on clover seed; paid Denny on Bond; cash to ward; paid Dr. Fuller's account; paid expenses to Maryland. Guardianship account recorded 20 Dec 1880.

Pages 335-337: Inventory and Appraisal of Property of Susan BRENT, dec'd., with B. NOONAN, Jas. N. BARNHART, John G. MILLER, Appraisers. Household items as walnut and mahogany bureaus, what-not, stove, wash bowles, feather beds, pillows. Total value: $44. Recorded Decr 18, 1880.

Pages 338-340: Estate of Godfrey MILLER, dec'd., in Account with John Abrm. MILLER, Admr. Begins Sept 1880 with Funds received from H. CONRAD, Trustee. Paid Admr. expenses, fees and Balance of Estate, $652.66, to be divided among 10 of his 11 children. Mrs. Sela S. GREEN has received her share. So $64.26-2/3 distributed to: George S. MILLER; W. S. MILLER; G. S. MILLER; Share of Mrs. Mary C. WOLFE, under assignment in writing of herself and her husband, Robert B. WOLFE, goes to Annie M. MILTON, Sidney O. MILLER, M. Emily MILLER & Sela S. GREEN; Bessie MILLER & Annie J. BELL, only children of Rebecca REA, dec'd.; J. A. MILLER; Sidney O. MILLER; M. Emily MILLER; J. S. CROSS; Anna M. MILTON. Recorded 19 Jany 1881.

Pages 341-342: Will of Mary B. WHITE. Has no debts. One-half of all property to each: brother, William Donagle WHITE, and father, R. B. WHITE, except that one-third of each portion goes to aunt, Juliet Opie WHITE and at aunt's death, "to my brother, Wm. D. WHITE". Cousin, Wm. M. ATKINSON, to be executor. 4 Sept 1878. Codicil, 4 Sept 1879. If aunt, Juliet O. WHITE, survives both father and brother, that portion of father and brother goes to her, unless brother has children. In that case, to his children. Proved 2 Feby 1881. As no witnesses to will, Mrs. Juliet A. McCAW swore to handwriting.

Pages 343-345: Estate of Ann H. TALBOT, dec'd., in Account with E. P. DANDRIDGE, her Admr. Begins April 1880 with receipts from rents and sale of real estate. Paid funeral expenses, crier, advertising, taxes, attorney's fee to Dandridge & Pendleton, "reserved for payment of collateral inheritance tax". Balance of estate, $2,215.19, due from Admr. to estate was forwarded, Decr 29, 1880, to C. S. WATROUS, the Admr. in Des Moines, Iowa, where testatrix died. Recorded in Court here, 21 Feby 1881.

Pages 345-351: Inventory and Appraisal of Estate of George JONES, dec'd. Adam WINDLE, T. C. WINDLE, Samuel EVANS, Appraisers. Personal property: Horse, wagon, wheel bearer, Horse Collars, Hames, saddles, whips, fodder, "1 lot of plunder in corn house loft" (purchased by Mr. CAPPER for $1). Appraisal recorded 21 Feb 1881. At Sale of Personal Estate of George JONES, most purchases by M. CAPPER. Some by John CAIN, G. WILLS, John JEFFERSON, Z. ADDISON, John BROOKS. Sale recorded Apr 9, 1881.

Pages 352-353: Estate of Thomasin SIDWELL, dec'd., in Account with J. Ed. WALKER, her Admr. Received from Claim against Estate of Richard SIDWELL, dec'd., $109.61. After paying expenses, the balance was distributed to Martha S. SIDWELL, Ann M. SIDWELL, E. J. PHILLIPS, Cornelia H. WALKER, Mary T. SIDWELL, in amount of $19.42-3/5 each. Recorded 18 Apr 1881.

Pages 354-357: Will of James KERN, 26 Jany 1881, "calling to mind the frail tenure of life". To wife, Sarah A. T. KERN, "brick house and lot on the corner which I now occupy"; another lot on Market Street and all Household property; rents from all my houses including 2 deeded to "my two daughters"; all books with her name written in them. Executors to sell rest of property and repay wife "for money I borrowed of her" and what is owed to Bently KERN and Frank WALLIN. Other bequests to Charles and Cora STEEL, daughter Eliza's two children. "I want them to have their 2/3rds shair." Also gives to sons, Thomas & Wilbur KERN. Wit: J. M. LUPTON, G. S. MILLER, Eben TAYLOR. Codicil, 4 Feby 1881, appoints Joseph M. LUPTON as one of executors. Will proved 18 April 1881, with Bentley KERN and Joseph M. LUPTON, as executors.

Pages 358-359: Will of Edward JONES, 24 Jany 1879. House and Lot on the corner of Kent & Cork to wife, Julie E. JONES and, "at her death, sell and divide to all children". Wife to be executrix. Wit: E. R. BICE, David HAMILTON, Chas. W. HOLLIS. Proved 21 April 1881.

Pages 360-361: Will of Harriet H. RUSSELL. Sell real estate and divide between brother, William G. RUSSELL, and children of brother, Isaac RUSSELL, dec'd. Nephew, James B. RUSSELL, to be executor. 26 May 1881. Wit: T. N. LUPTON, Clinton MAYNARD. Proved 22 June 1881.

Pages 362-364: Trust of Charles B. MEREDITH & Wife in Account with E. Holmes BOYD, Trustee. From Mar 1879 to April 1881, received payments on house and lot purchased by G. H. HAINES. Paid attorney's fees, advertising and other costs of selling house and administering estate. Trust Account recorded 26 June 1881.

Pages 365-366: Inventory and Appraisement of Estate of Mary THOMPSON, dec'd. 11 May 1881, with Geo. W. KURTZ, Geo. M ANDERSON, S. L. LAREW, Appraisers. Very short inventory: one each Bedstead, Straw Tick, Quilt, Bed clothes, rocking chair, lot of carpet, lot of dishes. Total value: $10.00. Recorded in Court 21 June 1881.

Pages 367-372: Will of Michel COPENHAVER, "being of sound and disposing mind and having the fear of God before me". To wife, Melissa E., $800 and 1 parcel of land (6 acres) on east side of Paper Mill Road, adjoining Thatcher land. After wife's death, remainder of above, if any, into 3 shares: (1) To children of dec'd. nephew, Michael B. COPENHAVER, of Clark County; (2) To children of Morgan BRANAN; (3) To children of John W. BYARLY. To wife, also, 1 large tin plate stove, one Beadstead & bedding, one small clock, one large sick chair, utensils and ½ of any live stock. Also she has exclusive use of "the back room downstairs in the brick house where I now live" and joint use of parlor, cellar, kitchen & furniture, yard, et cetera with nephew, John BYARLY, and his family. Gives to John BYARLY and his children "lot in the semetry as burrying place for his family after burying Malissa E." John Godfrey MILLER, Amos PIERCE, Execs. 5 July 1871. Wit: John B. T. REED, Sam'l. R. ATWELL, C. W. REED. Codicil, 21 Aprl 1874: Wife, Malissa has died so gives to daughters of dec'd. nephew, Michael B. COPENHAVER, of Clark Co. & to Michel CONROD. Additional to John BYARLY & family. Another codicil adds bequest to niece, Hannah, widow of Wm. HOLLIS, and to nephew, Morgan BRANNON, and to Hue BRANNON, son of nephew, Stewart BRANNON. Third codicil, Aug 1875: Henry S. SLAGLE to be executor instead of Amos PIERCE. Proved 18 July 1881.

Page 373: (very short will, for his & his heirs benefit) Will of James R. CONRAD. To Holmes CONRAD, Attorney at law, all real and personal property of every kind, he "being of the same name and kindred". 23 Octr 1875.
   Proved 21 July 1881. No witnesses so will proved by oath of Tilman SHUMATE that he was acquainted with testator's handwriting.

Pages 374-376: Inventory & Appraisement of Estate of Edward JONES, dec'd., 1 July 1881. C. W. HOLLIS, V. W. STRIKER, David HAMILTON, Appraisers. Among items: carpeting, chairs, parlor & cook stoves, churn, ½ interest in pair of scales, sausage grinder, tubs, baskets, steel trap. Total inventory value: $88.35. Recorded 2 July 1881.

Pages 377-378: Will of Catherine E. MILLER, widow of Godfrey MILLER. Gives everything except household & kitchen furniture, to 3 children: John A. MILLER, Godfrey S. MILLER (crossed out), Margaret E. MILLER, & Sidney O. MILLER. Household and kitchen furniture "to be kept for the use of the above named" or those that remain single. Sons, John A. MILLER, and George F. MILLER, to be executors. 12 Feb 1866. Wit: John G. MILLER, R. B. YEAKLEY. Proved 17 Octr 1881. George F. MILLER renounced any claim to qualify as executor.

Page 379: Will of Mary R. HUNSICKER. To sister, Rebecker A. LATHAM, if she survives, "all my intrust in the house and lot we own jointly" After her death, divide among the SLAGLE heirs then living. Apl 15, 1880. Wit: T. A. LATHAM, R. E. LATHAM. Proved 22 Novr 1881.

Pages 380-382: Appraisement of Walter BOWEN's Estate. Many misc. household items as pictures & frames, piano, mortar & pestle, bed clothing, straw & feather ticks, wood & coal stoves, harness, saddle & second-hand buggy. 15 Novr 1881. Appraisers: Oscar BARR, C. S. W. BARNES, John G. MILLER. T. W. HARRISON, Admr., accepts inventory.

Pages 383-387: Inventory and Appraisement of Personal Estate of C. B. MANN, dec'd., 16 Jany 1882. Among items: Bath Tub & Spickets, Boiler & Pipe to Bath Tub, 2 Barber Chairs, 86 Mugs & Brushes, combs, 4 Spitoons, Razors, Hones, Neck Dusters, pair Dumb Bells, Guitar, Bird & Cage, B. G. Board & Dice, Organ & Stool, Water Pail & Foot Tub, 6 pairs Turkey Red Curtains, 1 Croquet Set, 1 Davis Sewing Machine. Inventory recorded 19 Jan 1882. Joseph A. NULTON, Frederick BLANKNER, T. V. PURCELL, Dorsey WALTER, Appraisers.

Pages 388-391: Appraisal and Inventory of Personal Estate of Michael COPENHAVER. Some items: 1 set sofa bottom chairs, 4 Bedsteads, 2 feather beds, corn barrel, ten plate Stove, lot of Books, cash in bank of $1,000. Many bonds, notes and accounts. Among "good" ones: Bond of Amos PIERCE and Casper RINKER, at 10 days for $600, dated 22 June 1869, but subject to credits that made the amount due on same as of May 15, 1881, $315.45. One doubtful note, of John N. BELL & H. M. BRENT, dated 1865. Bond of N. M. CARTMELL, $1,043.02, due 1867, secured by Deed of Trust. Appraisers: Geo. F. MILLER, James H. BARNHART, John G. MILLER. Executor, John W. BRYARLY. Recorded in Court 26, Jany 1882. J. R. CARSON, Clerk.

Pages 391-392: Inventory and Account of Sales, Valley Female College, John J. WILLIAMS & Holmes CONRAD, Trustees under Deed of Trust from Valley Female College. Purchaser: Wm. R. DENNY; Price, $8,535.00, paid in cash. Recorded Feb 4, 1882.

Pages 392-394: Appraisement of Personal Estate of Mrs. E. W. LEYBURN, dec'd. Feby 14, 1882, with Dorsey WALTER, L. N. HUCK, Wm. BYRD, Appraisers. Bonds, City of Winchester, Note of P. W. BOYD, Bond of Mrs. Sarah SCHULTZ, Cash in hand of Barton & Boyd. After Inventory of Mrs. LEYBURN, E. Holmes BOYD, Admr. of Estate of E. W. LEYBURN, dec'd., asked that the foregoing appraisal be treated also as his inventory. 15 Feby 1882.

Pages 394-395: Appraisal of Personal Estate of Eliza J. L. CONVERSE, 14 Feby 1882. Only items: Jany 1880, her interest in Estate of Rev G. W. LEYBURN estimated at $1,000, and in the estate of Mrs. G. W. LEYBURN, $300. Appraisers: Wm. BYRD, L. N. HUCK, Dorsey WALTER. E. Holmes BOYD, Admr. for Eliza J. L. CONVERSE. Recorded 15 Feby 1882.

Pages 396-397: Inventory and Appraisal of Estate of J. Andrew BUSH, dec'd., Feby 11, 1882, with E. HOFFMAN, Adam WINDLE, Samuel L. LAREW as Appraisers. Total estate: 1 large clock, 6 chairs, 1 rocking chair, 1 side board, 1 lot of Planes, etc. Value: $36.50. Recorded 17 Feby 1882.

Pages 397-399: Will of Sarah FRENCH, "aged and infirm of body". After payment of funeral expenses "and any little debt that I may owe, of which I believe I owe none whatever". To niece, Sarah Ann SPENCER, all property (including house and lot on Clifford Street) to be held in trust for her only and exempt from any liability for the debts of any husband she may have. Thos. T. FAUNTLEROY, Jr., to be exec. 12 May 1875. Wit: T. T. FAUNTLEROY, Jr., Sam'l. R. ATWELL, Rob't. Wesley ROBINSON. Proved 21 March 1882. T. T. FAUNTLEROY, Jr. "relieved from responsibility of being executor". Sarah Ann SPENCER mentioned as being beneficiary and legatee.

Pages 399-401: Will of Thomas J. RILT. To Thomas Walter THOMPSON, minor child of Sarah F. THOMPSON, lot of ground. To Elma J. and Sarah Theresa THOMPSON, minor children of Sarah F. THOMPSON, other lots of ground, fronting on Market Street. Daniel THOMPSON, trustee for the 3 children. Add to trust, notes, bonds and any moneys. If trustee dies, appoints Evelina SETTLES, of Markham, Va. Expressly wishes "the father of said children has in no manner or form control over the property devised". 12 Jany 1882. Proved 20 March 1882. Daniel THOMPSON, Executor.

Pages 402-403: Will of Isaac Hite BALDWIN, of Frederick County, Va. To wife, Mary E. BALDWIN, whole estate, including House and Lot in Capon Springs, WVa. Mentions Deed of Trust to D. W. BALDWIN, Trustee for Grantor and wife, dated 12 Jany 1855 and 2nd Deed of Trust, dated 1 Feby 1859. 26 Feby 1879. Wit: J. W. PIFER, Joseph H. FUG?. Proved 21 March 1882. Mary E. BALDWIN, Exec. James H. WILLIAMS and J. F. KECKLEY made oath that they believed will to be in I. Hite BALDWIN's handwriting.

Pages 404-405: Appraisal of Estate of Thomas J. RILT, dec'd., Charles H. GRIM, Geo. W. RANDOLPH, T. C. WINDLE, Appraisers. Total inventory: 6 shirts, 3 pair pants, 2 pair shoes, 2 hats and coats, Socks and handkerchief, 1 bucket and bosier, 1 trunk, jewelry. Total value: $13.25. Recorded 5 April 1882.

Pages 405-406: Appraisal of Estate of James KERN, dec'd., with Eben TAYLOR, D. W. BROWN, G. W. SUMPTION, Appraisers. Among items: 1 new cart, 1 new plow, oak lumber, rough spokes, wagon rims, Blacksmith Tools, Coal, wagon wheels, scrap iron. May 2, 1881. Recorded 5 April 1882.

Pages 407-412: Inventory and Appraisal of Personal Estate of Harriet S. MARSTELLER, dec'd., by Wm. N. EDDY, Henry BAETJER, C. W. HENSELL, 23 Sept 1881. Among items: Sofa, Rocking Chair, 6 hair cloth Chairs, Cherry Table, Clothes Wringer, Spit Box, Rain Barrel, Tailor's Iron, Soap Kettle. Two notes of Huck & Neill dated 14 Octr 1857 and 9 Mch 1860. Recorded 14 Apr 1882. Total received from Sale Account of Personal Property, $126.40. C. W. WILSON, Admr.

Pages 413-418: Will of Silas BILLINGS, revoking former wills. He owes debts to 2 daughters, Mary E. and Cornelia F. BILLINGS. Often mentions his debts, which he estimates will require 3 to 5 years to pay off. Wife, Catherine, to have annuity of $250 each year, "charged on my property Fairfax Hall". Also mentions "the school at Fairfax Hall". Two daughters to have "property remaining unconsumed from estate of deceased son, Henry M. BILLINGS". Two daughters to pay to daughter, Clara K. SHEPARD, and George C. SHEPARD. Two daughters to be executrixes. 6 Jany 1880. Wit: R. T. BARTON, Eliza L. TRACY. Proved 17 Apr 1882.

Pages 418-419: Will of John W. GRIM, of Charles. All estate to wife, Ann Elizabeth GRIM and she to be executor. 11 Apr 1882. Wit: C. FUNK, C. W. ANDERSON, Samuel L. LAREW. Proved 18 Sept 1882.

Pages 420-432: Inventory and Appraisal of Estate of H. H. RUSSELL, dec'd., 30 June 1881, with Thos. N. LUPTON, Edwd. HOFFMAN, J. I. H. BAKER, and Geo. E. JENKINS, Appraisers. Among many items: 12 Chairs, Franklin Stove, Marble Top Tables, Glasses with Wax Flowers, Oil Paintings, Fancy Chairs, Liberia Curiosities, Coffee Urn, Gilt Frame Looking Glasses, Gold Watch & Chain, 2 Houses, Union Bank Stock, personal Bonds. Recorded 15 Sept 1882. Among purchasers at Estate Sale: W. G. RUSSELL, Sr., Isaac W. & Tillie M. RUSSELL, Randall MARTIN, Miss Annie BRIGGS, Mary TOLIVER, Jacob WARDEN, Miss Kate LAMBDEN, Mrs. Marshall WILLIS. Mrs. Bruce GIBSON.

Page 432:   Appraisal of Estate of Mary Ann SMITH, dec'd, 30 Jany 1881.
Appraisers: J. I. H. BAKER, T. N. LUPTON, George E. JENKINS.   Only items
are City of Winchester Bonds and personal Bonds of W. G. RUSSELL, Sr.,
J. S. JACKSON, Jas. H. BURGESS, Thos. S. SHADDEN, Jno. L. CARLIN.
Total: $4,746.67.   Recorded 15 Sept 1882.

Pages 433-435: Jas. B. RUSSELL in Account with Estate of Miss H. H. RUSSELL,
dec'd. Begins June 1881 with cash on hand; received interest and proceeds of
Sale of Personal Estate and Sale of two Houses (to Mrs. John LINN and W. G.
RUSSELL, Sr.). Among expenses paid: medical bills, funeral expenses, house
cleaning, taxes, fees. Executor's account recorded Novr 20, 1882.

Pages 436-437: Estate of Mrs. M. A. SMITH, dec'd., in Account with Jas. B.
RUSSELL, Admr. Begins Aug 1881 with such receipts as "in part and in full
judgment on Jas. H. BURGESS", Dividends, interest, Bond Principal. Cash paid
to Attorneys, to Rev. H. M. WHITE, Pastor of Presby. Church; to Dr. D.S.,
Hattie T., Edwin L., Tillie M., Isaac W., James B., and W. G. RUSSELL, Jr;
Other legatees: Mrs. Mary E. GIBSON, Mrs. Mary E. WILLIS; Selia WILSON.
Admin Account recorded 20 Nov 1882.

Pages 438-439: Estate of Godfrey MILLER, dec'd., in Account with Jno. Abra-
ham MILLER, his Admr. Begins Nov 1881 with such receipts as that from Kate
WOLFE, executrix of R. B. WOLFE, dec'd., Bonds and interest received. Paid
for Grave for Mrs. MILLER; paid H. BAETJER & Co. for funeral; paid G. W.
KURTZ & Co. for coffin, etc.; paid for tombstones, taxes, attorneys fees.
Balance for distribution, $4,213.97, to ten legatees as named in will.
Estate account with Jno. Abr. MILLER, Admr., recorded 19 Jany 1882.

Pages 440-441: Will of Eliza Jane STRIKER. All property to sister, Elizabeth STRIKER and her husband, Vance W. STRIKER, except household furniture
or its value to sister, Alice T. McCARTEY. ___ Dec 1881. Wit: Dorsey
WALTER, David HAMILTON. Proved 18 Sept 1882. Vance W. STRIKER, Admr.

Pages 442-444: Will of George W. CROCKWELL. All property to wife, Mary. At
her death, to son, Wm. C. CROCKWELL. Dr. G. S. MILLER, trustee, to hold and
apply proceeds of estate for maintenance of son, William C. CROCKWELL, during
his lifetime. After death of wife and William C., the rest to his children.
Lot and House on Clifford Street to Charles E. CROCKWELL, in trust for daughter, Catherine C. CARRIGAN, free from control of her husband. Other lots on
Clifford & Braddock Streets to sons, Charles E. and John R. CROCKWELL. Wife,
Mary, to be executrix. 22 May 1875. Proved 18 Dec 1882. James H. MARKELL,
Admr.

Pages 445-460: Report of Sales Account by Jno. J. WILLIAMS, Admr. of Mrs.
Harriet A. MILLER, dec'd. July 13 & 14 1878. Long list of items sold and
purchasers, some of which are: J. H. BITZER, wash tub & Bread tray; Rob't.
WEBB, lumber; Joe HEITT, 3 jugs; F. W. KOHLHOUSEN, Demijohn; C. A. B.
COFFROTH, Clothes Horse; H. BESORE, Hod; Mrs. Wm. JENKINS, Lamp Shade.
Estate account inspected and approved 2 Augt 1882.

Pages 461-463: Estate of Mary B. WHITE, dec'd., in Account with Wm. M.
ATKINSON, her Exec. Begins Feby 1881 with investments in Union Bank Stock
and in Bowley & Hensel Bond; paid R. B. WHITE, expenses for Miss Mary B.
WHITE; paid Mrs. Lucy PAYNE board bill; paid Wm. M ATKINSON his expenses
to go to Staunton & bring trunk to Winchester; paid burial permit. Account
recorded Jany 19, 1883.

Pages 464-465: Inventory and Appraisement of Estate of Andrew J. HOUCK, dec'd., with appraisers: Henry KENZIL, H. M. BAKER, P. W. BOYD, 23 Jan 1883. Total Appraisal: Cash in Bank, Shares in Shen. V. N. Bank, Shares in Wm. Buildg? (Mutual), and Bond of Oscar BARR. Recorded Jan 31, 1883.

Pages 466-469: Will of E. S. W. TAYLOR, Clermont, Clarke Co, Va. Elizabeth S. W. TAYLOR appoints John J. WILLIAMS, her executor. Not provided for is Miss Patsey FROST's annuity. From Dearmont and Grim "debts due me" pay in equal shares to Mary M. SULLIVAN, wife of A. S. SULLIVAN, and their son, George H. SULLIVAN; to Thomas B. & Harriet M. HAMMOND and Florinda TILFORD, children of George W. & Sarah A. HAMMOND; to Bessie T. & Frank V. TILFORD; to Alice KOUNSLAR, B. Taylor and Edward M. STRIBLING, children of John & Ann STRIBLING. When collect on Note of Wm. TAYLOR, give to Mrs Bettie LUPTON; Mary & Florinda MILTON; Wm. TAYLOR and his daughter, Anna MOSS; Eliza TUCKER, widow, and her son, Alfred B. TUCKER. From Dr. Bushrod TAYLOR's Note: to niece, Sally HOLLIDAY, daughter of Sarah C. & Robert HOLLIDAY. 31 Aug 1881. Wit: E. S. McCORMICK, S. Scolly MOORE. Codicil, 31 Aug 1881. "I have often and for months at a time lived with Mrs. Mary SULLIVAN, wife of Algernon SULLIVAN." Wishes to pay her "such sum as she may think right". Adjusts her bequests so this change has priority. Wit: E. S. McCORMICK, A. R. BROWN. Proved 21 Feby 1883.

Pages 470-471: Estate of Harriet S. MARSTELLER, dec'd., in account with C. W. WILSON, her Admr. Begins 1881 with cash paid in suit in Baltimore County, Md. Among other payments are for shingles to cover house, new hydrant and pipe, auctioneer, Albin & Bros. for Tombstones, commissions. Receipts did not cover expenses. Recorded 21 May 1883.

Pages 472-475: Estate of C. B. MANN, dec'd., in Account with Geo. T. Mann, his Admr. Begins Jany 1882 with receipts of cash of Mary MANN, widow (cash in hand at death), Bank Deposits, Shop Fixtures sold, Furniture etc sold to widow at appraisement, Wagon, Harness and Barber Tent sold, collected on Notes and Accounts. Among expenses paid were to B. NOONAN for hacks at funeral, G. W. KURTZ funeral bill, Gas bill, appraisers fees and city & state taxes. Distribution share in estate: to Mary MANN, widow, and to Emma MANN, only child paid to her trustee. Payment of $139.55 to widow was overpayment so reduced it to $120.43. Recorded 19 Feby 1883.

Pages 476-477: Will of Tilman SHUMATE. To sister, Elizabeth, shares of stock in each Shen. Valley Natl Bank and Winchester & Strasburg R. R. To sister, Rebecca, shares of stock in Potomac R. R., in Shen. Valley Bank & Union Bank of Winchester. To sister, Martha, house & lot on NE corner, Washington & Amherst Streets, etc., Books etc, without appraisement. Law library to E. P. DANDRIDGE. Gold watch & Chain to Wilson L. BROWN. Executor to be John J. WILLIAMS. 9 Nov 1882. No witnesses. Proved 21 May 1883.

Pages 478-479: Will of Frederick WULFERT. All estate to wife, Sophia, and she to have full control. At her death, all to father, Henry WULFERT, and mother, Gertrude, of New York state. If wife and parents die, then all to brothers and sisters. Sophia to be executrix. Apr 29, 1880. Wit: J. D. KIGER, J. C. REILY. Proved 21 May 1883. Note at bottom of Page 479, in different handwriting, mentions appraisers appointed: T. M. BAUTZ, Jno. R. JONES, John C. SEABRIGHT, Charles BOXWELL, Eugene BLOCKLEY. May 22, 1899.

Pages 480-481: Estate of Ann RANDOLPH, dec'd., in Account with S. N. HUCK, her Admr. Sept 1880, cash paid for bond, taxes, fees & commission for Admr. Jany 1881, Cash received from B. RANDOLPH's estate. Balance shows total due Admr which has been assigned to Byrd HUCK. Recorded 17 Apr 1883.

Pages 482-486: Will of Sarah FIELDS. Revokes other wills. Three sons, Robert, Raph, Charles to have all personal property at its appraised value, except Charles to have best bed & bedding. Brick house & lot, Kent Street north of the Baltimore & Ohio R. R. depot, to three sons subject to their payment of legacies of $275. House & lot on Cecil Street to daughter, Sarah COURAGER, if she or her heirs pay legacies of $175. To daughters, Felicia WASHINGTON, $25; Susan MITCHELL, $100; Jane BRIGHTON, $100. To four children of Cornelia TOCUS, $100; to granddaughter, Sally, child of Abraham FIELDS, $25; to sons, William & Aaron, $25 each. William M. ATKINSON to be executor. 22 Nov 1877. Wit: John R. JONES, Geo. E. WILLIS. Codicil, 8 July 1881 (at end of codicil, the date is 8 Nov 1881). Changes legacy given to son, William, now deceased, to son, Charles and legacy left to daughter, Felicia, to go to son, Charles. Wit: John H. CREBS, J. C. SEABRIGHT. Proved 21 May 1883.

Pages 487-489: Estate of Edward JONES, dec'd., in Account with Julia E. JONES, his Executrix. Sept 1881 to Jany 1883: some receipts for selling sausage machine and stuffer, pair of scales, lot of land; payments for clerk's and attorney's fees, taxes, and "swearing apprasers". Not enough funds to pay debts. Most of property exempt under the "poor law". Widow and children sold portion of lot where decedent had lived and applied that to paying debts. Recorded June 18, 1883.

Pages 490-493: Inventory and Appraisement of Estate of Tilman SHUMATE, dec'd. Appraisers: W. B. BAKER, Bentley KERN, Dorsey WALTER. Among items: Bond of Oscar BARR, shares of Stock in Winc. Strasburg R. R. and in Winc. & Potomac R. R.; Corp. of Winchester Bonds; Bank Stocks; Bonds of Robert P. & Sarah S. GLASS. Appraisal signed June 30, 1883. Recorded 5 July 1883.

Pages 494-495: Appraisement of Estate of John W. MARVIN, dec'd. Among items: 3 long School Desks with Benches, 4 short School Desks with Benches, School Benches with and without Backs; case of Philosophical & Chemical Apparatus, Cabinet of Minerals, Blackboard. 21 Nov 1882. Appraisers: O.M. BROWN, R. Wm. WALTER, J. C. MAXWELL. Recorded 11 July 1883.

Pages 496-498: Sale Account of Jno. W. MARVIN with Dorsey WALTER, Admr. Examples of Sales: 2 short Desks purchased by Miss BURNSIDE for 40¢; Globe by Miss E. BROWN, 13¢; Long Desk by J. C. WHEAT, 45¢; Acorn Bedstead by J. W. KREMER, 50¢; Dinner Bell by R. R. BROWN, 15¢. Recorded 11 July 1883.

Pages 499-501: Will of J. H. GIBBENS, who presently owns small brick storehouse, west side of Loudoun Street, dwelling house & lot on east side of Loudoun Street adjoining Henry EVANS, a 4-acre lot with 3-story brick house on west side of Martinsburg Turnpike. All of these to C. W. GIBBENS, his nephew, as trustee, to manage, sell, use funds any way for maintenance, education and general advancement of his children. Mentions real estate in Indiana. "To wife, Mary, rest of it and whatever or elsewhere." 1 Aug 1882. No witnesses. Proved July 16, 1883 by oaths of J. P. BROWN and Douglas FULLER, who recognized handwriting of decedent. Wife, Mary, renounces her right to qualify as Administratrix.

Pages 502-503: Estate of George JONES, dec'd., in Account with C. W. REED, Sergeant & Commr. Admr. Begins Jany 1881 with receipts of rent from T. BANNISTER and C. CHANDLER; proceeds from Sales; paid for coffin, $20; paid Bell Bros for Crape and Henry BESORE, cryer. Recorded July 16, 1883.

Pages 504-510: Estate of Andrew J. HOUCK, dec'd., in Account with Chas. W. HOUCK, his Admr. Begins with cash in Bank; collected rent, interest and dividends; paid for coffin, hearse, hacks for funeral, cemetery grave, and retained $200 for tombstones. Distribution of estate: "the decedent was intestate, unmarried and childless" so $9,011.12 to be divided equally among his six brothers and sisters: Charles W. HOUCK, Mrs. Mary F. RIDENOUR, Mrs. Mary Ann SLAGLE, wife of Wm. I. SLAGLE, Harrison HOUCK, Mrs. Jane MILLER, James HOUCK. Recorded 16 July 1883.

Pages 511-512: Inventory and Appraisal of Estate of E. S. W. TAYLOR, dec'd., in Hands of her Executor, John J. WILLIAMS. No appraisers named. Bonds of Jane E. DEARMONT, Bond of Bushrod TAYLOR (believed to be uncollectible), Bond of William & Hannah TAYLOR (of doubtful solvency). Signed by Jno. J. WILLIAMS, Exec. Recorded 7 July 1883.

Pages 512-513: Inventory and Appraisal of Estate of Frank WASHINGTON, dec'd., with appraisers: Raw? MARTIN, George W. NICKENS, Robert ORRICK. 12 May 1882. Lucy WASHINGTON, Admr. Among items in small inventory: two featherbeds, Stool, Wash Stand, 4 chairs, 3 Hogs, 3 pictures. Recorded 19 Nov 1883.

Pages 514-519: Will of Almira E. SHARP, of Baltimore, Maryland. To cousin, Richard BROWN, Jr., all property, in trust, for benefit of sister, Florence V. SHARP. At her death, divide equally "among my heirs at law". Richard BROWN, Jr., to be executor. 29 Dec 1880. Wit: Louis DOHANE, John A. WELL-INGTON, Joseph BLUM, Rob't. T. PETZOLD. Almira E. SHARP died 27 Dec 1883. Will proved 4 Jany 1884. Many papers from Baltimore signed by Robert T. BANKS, Register of Wills. 8 Jany 1884. Dated in Winchester Jan 21, 1884.

Pages 519-522: Will of S. F. GAENSLEN. Executor to sell "as soon after my death as he can" all real estate. House and Lot on East side of Loudoun Street (in which testator lived for many years and in which the Post Office is now kept). Also House and Lot on Water Street between Braddock and Washington, known as the Slagle Brewery property. All property plus proceeds from Sales to four grandchildren: Frederick B., Mary Cornelia, George R., and Bessie, children of my deceased son, Dr. John Jacob GAENSLEN. During their minority, to be held by Samuel L. LARUE as trustee and Executor. (Mother of the grandchildren is now living). 2 Dec 1882. Wit: C. M. GIBBENS, T. A. LATHAM. Proved 21 Apr 1884. On 16 June 1884, S. L. LAREW qualified as Executor and Trustee.

Pages 523-524: Will of R. R. BROWN. To two sisters, Sarah Ann BROWN and Margaret H. BROWN, one-half rent of Brick House on the hill on East Lane. To son, Richard R. BROWN, corporate Stock; to son, John, corporate Stock; also to these two sons, stock in the Tanyard. To three daughters and son, Charles, corporate stock. To wife, Elizabeth J. BROWN, all property except above. Property given to daughters is "to them and no other person". Wife to be executrix. "The sixteenth of the third month, 1881" Proved 22 Apr 1884. No witnesses so S.T. MOORE proved handwriting.

Pages 525-527: Will of Virginia M. BURNS. Executor to sell real estate: undivided one-half interest in 2 houses and lots in Higgonsville, Mo. held jointly with sister, Mrs. A. M. EARLE. Also vacant lot in same place. Collect money held or invested by Geo. O. WASHBURN, of Blackston, Mo. Also collect what due from A. M. EARLE. Pay funeral expenses plus marble slab and lot in Mr. Hebron Cemetery. Makes bequests to Miss Fannie M. EVANS and G. Washington BURNS, "my uncle"; to Mary Gertrude CAMERON, of St. Louis.

To brother, Oliver M. BURNS, of Higginsville, Mo., rents and interest that accrue each year for 6 years. To Fannie A. CASTLEAR, to educate her daughters, Eloise, Bessie and Fannie. At end of 6 years, above to go to Rev. J. R. GRAHAM, Rev. C. W. HOLLIS, and Holmes CONRAD to dispose of as they think proper. Gives to two sisters, Mary E. EARLE and Fanni A. CASTLEAR. James B. RUSSELL to be executor. 14 Mar 1884. Wit: Holmes CONRAD, Sarah C. McCOLLUM. Proved 19 May 1884.

Pages 528-530: Estate of Thos. J. RITT, dec'd., in Account with Daniel THOMPSON, his Exec. Jan 28, 1882 to May 1883 with such expenses as paid Appraisers: C. H. GRIM, F. C. WINDLE, G. W. RANDOLPH; paid for coffin and hack; paid Dr. HENKEL's account; paid Jane LUCAS for washing; paid freight on clothing; paid several fees and commissions. Recorded April 17, 1884.

Pages 531-539: Will of John M ROSS. "I, John M. ROSS, of the United States Army." All property to wife, Gertrude V. ROSS. At her death, to "our daughter, Gertrude C. ROSS". Wife is appointed executrix and she to manage estate and settled without intervention of probate court, according to Code of Washington Territory. Wife to be guardian of the daughter. 4 Aug 1883. Wit: N. H. BLOOMFIELD and W. Byron DANIELS, of Vancouver, Clark Co., W.T. Proved 3 June 1884 by depositions from Probate Judge of Clarke Co., Wash. Terr. N. H. BLOOMFIELD, 33 years old, occupation: attorney, said at time of signing the will, decedent was 21 years old. W. Byron DANIELS, 35 years old, attorney. Wife qualifies as executrix, June 16, 1884.

Pages 540-545: Will of Isaac KREBS. "Wife being dead, I have no provishun to make for her." Four sons and two daughters now living: William Francis, Rufus Isaac, Walter Edmond, Henry Clay, Louisa M., wife of C. W. COONTZ, Joanna B., wife of Camillus S. HART. All estate to be divided into six equal parts. "Against all of these children I have charches and notes to come first out of their share." Interest at 6% must be "charched on said debts". To Louisa: had already made donation to her of $1500 to buy lot to make brick on and carry on business to make a living for herself and children. After these debts paid out of her share of estate, any left, paid to Henry Clay KREBS, her trustee, for her sole use and of her children. As for Joanna B. and husband, C. S. HART, "charches paid first". Remaining to her brother, Walter E. KREBS, in trust for her sole benefit. She can change trustee to anyone she wishes but not to husband. Son, William F., has but one child named Kate E. Henry C. KREBS and Walter E. KREBS to be executors. Bulk of estate probably will be Bonds, Notes and Cash on hand. 4 Feb 1876. Wit: W. T. GILBERT, Geo. F. GLAIZE. Codicil, 11 June 1876. Since making will, daughter, Louisa M. COONTZ, wife of C. W. COONTZ, "dide", left 3 children: Walter K., Emma V. and Jo. Esther. He provides distribution of their mother's share to them. Wit: Bentley KERN, J. W. BARR. Codicil, Feb 13, 1878, adds: William F. KREBS, son, to be executor. Wit: W. T. GILBERT, Geo. F. GLAIZE. Proved July 21, 1884.

Pages 546-549: Inventory and Appraisement of Estate of S. F. GAENSLEN, dec'd., with Appraisers: John G. MILLER, C. W. HOLLIS, C.W. REED, Lewis N. HUCK, D. H. BRAGONIER. 12 July 1884. Among items: Cash in Bank, $2,798.50; Bonds of N. ROUTZHAN, John J. ANDERSON, Hunter B. GRIM, Philip W & Holmes BOYD, August GRAICHEN, Eliz. A. & J. W. SCHULTZ, Jas. B. & Anna V. STREIT. Houses & Lots on Main Street and on Water Street.

Bonds appraised at worthless: Jno. W. BELL, Wm. H. STREIT, W. I. SLAGLE, P. HANSUCKER. Recorded 17 July 1884.

Pages 550-552: Inventory and Appraisement of Estate of Eliza SHUMATE, dec'd. Appraisers: Bently KERN, Henry KINZEL, S. H. HANSBROUGH. 25 July 1884. Among items: 3 doz. fruit jars, 2 rocking chairs, 1 towel, ten plate stove and cook stove, many bonds of Corporation of Winchester. Recorded 5 Aug 1884.

Pages 553-554: Inventory and Appraisement of Estate of Catharine GRAICHEN, dec'd., with appraisers Geo. W. HILLYARD, James HODGSON, James LOWRY. 26 May 1884. Total inventory: 2 bonds of J. A. GRAICHEN, $2,000. Recorded 7 Oct 1884.

END OF WILL BOOK NO. 3

Page 1: Will of Elias A. HIBBARD, born 17 Augt 1801, Concord, Vermont. After paying debts "and fulfiling the contract entered into between me and my wife previous to marriage", gives to daughter, Emily A. SMITH and husband, Wm. A. SMITH, both of Boston, Mass., all property. Wm. S. CLARK, now mayor of Winchester, executor. 22 Feby 1879. No witnesses. Proved by Samuel L. LAREW and John H. CREBS, Oct 22, 1884.

Pages 2-3: Will of Caroline M. HIBBARD. To niece, Helen S. STEPHENS, all real estate including testator's one-half interest in house where " I now reside which was willed to me by my late husband, Elias A. HIBBARD, on Main Street". Niece not to sell house but to hold it "to prevent it from falling into the hands of outside persons". 10 June 1884. Wit: P. H. REARDON, J. P. WHITACRE, Elizabeth REARDON. Proved Oct 21, 1884. James P. WHITACRE, Admr.

Pages 3-4: Will of Eliza GLENHOLM. Pay debts, funeral expenses and stone at grave. All property to daughter, Annie E. NOAKES, widow of Samuel G. NOAKES. Daughter to be executrix, no security required. Daughter to keep grave and lot in good condition. 29 July 1880. Wit: D. H. BRAGONIER, Daniel BUSH, George E. JENKINS. Proved 17 Nov 1884.

Pages 4-5: Will of Elizabeth M COFFROTH. To son, Edwin M. COFFROTH, $600. To daughter, Gertrude V. ROSS, all estate of every kind including moneys, bonds, investments, except certain household and kitchen items on a written list in possession of friend, C. S. W. BARNES. Articles on list willed to daughter only so long as she lives or as long as she resides and keeps house in Winchester or vicinity. At her death or change of residence or breaking up housekeeping, articles to persons named in list. Daughter to be executrix. 27 Oct 1884. Wit: T. P. SPOTTS, C. S. W. BARNES. Proved Dec 15, 1884.

Pages 6-12: Estate of Tilman SHUMATE, dec'd., in Account with Jno. J. WILLIAMS, his Exec. Begins May 21, 1883 with Balances in Union and SVN Banks; Dividends from W&P R R Stock & Bonds; Cash on Bonds of Mrs. Sarah S. GLASS; Cash from Life Insurance Policy; Paid items as S. P. STACKHOUSE, Undertaker; Safe Dept & Trust Co.; Martha SHUMATE, rent rec'd. of E. P. DANDRIDGE; Rebecca SHUMATE, Legatee; Loaned to Josiah RINKER; paid State tax on Estate of Eliza SHUMATE, dec'd. Final Distribution to: Elizabeth, Rebecca and Martha SHUMATE. Recorded 13 May 1885.

Pages 13-14: Will of Alfred SEAL. Wife, Catherane M. SEAL, all property, to have and control. At her death, to son, Henry SEAL. Son, John M. SEAL, "long since received his share of my estate by deed to a lot adjoining where I now reside, west of mine". 1 Feby 1883. Wit: S. M. MULLIN, M. H. SPOTTS. Proved May 18, 1885. May 19, 1885, Catharane M. SEAL, widow, waived her right to be Admr. Samuel L. LAREW, appointed.

Pages 14-15: Will of Elizabeth B. MEREDITH. Aug 9, 1880. All to daughters, Elizabeth H. SMITH and Virginia I. BRAGONIER, equally except to Virginia, Butter Dish, Cake Knife, 6 tablespoons, 7 teaspoons, all silver and one silver-plated coffee set. Wit: J. R. GRAHAM, Robert A. DENNY. Proved May 19, 1885. Handwriting proved by Joseph H. MEREDITH and he appointed Admr.

Pages 15-16: Estate Account of Elizabeth WALL, dec'd., in Account with
James W. BARR, her Admr. (No date) paid Kern, Barr & Co. in full; paid
Mattie WALL and Miss Virginia WALL, legatees. Jany 19, 1880, amount
received of S. T. MOORE, Admr. of Mathias RITTER; received of T. T. WALL
Note; received of Mrs. Rebecca HARDY; received of Appraisal of personal
property & household goods/furniture. Appraisers: P. O. FISHER, E. M.
BARR. Recorded 15 June 1885.

Page 17: Will of Rosa HAYMAKER. To Sophia E. HAYMAKER, all property including House & Lot on Kent Street. 3 Apr 1885. Witnesses, who called her
Rosanna HAYMAKER: S. T. HOLLIDAY, Lafayette JACKSON, L. N. HUCK. Proved
18 June 1885.

Pages 18-21: Inventory and Appraisement of Estate of J. D. GOSHERT, dec'd.,
with Emma C. GOSHERT, Admr. Appraisers: S. L LAREW, T. F. GRIM, Jacob
HOOVER. 22 June 1885. Among items: 8 Hogs, several Safes, Four Horse Stage,
Old Hack, Sleighs, Spring Wagon, 2 Buck Board Wagons, Buggies. Mention is
of Boyce Stage, Martinsburg Stage, Berryville Stage and Berryville & River
Stage. Other items in Inventory are Stage Office & Fixtures, Harnesses and
many Horses. Among Bonds held are those of Jas. T. RIELY, Geo. W. KAUFFMAN,
Jno. HUBER, C. E. GOSHERT, Henry HUSER & Son. Recorded July 11, 1885.

Page 22: Will of B. NOONAN (Bartholemew). All estate after paying debts, to
wife (unnamed) to do with as she deems best. Apr 6, 1885. Wit: Jas. P.
RIELY, R. G. SMITH. Proved 21 Sept 1885. Isabella NOONAN, Executrix.

Pages 23-25: Estate of Mrs. Eliza SHUMATE, dec'd., in Account with Catharine
BROWN, her Admr. Begins July 24, 1884 with paying taxes and attorney's fees.
Other items: Received cash for coupons on Bonds of City of Winchester and on
US Bonds. Made distribution of cash and furniture to Elizabeth, Rebecca and
Martha J. SHUMATE. Paid commissioners and clerks fees. Account recorded
19 Oct 1885.

Pages 25-39: Inventory, Appraisement and Sale Account of Estate of Mrs.
C. M. HIBBARD, dec'd. Appraisers: E. S. HODGSON, David DAVISON, W. M.
ROBINSON, appointed 30 Oct 1884. Some items in large inventory: Lot of
Pictures in Parlor, 6 cain seat Chairs, Spittoons, Lamp & Lantern, sheet
iron Stove, Feather Beds & Straw Ticks, many Bed Clothes, 5 bags Soap,
1 box Bottels, many Sundries, lot of Sawed Wood, contents of Coal Celler,
4 Window Blinds, Certains & Strings. Account by J. P. WHITACRE, Admr.,
ordered to lie for exceptions, 19 Oct 1885. No exceptions, so recorded
21 Dec 1885. Among purchasers at Estate Sale: James STOTTLEMYER, John
DARLINGTON, Henry WULFERT, John VILWIG, James WHETZELL, Wm. STRONG. Estate
Sale recorded 21 Decr 1885.

Pages 40-45: Estate of Henry M. JAMESON in Account with A. R. PENDLETON,
Admr. Begins Jany 31, 1885 with cash received of S. WILLIAMS and cash from
W. & J. HOTTEL on Bond. Expenses paid: Attorney for services as to assignment in Pennsylvania; Attorney fees for suit vs W & J HOTTEL; Attorney fees
for advise as to House & Lot and proceeding to get the whole of it; Attorney
fees for suit in chancery to sell lot in Shenandoah; paid Sheriff, Shenandoah County; paid C. B. HANCOCK, Sheriff; paid Clerk & Sheriff, Rockingham
County. Estate of Henry M. JAMESON in Account with E. P. DANDRIDGE, former
Admr., begins Feby 10, 1883, with cash received of W. & J. HOTTEL; paid for
affidavit, clerks and appraisers fees; paid attorneys fees. Paid for telegram. Paid Mrs. Mary A. JAMESON, Assignee of Susan HINKS (later called HINKINS)

$50. Final Distribution of Estate of Henry M. JAMESON: To Mrs. Mary A. JAMESON, $102.33½. To the following, $20.46-3/5 each: J. B. JAMESON, Ellen SHERMAN & husband, Amelia LEVER & husband, Rush JAMESON's Estate, Nancy WEAVER's Estate. Recorded 21 Dec 1885.

Pages 45-49: Will of Portia L. BALDWIN, of Frederick County. Executor instructed to collect all claims, including debt due Estate of son, R. T. BALDWIN, and pay legacies: To grandson, Lawrence CLARK, to Nephew, Wm. E. JACKSON, to Niece, Philippa JACKSON, to granddaughter, Portia Lee MORRISON (as stipulated by her father, Rev. Dr. ATKINSON, re land in Buffaloe Marsh Tract in Frederick County). If any funds left, put in trust for benefit of grandchildren, William Ludwell and Portia BALDWIN. Mentions land in Frederick County, devised by deceased son, John H. BALDWIN, about 296 acres, to set up trusts for grandson, Robert Lawrence CLARK, Imogen & Peyton CLARK, sister and brother of Lawrence. William Ludwell and Portia BALDWIN are children of deceased son, William Ludwell BALDWIN, who owed debt to deceased son, John H. BALDWIN. There is now a suit in Chancery Court, Frederick County, with Portia L. BALDWIN, plaintiff, and Cornelia HOLPHINS, devisee, and others as defendants. Nephew, D. F. LEE, Jr., to take charge of all furniture and household effects and distribute. Nephew, Cassuis F. LEE, Jr., of Alexandria, Va. to be executor. 15 Oct 1883. Wit: E. R. MILLER, Jno. M. MILLER, W. W. MILLER. Proved 21 Dec 1885.

Page 50: Will of Henry KINZEL, Febr 10, 1886. (very short will, no witnesses) Wife, Lucy C. KINZEL, to have all personal and real property of every description and wherever located. Mentions "my children". Wife to be executrix, without security. Requests she make provisions for unmarried daughters "to have comfortable support and will further request her not to endorse for anyone". Proved Monday, 15 March 1886, by oaths of E. Holmes BOYD and M. H. G. WILLIS, who deposed they were well acquainted with the handwriting of the deceased. Bond for Lucy C. KINZEL to be executrix set at $40,000.

Pages 51-53: Will of Samuel L. LAREW. Executor to sell on best terms he can, the following real estate: Houses & Lots at 160 E. S. Cameron St., 40 E. S. Cameron St., 42 E. S. W&M Pike, E. S. Kent St., 9 N. S. Wolfe St, and Lot 45, S. E. Picdy. St. and E. Lane. Executor to collect all tax bills, notes & debts due, except those he regards as investment. Funds collected to be invested in good real estate or other securities. Two Bonds against Jos. S. DAVIS Estate and others against Constantine ORK not to be collected until after death of Mrs. Mary DAVIS and "my sister, Sarah ORK". When collected, pay to son, Sam'l. L. LAREW, Jr. Rest to wife, Sarah S. LAREW and at her death to son, Samuel L. LAREW, Jr. and his children. If he dies without surviving children then all "to my brothers and sisters, equally." C. M. GIBBENS to be executor. 8 Jany 1886. Wit: T. A. LATHAM, G. S. MILLER, Wm. M DESHON. Codicil, 9 Feby 1886, to bequeath to nephew, Milliard ORORK, "for his faithful attention to me in my sickness, tract of land in Frederick County on which he and his mother now live". Wit: G. S. MILLER, C. W. REED. Proved 15 Mar 1886.

Pages 53-55: Will of William Henry FAIRFAX. Executor to collect money due and from this pay funeral expenses, erect tombstone and pay debts. To William ORRICK "the first room I built" and specific furniture. To

Ida "the other room I built", forks and things I have given to her. To
Robert ORRICK "the things at Robert ORRICK's ". To George NICKENS, large
hickory rocking chair and small clock. To Chanie, "the chair I loaned her".
Other bequests to Ned MONTGOMERY, Maria BROWN, Isham & Mark WILLIAMS,
Misses Lucy & Sallie WILLIAMS. To Nancy TURNER, "the prettiest clock";
to Thomas REARDON (Little Tommy) "my gold watch"; to Willie REARDON
"my silver watch". Many other bequests. 25 Jany 1886. Wit: P. H. REAR-
DON, W. C. REILY. Codicil, Feby 2, 1886, directs Sarah STRANGE to have
dressing table & mirror and M. P. REARDON to be executor. Wit: L. D.
WILLIAMS. Proved 22 April 1886. Appraisers appointed: John RAY, T. C.
WILLIAMS, J. P. SILER, T. V. PURCELL.

Pages 56-59: Appraisal of Estate of Samuel F. GAENSLEN, dec'd. 18 March
1886. Appraisers appointed: John J. WILLIAMS, Alex R. PENDLETON, Wm. R.
ALEXANDER, Dorsey WALTER, R. T. BARTON. Some of the inventory: Certifi-
cate for 20 Shares Stock in Shenandoah Valley Nat'l. Bank; Bond of N.
ROUTZAHN, dated Oct 9, 1877; Bonds of John J. ANDERSON & Others, of Hun-
ter GRIM, Henry B. BROWN, Geo. P. & C. S. BAKER, Philip W. & E. Holmes
BOYD, James B. & Annie V. STREIT. Notes of W. T. NOTT, F. August GRAICHEN,
Elizabeth A. & J. W. SCHULTZ, and of Hiram Lodge No. 21, Free & Accepted
Mason of the Town of Winchester, dated 1 May 1867. Three Notes of B. F.
HARPER and Bonds of Samuel G. NOAKES, of Lucy, Annie & Jennie BRIGGS, of
the United States, and of John C. COE. Considered worthless are Bonds of
John N. BELL, of Wm. H. STREIT, and of Wm. I. SLAGLE. 29 March 1886.
Appraisal recorded 19 Apr 1886. Lewis N. HUCK, Admr.

Pages 60-62: Appraisal of Estate of Henry KINZEL, dec'd., Mar 10, 1886.
Appraisers appointed: John W. RICE, Geo. E. JENKINS, James W. BARR, T. T.
WALL, H. Clay KREBS. Total Inventory: Stock and Fixtures in Store &
Bakery; Furniture in 2-story dwelling; 1 Buggy; 12 Bonds of Rockingham
County; Bonds of US, Corporation of Winchester; Notes of J. E. & E. D.
LAWS, Wm. H. HARDY, T. T. WALL, J. Miller LONG, Dawson McCORMICK, Geo. C.
NEVILLE; Cash in Banks; Drafts on Bank of America, N. Y. Lucy C. KINZEL
added Stock in Citizens Building Assn. Recorded 17 May 1886.

Page 62: Appraisal of the Estate of Adam FORNEY. Appraisers: R. M.
PARKER, John R. MESMER, Wm. R. JONES appeared before D. H. BRAGONIER, a
Commr. in Frederick County, 22 March 1886. Only item in Inventory is
Money on deposit, Union Bank. Recorded 17 May 1886.

Page 63: Appraisal of the Estate of Nancy FORNEY. Appraisers appointed
by Frederick County, 22 March 1886, are same as those for Adam FORNEY's
Appraisal. Only item in this Inventory: 15 shares of Winchester & Potomac R. R. Stock & Dividends. Recorded 17 May 1886.

Pages 64-65: Appraisal of Estate of Wm. Henry FAIRFAX, 3 May 1886.
Appraisers: T. V. PURCELL, J. P. SILER, T. C. WILLIAMS. Part of Inventory:
Gold & Silver Watches; metal, wooden and round clocks; household wares &
furniture; Bonds of Mary J. J. & P. WILLIAMS Estates. Doubtful accounts:
John I. BAKER, Bettie TURNER, George PENN, Gabe FESTUS, Alfred HORNEY, Alex
CAREY, Robert SMITH, and Methodist Church. Appraisal recorded 17 May 1886.

Pages 65-66: Appraisal of Estate of H. Benton WILLIS, dec'd, with S. L.
LAREW, Admr. "No property belonging to said estate has been produced to us
for appraisal." D. H. BRAGONIER, C. W. HOLLIS, L. T. MOON. Appraisal
recorded 17 May 1886.

Pages 66-67: Will of Evan P. ANDERSON, "in feble health". After payment of honest debts, his remains to be buried in Mt. Hebron Cemetery in lot of Nancy ALEXANDER's estate, with suitable tombstone. All estate after payment of $50 to J. Gus GREEN, to be divided equally between J. Gus GREEN and Sadie KERFOOT, daughter of Jack KERFOOT. Jas. B. RUSSELL to be executor. 25 March 1886. Wit: Daniel BUSH, Isaac K. ANDERSON. Proved 17 May 1886. Jas. B. RUSSELL "refused to take upon himself the burthen" of the execution of this will. John H. CREBS to administer.

Pages 67-74: Appraisement of the Estate of S. L. LAREW, dec'd., Frederick County. Appraisers appointed by City: R. M. PARKER, C. W. REED, Wm. H. CALVERT, N. A. BRENT. 19 March 1886. Among items in the Appraisement of House Hold "Stuff devised to the widow, Sarah": one double heater stove, one organ, 2 ottomans, parlor furniture, Bookcase, Bureaus & Bed Room Furniture, 3 horses, saddle, wagon & harness, 9 new doors, two hunting case gold watches. At "Wall" place: harrow, hay rake, plow, two-horse plow (oliver chilled) & other things. Among things in the "Treasurer's Office": desk, table, chairs, 6 pieces real estate to be sold. More than 100 Notes of which these two are doubtful: Stock of Winchester Gas and Stock of Shenandoah Valley Agricultural Society. Not reported are certificates for shares of Stock in Winchester & Martinsburg Turnpike in the names of other parties found among Mr. Larew's things. Recorded 21 June 1886. C. M. GIBBENS, Exec.

Pages 75-76: Appraisement of Estate of Andrew J. FRANK, dec'd., 18 May 1886. Appraisers: John R. MESMER, Richard M. PARKES, Wm. R. JONES and M. D. ALBIN who was appointed but did not serve. Among items in short inventory: Notes of ASHBY and of C. W. & Wm. H. FRANK; 2 tables, 6 chairs, lounge, cow, 2 stoves, safe, churn, 2 pigs. Recorded 21 June 1886.

Pages 76-78: Appraisement of Estate of Evan P. ANDERSON, dec'd. Appraisers appointed: J. Vance BELL, Wm. LEWIS, Henry DICK, J. M. COBB. Total inventory in Clarke County, 11 June 1886: 1 parlor stove, 2 two-year old cattle, 50 acres wheat, 1 Hair Brush. Winchester Appraisal, 19 May 1886, by Meredith FORNEY. Some items in small inventory: 1 Bed, bed clothes & bedroom furniture; 1 wash stand; 1 candle stand; 1 rocking chair and 2 hickory chairs, 1 sewing machine. Recorded 21 June 1886.

Pages 78-79: Appraisement of Estate of Alfred SEAL, dec'd., 30 May 1885, with C. W. HOLLIS, George V. OYLER, J. C. RIELY, Appraisers. A part of the small inventory: 1 Oriental stove, 3 bird cages, 1 wheel barrow, 1 shaving horse, 1 grind stone, 2 trussels, 1 chicken coop, 1 lot rubbish, 1 bathtub, 2 hogs, lard press. Recorded 21 June 1886.

Pages 80-83: Sale Account of Samuel L. LAREW Estate, Apr 3, 1886. Many items purchased by: N. J. MORGAN, Wm. CALMES, C. L. CARPENTER, A. CRIM, Samuel CHILES, John STAUB. M. O'ROKE and Philip BRENT each bought pistols; D. SHAULL bought "gee stick" for 13¢; Rob't. FARQUHARSON bought white faced colt; Josiah L. BAKER bought a shovel. Hay, at Wall Place sold to Wm. L. CLARK. Sale account recorded 21 June 1886.

Pages 84-85: Estate Account of E. A. HIBBARD, dec'd., with John H. CREBS, Comee. Admr. Begins July 29, 1885, with money received from Wm. L. CLARK, Atty., on Holliday Note. Some other items: Collected from Jas. P. WHITACRE, Admr. of C. M. HIBBARD. Paid for proving will; paid John H. CREBS commission; paid Chas. H. BROWN for funeral. Balance paid to Wm A. SMITH and Emily SMITH, one half each. Account settled Nov. Term, 1885.

Pages 86-89: Estate of Alfred SEAL, dec'd., with S. L. LAREW, his Admr.
Begins May 30, 1885. Among payments: to appraisers, to auctioneer, E. L.
HODGSON; to Dr. Wm. A BELL for attending deceased in his last illness
(during 1884); paid many taxes, including Henry SEAL's state tax; paid
clerk's fees for taking bond, recording and proving will, recording appraisal; paid balance on Henry SEAL's Corporation. Administrator's accounts
for settlement of this estate "were posted at the front door of the Courthouse for 10 days". Balance due Admr. from estate was $4.28. June 21,
1886.

Pages 89-90: Appraisers named for the Estate of Elizabeth GARNER, dec'd.,
22 June 1886: E. L. HODGSON, H. K. PRITCHARD, R. M. PARKER. Total inventory: 6 chairs, 1 stove. Recorded 29 June 1886.

Pages 90-91: Will of John R. CARSON. To sister, Josephine W. CARSON,
land in Tennessee, Morgan and Fentress Counties. Also certain interest in
"Cincint" & Great Northern R. R. Co., in stock and accrued dividends. Also
all personal property and "all dues, fees, fines and cost due me as Clerk
of Corporate Court of Winchester". 7 May 1883. Will proved 21 June 1886.
As there were no witnesses to will, handwriting and signature were proved
by J. P. RIELY and O. W. HOLLIS. Josephine W. CARSON to be executrix.

Pages 91-94: Estate of E. S. W. TAYLOR, dec'd., in Account with John J.
WILLIAMS, her executor. Begins April 7, 1883, with cash received from
Mrs. M. M. SULLIVAN, cash in her hands at death of Mrs. Taylor. Other income: cash from rent, L. T. F. GRIM; cash from J. J. WILLIAMS, Trustee
in Hahn & Wife vs Dearmont; proceeds of Jane E. DEARMONT's bond received
by Alice M. KOWNSLAR as advancement on her legacy. Among payments: for
grave and walling of grave; to M. D. ALBIN for gravestones; paid telegram to Berryville, 30¢; paid witness to will; paid undertaker's,
physician's and drug bills. Legatees named: Alice M. KOWNSLAR, Mary M.
SULLIVAN, George H. SULLIVAN, Thos. B. HAMMOND "cannot be found",
Harriet M. HAMMOND, Florinda J. TILFORD, Bessie T. and Frank V. TILFORD,
Edward M. & B. Taylor STRIBLING. Account confirmed in court 21 June 1886.

Pages 94-97: Estate of Charles HARDY, dec'd., in Account with Henry
KENZEL, his Admr. Begins July 20, 1874 with paying Clerk's fees, corporation tax, state, county and township taxes. Also payments to Mrs. Hardy.
Similar payments made, each year, through 1885. Funds received for the
same years from Dividends, Winc. & Potomac R. R. Co. Jany 3, 1885, Amount
paid for tombstone for Chas. HARDY being paid by his daughter, Hattie, from
amount received by her from the Corporation Skinplaster? Bond. At end of
this account, Balance due, H. KENZEL, late Admr., $245.23. Note along margin:
Balance of $245.23 was settled by Deed of Release dated 15 Jany 1895.
Account of George W. KURTZ, undertaker for burial of Mrs. Lucy HARDY paid by
her son and family. Administratrix of Henry KENZEL, dec'd., brought to
Court papers pertaining to Estate of Charles HARDY, dec'd. Example: 54
shares Winchester & Potomac R. R. Stock, Bonds & Notes of Harrison BOWERS
(deemed worthless), Bond of Joseph DENNY. Admn. of Account of Henry KINZEL
confirmed Sept 22, 1886.

Pages 98-99: Estate Account of Wm. C. MEREDITH, dec'd., with A. M. SMITH,
Admr. (No dates) Cash paid "per last settlement being 50½% to Dunlavy
JONES". Many other payments, including those to: J. Smith GILKESON, Wm.
KNABE & Co., Mrs. Hugh McGUIRE, S. S. HOUSE. Paid Barton & Boyd, Atty for
Jos. L. LOGAN. Jany 30, 1886. Confirmed in Court, Sept 22, 1886.

Pages 100-101: Will of Martha C. BENT. To sister, Heriot R. ANNAN, all property and on her death, to niece, Mrs. Hattie HILLEARY, of Warrenton, Va., $300, and her choice of personal estate. On death of sister, Heriot R. ANNAN, give rest and residue of estate to brother, James R. ANNAN and nephew, William L. ANNAN. "It is distinctly understood, that my will is, that my sister shall have an estate for her own life." 30 July 1886. Wit: W. B. BAKER, C. S. BAKER, W. W. WALL. Proved Oct 18, 1886. Legatees were: H. R. ANNAN, James R. ANNAN, Wm. L. ANNAN, Heriot J. HILLEARY, R. W. HILLEARY. E. Holmes BOYD appointed to administer will.

Page 101: Estate of Josephine J. DAVIS, dec'd., in Account with S. L. LAREW, her Admr. Begins March 1878, with amount received from John J. WILLIAMS. Paid J. H. YEAKLEY for coffin, $6.00; paid Clerk's and Commissioner's fees and recording this settlement. Admin. Account settled 15 Nov 1886.

Page 102: Estate of Evelina STREIT, dec'd., in Account with S. L. LAREW, her Admr. Begins Oct 27, 1877 with payments made "Under report of Comr. POWELL of Oct 1877" to Anna STREIT, Emma C. BAKER, Portia B. BAKER, Mrs. O. M. BROWN. Paid for Deed of Release, fees, and recording this report. Account settled and recorded Novr 15, 1886 with balance due Admr., $5.50.

Pages 103-105: Estate of James W. WATSON, dec'd., in Account with S. L. LAREW, his Admr. Begins May 9, 1882 to 1884. Among items: Cash on hand and check of R. D. HARDESTY; cash of Albert TAYLOR, surviving partner of the firm of WATSON & TAYLOR; paid Mt. Hebron Cemetery; paid one half of J. D. CROWN's account against WATSON & TAYLOR and one half of several other accounts of the firm. Paid R. P. PAGE medical account and F. P. SPOTTS store account. Scheme of Distribution: pay to R. P. PAGE, J. L. DAVIS, B. N. SEABRIGHT and George W. KURTZ. Filed in Clerk's office, 28 Sept 1886.

Page 105: Will of George Washington ANDERSON. "I George Washington ANDERSON, in view of the uncertainly of life, do make this my last will". Has already by Deed conveyed the house where he now lives to his wife, in Trust for her use. At her death, "to her children, Charles and Virginia". All personal property to wife, Nancy. Friend, George E. JENKINS, to be executor. 19 March 1886. Wit: George E. JENKINS, R. J. STEPHENS, Jno. J. WILLIAMS. Proved 20 Dec 1886.

Pages 106-107: Will of Sarah Ann CLAYTON (was Sarah Ann SPENCER). Mentions certain House & Lot on Clifford Street "devised to me by will of Sarah FRENCH". After paying all debts, income from rent and pay to go to Chas. SPENCER, son of brother, John SPENCER, now of Alleghany City, Penn. In case of death of Charles, to nephew, Willie SPENCER, son of John SPENCER. In case of death of Willie SPENCER and brother, John SPENCER, rents to go to "male child or children begotten in legal matrimony". Three tables "downstairs" to John F. GRAY and yellow wardrobe to brother, John SPENCER. Also gives to Mary, Gertrude and Ida GRAY, daughters of John GRAY. Ice cream bowls to Maria HOWARD. 5 Nov 1886. Wit: R. Wm. WALTER, Wm. M. ATKINSON. Proved 20 Dec 1886.

Pages 107-109: Inventory & Appraisement of Estate of Mrs. Martha C. BENT, dec'd., with Appraisers: C. F. EICHELBERGER, Frank G. WALTER, John N. BELL. 19 Oct 1886. Henry W. HYDE, Notary Public. Part of inventory: 1 box Coal, 1 Parler Cook Stove, pair Scales & Weights, Bed Pan, Flour Bucket, Waffle Iron, Argand Stove, pair Lambrikins, 50 shares Winc. & Pot. R. R.

Stock, Bond of A. H. MILLER, Cash in Shen. Valley Bank. Inventory recorded 17 Feby 1887.

Pages 110-111: Sale of Personal Property of Mrs. Martha C. BENT, dec'd., by E. Holmes BOYD, Admr. Oct 19, 1886. Part of sale & purchasers: Rainbarrel, Conrad KREMER; Spittoon, Wm. M. ATKINSON; Sugar Dishes, F. KOHLHOUSEN; Cups & Saucers, Tilden REED; Kitch. Table, Tilde ROBINSON; Small Table, Miss Kate SHAULL; Picture, Harry MULVERHILL; Chairs, Miss Ellis A. BROWN; Piece of zinc, Pat MURPHY; Stove, Miss Kate McVICAR. Sale recorded 17 Feb 1887.

Page 112: Inventory & Appraisement of Estate of George W. ANDERSON, dec'd., with Appraisers: Henry M. BAKER, Chas. S. JENKINS, Edward J. EVANS. 28 Dec 1886. Total inventory: Garden Tools, Chairs, Press, Lamp, Iron, Carpet, Stand, Looking Glass, 4 quilts, 4 Books, Lounge & Table, Picture, 2 copper Kettles. Recorded Feby 26, 1887.

Page 113: Will of Solomon HORN. To wife, Hannah HORN, all personal property, house & kitchen furniture, all provisions on hand and 2 shares of Bank Stock. She also to have houses and lots with rent and interest during her life. After her "deth", real estate to John G. MILLER, in trust "for the wright and use of my daughter, Elizabeth A. BURK, living in Green Castle, Penn". Appoints Perry HORN, of Rockingham County, his Trustee. 17 Dec 1861. Wit: W. B. MILLER, James H. BARNHART, Wm. MILLER. Proved July 6, 1863. Above certified copy of will produced in Winchester Court, Feby 21, 1887.

Page 114: H. S. SINGHASS Settlement, in Account with R. E. TRENARY, Com. Admr., 23 March 1887. Amount on deposit in Shenandoah V. N. Bank, $35.10; paid attorney's fees, clerk's fees, 10% commission, D. H. BRAGONIER's comr. fees, and paid C. M. GIBBENS, Exec of S. L. LAREW, dec'd. Total payments: $35.10 so Balance in Account is ZERO. Settlement recorded Mar 24, 1887. Richard L. GRAY, Clerk.

Page 115: Samuel WEIR's Estate Settlement in Account with R. E. TRENARY, Admr., 23 March 1887. Amount on deposit in Shen. V. N. Bank, $61.60. Paid Attorney's and Clerk's fees, 10% Commission, BRAGONIER's Comr. Fees and C. M. GIBBENS, Exec. of S. L. LAREW, dec'd. Total payments: $61.60, so account balance is ZERO. Recorded Apr 25, 1887.

Pages 115-116: Will of John PIRKEY. Executor, as soon as possible after "my death, pay all expenses, and to proceed as rapidly as he may be able to do so" to collect and pay debts. Gives all estate to son, Frank, "for care and attention he has given me and if he continues this care and be faithful until age of 21". Wishes care and diligence in disposing of his many and valuable books. Thos. J. COOPER, to be exec. Testator bequeaths his soul to Him who gave it with faith "that He will give me an inheritance that will be incurruptable, undefiled and that will not fade away". 12 May 1887. Wit: T. J. COOPER, Obed FUNK, B. M. KNIGHT, J.P. Proved, in part, 20 June 1887, by Thos. J. COOPER and on 21 June 1887 by Obed FUNK. Appraisers appointed: J. E. COOPER, W. R. WILLIS, J. F. BROWN, H. BAETJER, G. G. BAKER.

Pages 117-118: Estate of Catherine GRAICHEN, dec'd., in Account with F. August GRAICHEN, her Admr. Begins June 1, 1885 with receipt of Rent of Dwelling and Bond interest. Paid expenses to finish house, state and corporation taxes, clerk's costs, commissioners, Tax on Suit. Balance due Admr.: $50.50. In 1886, received rent and interest and paid taxes, for painting house and Balance due Estate, $117.09. Received same income in 1887 and made payments to Anne, Carrie and Fred A. GRAICHEN. Account recorded July 18, 1887.

Pages 118-119: Estate of Susan BRENT, dec'd., in Account with N. S. BRENT, her Admr. Begins 23 Sept 1880, with payments: to P. C. BOYD for grave; S. P. STACKHOUSE for hearse; J. H. CREBS for qualifying Appraisers; paid taxes. Paid to Legatees $57.50 each: N. T. BRENT (in full of legacy & Share of Personalty); Mrs. Mary A. SHEPARD (in full of legacy & Share of Personalty); Geo. A. BROWN, plus Bureau & Walnut Chest; Mrs. A. C. COOPER, plus Bureau; N. T. BRENT, plus bed clothes, silverware and gold spectacles. Testator devised house & lot, Braddock Street, to Nathan C. BRENT to pay expenses and legacies. Court believes all has been done except legacy to Mrs. Sallie A. METZGER. Will wanted it in trust but court believes it should go to her personally. Also Bond of Lloyd LOGAN, beqeathed to Mrs. Susan H. BRENT now in hands of R. T. BARTON as compensation for services. Estate account recorded July 18, 1887.

Page 120: Estate Account of James KERN, dec'd., with Joseph M. LUPTON and Bentley KERN, executors. Begins Mar 1881 by cash received for plow sold. Many collections on Notes & Accounts due. Received also from sales of Benches in Chapel and Blacksmith Tools. Paid Wm. EVANS, hack hire; paid funeral expenses, Dr. G. S. MILLER, Medical Bill; paid Appraisers & fees; paid cash to Sarah F. KERN and paid T. A. LATHAM note. Recorded July 18, 1887.

Pages 121-124: Inventory, Appraisement and Sale Account of Estate of Wm. T. GILBERT, dec'd. Appraisers: John GLAIZE, H. M. BAKER, George E. JENKINS. June 23, 1887. Long list of Inventory, including household furniture, sewing machine, fancy chairs, lot of jugs & barrels. Claim vs B. CRAMPTON and Note of C. W. McVICAR and of N. W. & Barbara A. SOLENBERGER. Inventory returned 2 July 1887. Among purchasers and purchases, at Sale: A. H. BOX-WELL, Baking Dish; Till REED, Cherry Seeder; Warner SWIFT, Stew Pot; Wm. McDONNELL, 2 Cribs; C. S. W. BARNES, Writing Table; Thos. TAYLOR, Sugar Bowl; Patsy WEBB, Bureau; J. G. REDMOND, Secretary; Millie JENKINS, Wash Stand. Sale Account recorded July 18, 1887.

Page 124: Report of Sale, under Deed of Trust, dated Dec 15, 1886, by R. T. BARTON, Trustee, to L. N. HUCK, Commr. of Accounts. Deed of Trust executed by Wm. T. GILBERT and wife to Trustee, who proceeded to advertise The Foundry Property and such personal property connected therewith, to sell at Public Auction. Sold, Apr 25, 1887, to Charles B. HANCOCK. Recorded July 18, 1887.

Pages 125-126: Trust Account of R. T. BARTON in Deed of Trust of Wm. T. GILBERT & Wife. Begins Dec 15, 1886 with some activities as: paid tax & for recording deed, paid insurance, Notary, stationery, stamps. Received of John GLAIZE for sale of old iron. Paid John GLAIZE for wages of foundry hands; paid James H. BARNHART interest due Jacob BARNHART, dec'd. Paid Union Bank note with German SMITH as indorser. Received of T. H. GOSOM, rent of building and from Mrs. E. A. GILBERT "to be applied in aid of Trust Fund to satisfy prior Judgt." Paid debts due Miss Mary TIDBALL and Dr. W. S. LOVE. Paid E. Holmes BOYD, Admr. Recorded July 29, 1887.

Page 127: Sale Bill of Personal Property of Evan ANDERSON, dec'd., returned by John H. CREBS, Admr. Purchasers: Amos COOPER, A. J. KERFOOT, G. W. HADDOX, Theo KENZELL, W. H. WRIGHT, J. G. GREEN. Total Sales, $45.50. Recorded July 18, 1887.

Page 127-128: Appraisal of Estate of Miss Harriet E. BOWERS, dec'd., with appointed Appraisers: M. H. G. WILLIS, L. H. BARTON, H. K. PRITCHARD, Dorsey WALTER. 21 June 1887. Only item: cash on deposit, Union Bank of Winchester, $150. Recorded July 18, 1887.

Pages 128-132: Inventory and Appraisement of Estate of Frank P. SPOTTS, dec'd., with George M. ANDERSON, appointed Admr. His bond $550 with Levi T. F. GRIM as Securety. Appraisers: C. W. ANDERSON, M. KINGSBURY, C. S. W. BARNES. Some items in large inventory: Dozens cans each peaches, tomatoes, corn, pumpkin; Boxes of hominy grits, dozens of Vanilla & Lemon Extract, lamp chimneys, 2 gross wicks, 7 reams wrapping paper, 26 tin coffee pots, nutmeg graters. Many book accounts with some called "good": John C. ANDERSON, Isaac BAKER, Mathew FINLEY, John HAINES, Sydney HENRY. Inventory of Stock of Goods & Wares appraised at cost less 30% for depreciation. Entire stock sold to Lewis H. ANDERSON, Apr 13, 1887, for $200. Estate account recorded July 18, 1887.

Pages 133-135: Estate of Jacob D. GOSHERT, dec'd., in Account with Emma C. GOSHERT, Admr. Begins 25 June 1885 with draft to Youngstown Carriage & Wagon Co. Paid Samuel GOLD for corn; paid repairs to Fugitt's House; paid Winchester Times; many payments to names only. Account recorded Oct 17, 1887.

Pages 136-137: Estate Account of Evelina SMITH, dec'd., with William M. ATKINSON, Admr. Begins Sept 25, 1885 with income from deposit in Union Bank and rents of C. W. HENSELL and general receipts of Wm. L. CLARK. Then back to Dec 1855 for expenses paid as for funeral & grave costs; paid Wm. L. CLARK, Atty for Wm. SEEMER in full of his claim; paid commr. & court fees and attorney fees. Scheme of Distribution: Mrs. Mary A. STANSBURY, Georgiana E. MERCER, Frank SMITH, $33.92-2/3 each. Recorded 23 Sept 1887.

Pages 138-141: Estate of Portia L. BALDWIN, dec'd., with C. F. LEE, Jr, her Executor. Begins Dec 1885 with such items as Cash paid for digging grave and for attending court for probate of will. Paid 1884 Frederick Co. taxes; paid R. T. BARTEN's bill for rent and J.C. VAN FOSSEN's bill. Paid Phillippa L. JACKSON legacy and W. L. CLARK, Jr., Guardian, legacy due to Lawrence CLARK. Paid expenses of Executor to Winchester and return. Cash "found in house at death" and cash from U.S. Pension Agent; also cash from F. L. BEELER for hay & corn sold. Paid Portia L. MORRISON, her legacy. Executor had posted notice at courthouse door, 1 Oct 1886, stating any debts or demands against estate should be made known. None appeared but records show creditors holding up settlement of estate. Recorded Feb 21, 1888.

Page 141: Will of J. John WEDLOCK. (very short) All property to brother, Polk FLETCHER, no appraisal required. 5 April 1888. Wit: Wm. M. ATKINSON, John M. FRYE. Proved 20 April 1888.

Pages 142-143: Will of William N. EDDY, revoking all other wills. To wife, Mary E. EDDY "so long as she remain my widow", all real estate: Residence & household furniture on Fort Hill, Lot thereto; Brick Store room & Warehouse and all fixtures on Market Street; farm on Abram's Creek known as Valley Mills Farm; Mill and all other fixtures & Machinery thereto; Farm adjoining Valley Mills Tract on the west known as Rose Cottage. Other property: Stocks, Bonds, Book Accounts, Store Goods, Stock in Mill & Warehouse, proceeds from insurance policies, cash on hand, divide into 3 parts with one third to each: widow and two sons in law, Geo. J CUNNINGHAM and L. H. McKINSTER. Whatever wife may accrue during her widowhood shall be given to 2 daughters, Harriet E. CUNNINGHAM and Alice M. McKINSTER and it shall be free from control of husbands. Daughter, Alice M. McKINSTER to have Fort Hill residence. 15 Feby 1888. Wit: G. O. SNAPP, J. W. KELLEY. Proved 18 April 1888. Appraisers appointed: Henry BAETJER, Oscar BARR, Wm. H. BAKER, of Wm., James W. BARR, Thomas J. COOPER.

Page 144: Will of Sarah SCHULTZ, widow of Frederick SCHULTZ, dec'd.
All property to be divided equally "among my children". Any that
cannot be divided, should be sold and proceeds divided. Portion to
daughter, Catherine M., to be paid to her. Part to daughters, Mary E.
MILLER and Sallie F. BOYD for their sole support and then to their child-
ren. Leaves Sallie F. BOYD $200 more than Catherine M. SCHULTZ? and
Mary E. MILLER. "I think Philip W. BOYD paid two much for the lot he
purchased of me." Lewis A. MILLER & Philip W. BOYD to be executors.
Aug 1, 1882 (or 3). No witnesses so will proven, 18 June 1888, by oaths
of M. H. G. WILLIS & Isaac W. RUSSELL as to handwriting of Sarah SCHULTZ.
Lewis A. MILLER & Philip W. BOYD declined to qualify as executors so
James B. RUSSELL was appointed to administer. Appraisers appointed: John
G. MILLER, Chas. B. HANCOCK, Holmes CONRAD, Thos. N. LUPTON, Henry BAETJER.

Page 145: Appraisement of Personal Estate of Wm. N. EDDY, dec'd., 7 May
1888. Total inventory: Deposit in Bank ($8,166.75) and Bank Stock;
Stock in merchandise and in Mill & W. House; Scales in Mill; Cart and
Mower on Farm; Bills Receivable and Book Account. Oscar BARR, J. W. BARR,
T. J. COOPER, Appraisers. Household furniture left to widow during her life-
time was not appraised. Recorded May 28, 1888. George J. CUNNINGHAM and
L. H. McKINSTER, executors.

Page 146: Will of John HODGSON. To wife, Ann Elizabeth HODGSON, house and
lots on Washington Street with all personalty of every kind as long as she
lives. At her death, all to "my dutiful daughter, Ann Elizabeth and her
heirs". If said daughter has no issue, said property to be sold & divided
"among my several children and their heirs". Wife to be executor with no
security required. 18 Apr 1879. Wit: Wm. N. EDDY, J. A. BARTLETT, W. G.
RUSSELL. Proved Sept 17, 1888.

Page 147: Will of Cornelius GRIM. To sister, Mary Ellen ANDERSON, wife of
John C. ANDERSON, all real estate and personal property, to wit: House and
Lot known as Woods Addn., Lots #23 & 24, and adjoining that recently sold
to niece, Mrs. Lillie C. YEATMAN. After death of sister, to nephew, Rob't.
E. Lee ANDERSON. 15 July 1886. Wit: Vance W. STRIKER, Charles A. McCARTY.
Proved Sept 17, 1888. Mary E. ANDERSON appointed Admr.

Page 148: Will of Marsha WEAVER, March 5, 1879. All to two children,
James W. WEAVER and Sarah E. LOVETT. Wit: George F. MILLER, John G. MILLER.
Codicil, June 30, 1880. House & Lot in Winchester to son and house and lot
recently purchased in Harpers Ferry, Va, to daughter. Witnesses same as to
will. Proved 21 Sept 1888.

Pages 149-152: Will of William B. BAKER. (very long will) To wife, Elizabeth, house & lot on Market Street (present residence). At her death, to be
disposed as directed in will. If she has no will, executors to sell this
property and divide as directed "in the 14th section of this will". To wife
all household furniture & silver and plate ware, paintings, books, and provisions on hand. Also to her $40,000 of interest paying stocks & bonds,
now held in testator's name or in the firms of Baker & Co., & W. H. BAKER
& Co. Interest to be spent by her as she wishes after maintenance of
daughter, Sophia. If she marries, not for the use of her husband. Gives
to three sons, $15,000 in trust for daughter, Ella (now Mrs. C. R. PAGE)
for her sole use and not subject to debts of husband. To three sons,
house and lot No. 467, Prospect Street, Cleveland, Ohio, to be held by
them in trust for daughter, Emma (now Mrs. H. H. POWELL). Gives to sons
"my Steam Flouring Mill & Machinery purchased by me in 1872 of my brothers
George P. & Christian S. BAKER. Bequest to Rev. T. W. DOSH "as a slight

testimonial of my appreciation of his assiduous attention and kindness during my protracted illness in 1862". Mentions his interest in land devised by his father to "6 of his sons". "Through the goodness of God, I have enjoyed throughout my life many spiritual blessings, not the least of which were the instructions and example of my sainted father and mother." 30 Apr 1887. Two short codicils. No Witnesses. Proved 21 Sept 1888 by oaths of William M. ATKINSON & Dorsey WALTER. Three sons, Albert, A. M., and Wm. H. BAKER, qualified as executors. Appraisers appointed: H. S. SLAGLE, John W. RICE, E. Holmes BOYD, Wm. M. ATKINSON, Dorsey WALTER.

Page 153: Will of Chas. Michael CONRAD. All property to wife, Ellen, for and during her natural lifetime. At her death, to daughter Mary G. CONRAD. Gives $125 to each grandchild: Lucretia & James W. CONRAD, children of son, James W. CONRAD, dec'd. 14 Feby 1888. Wit: J. Wm. CONNER, J. M. STEELE. Proved 29 Sept 1888.

Page 154: Will of George M. ANDERSON. All property to wife during her lifetime and then equally "among my children". Nov 26, 1888. Wit: G. L. MILLER, Wm. A BELL. Proved Decr 21, 1888. Mary M. ANDERSON (wife) made executor.

Pages 154-155: Inventory and Appraisement of Personal Estate of Wm. B. BAKER, dec'd. Estimated interest and capital in Firms of Baker & Co. and W. B. BAKER & Co.; Interest in 75 acres of outlots near Winchester; Shares in Bank Stocks, land companies, gas & railroad companies. Total appraised value: $99,888. Appraisers: E. Holmes BOYD, H. S. SLAGLE, John W. RICE. Recorded Decr 17, 1888.

Pages 156-157: Will of Henry S. BAKER. To wife, Aletta BAKER, during her natural life, House & Lot in Winchester, with all household furniture, Books, Silver, Glass, Plate, China & other moveable articles, including the Piano. Also to wife income of $40,000 for support of herself and daughters, Gertrude and Lely?. Sets up trust for daughters, husbands not to have any control over. Son, Harry H. BAKER, to have interest in warehouse property & adjacent lots at railroad Depot in Winchester; Son, Robert W. BAKER, house & lot on corner of Water & Market Streets (part now occupied by Times Newspaper Co.); Son, William W. BAKER, Store House property & lot known as the Streit Property, on Loudoun Street opposite the Court House. Five lots of ground in Keokuk, Iowa to trustees of Grace Evangelical Lutheran Church, of Winchester. Deed to be executed to J. M. BEUTELL for property where he now lives in Frederick County. Sons, Harry H. and Robert W. BAKER to be execs. 23 Dec 1888. Wit: S. T. HOLLIDAY, E. Holmes BOYD, Albert BAKER. Proved 18 Feb 1889.

Pages 158-159: Will of Julia Ann JENKINS. All property to husband, William JENKINS. At his death, property on northeast corner, Loudoun & Cork Sts, to son, William M. JENKINS. Property on north side of West Cork Street to daughter, Kate Kurtz ROSENBERGER, wife of John ROSENBERGER, never subject to control of her husband. Husband to be exec. 11 Sept 1885. Wit: T. V. PURCELL, H. N. CORRELL. Proved 21 Feby 1889. H. N. CORRELL not now a resident of the state, his brother, C. Ed CORRELL testified to handwriting. Appraisers appointed: James W. ANDERSON, M. T. REED, C. W. REED.

Pages 159-160: Will of Bettie A. WADE, widow of Daniel WADE. To daughter, Virginia A. WADE, all personal property plus house & garden purchased of Mrs. Mary E. HOCKMAN, on Bradet Street. To daughter also bonds held against H. R. M. HOUT & Urilla V. HOUT. Jany 30, 1889. Wit: W. J. BEST and Wm. S. LOVE. Proved 27 March 1889. Daughter, Virginia A. WADE is executor. Mentions codicil proved by Nannie FLANNIGAIN & Wm. J. BEST.

Pages 160-161: Will of Hon. Joseph H. SHERRARD. To two unmarried daughters, Virginia B. & Elizabeth K. SHERRARD, in equal ownership, all real and personal property, subject to payment of funeral expenses and debts, if any. Said daughters, or the suvivor of them, to be executors without security. Requests no public sale of any part of property unless necessary to pay debts or funeral expenses or the need of these two daughters. Other children will understand the giving only to two daughters who are unmarried as the estate, if divided among all, "would be utterly inadequate". 16 March 1881. Proved Apr 15, 1889. As there were no witnesses, will & signature were proven by oath of A. R. PENDLETON.

Pages 161-162: Inventory & Appraisement of Personal Estate of Henry S. BAKER, dec'd., and of his Real Estate not specifically devised. Shares of Stock in Banks: Shenandoah Valley Nat'l., Union & Front Royal Banks; Shares in Winchester Gas Co,. Winchester & Potomac R. R.; Winchester City Bonds, "Virginia Reddlebergers, $1,720.16". Many personal bonds as those of J. M. MILLER, C. M. PEERY, Mrs. M. J. CLOUSER, T. M. NELSON. Note of J. E. KERFOOT. Estimated total inventory: $99,879.40. Appraisers: Wm. H. BAKER, Albert BAKER, Jno. W. RICE. 21 March 1889. Executors: H. H. & R. W. BAKER.

Pages 163-164: Evan P. ANDERSON, dec'd., Estate Account with John H. CREBS, Commr. Admr. Begins May 1886, with paid Appraisers: R. M. PARKER, J. R. MESMER, M. FORNEY. Also paid Appraisers in Clarke County: J. V. BELL, Henry DICK, Wm. T. LEWIS. Paid E. L. HODGSON, Auctioneer, and R. L. GRAY, Clerk. Distribution: To Admr. of J. R. CARSON, late Clerk, for recording will, and to C. S. W. BARNES, late Clerk of Corporation Court, for recording appraisal and swearing appraisers. To R. L. GRAY, Clerk, for recording settlement. Preferred debt paid to Dr. Wm. P. McGUIRE for services in last illness. Paid Baker & Co. for timothy seed, for sugar and coffee. Paid A. L. SHEARER's Account for one dozen sheepskins; paid Wm. R. ALEXander for Alley fee. Paid Winchester Times Company, March 1886, for three years, twenty-four days subscription. Settlement accepted April 15, 1889.

Pages 165-167: A. J. FRANK, dec'd., with John H. CREBS, Admr. Begins May 1886, with income received from Ashby & W. H. FRANK and from A. L. W. HODGSON for wheat. Some expenses were: paid Wm. L. CLARK, Jr., Atty. and Appraisers: R. U. PARKER, J. R. MESMER, Wm. R. JONES. Paid Faulkner & Co. funeral costs. After paying Court Costs, balance of $28.22 was distributed: Creditors to receive 20% of each claim of Baker & Co., Wm. BROWN, Admr. of Jas. GIFFIN, and Meredith CAPPER. Settlement of Estate Account confirmed by Court, Apr 19, 1889.

Pages 167-168: Will of Margaret PRITCHARD, 10 February 1877. All property to two daughters, Harriet Ann & Ida Maria PRITCHARD. If either marries, "her life estate in the property terminates". If both marry, estate is to be sold and equally divided "among all my children then living". House & Lot on corner Loudoun & Cork Streets. If two daughters decide to sell the House & Lot, proceeds to be divided among all children. Son, Housen K. PRITCHARD, paid taxes for testator and repairs to house and should be reimbursed. Wit: Wm. L. CLARK, Wm. M. ATKINSON. Proved 20 May 1889.

Pages 168-172: Estate of Samuel F. GAENSLER, dec'd., in Account with L.N. HUCK, his Admr. Begins Mar 1886 with such expenses as: Paid C. B. HANCOCK, Sheriff fee; paid C. M. GIBBENS, Treasurer, Tax; paid J. R. T. GRIM for building privy; paid Mrs. BRIGGS on Bond and C. W. HOLLIS for writing will. Estate had shares in Shen. Valley Natl. Bank, Bonds of N. ROUTZAN and of P. W. & E. H. BOYD. Account of L. N. HUCK, Admr. of S. F. GAENSLER, recorded in Frederick County, 29 June 1889. Joseph A. NULTON, Clerk.

Page 173: Annie Jane CARPER, dec'd., Appraisal of Estate by C. M. GIBBENS, C. W. HOLLIS, D. H. BRAGONIER. Total Inventory: 1 pair Bedsteads; 1 Bond of P. P. CARPER & C. A. GRIM, dated 29 Sept 1887; 1 Bond of Jefferson WATERS & P. P. CARPER, dated 29 Sept 1887; Cash on hand, $16.55. Recorded 25 July 1889.

Pages 173-177: Will of Benjamin WILLIAMS, "now advanced in years". Has real estate in Frederick County. Is "eaquel owner with my sons, Philip B. & James W. WILLIAMS', of The Stonewall Factory Property, The Falling & Carding Mill and 100 acres of land. Personal property to be appraised and "my devicees take as they desire". Pay from sale of property: $100 for each year lived with daughter, Mary E. EDDY, wife of Wm. N. EDDY (from May 9, 1874); pay medical & funeral expenses & buy stone similar to one at wife's grave. Rest to children, one-fifth to each: Philip B., James W., Harriet, wife of Jacob W. RICHARDS, Mary E. EDDY, and Margaret E. REED, wife of Wm. E. REED. Son in law, Jacob W. RICHARD to be executor. 10 Dec 1884. Wit: J. W. KELLEY, Henry BAETJER. Codicil, 16 July 1886, revokes part giving Mary E. EDDY $100 per month. Now provides "by bond in the penal sum of $5,000, payable to Wm. N. EDDY or his assignees". Executor may sell Stonewall Factory and Duck Run Factory with land. Will proved July 15, 1889 by J. W. KELLEY & Henry BAETJER. J. W. RICHARDS declined to be executor, so Jas. P. WHITACRE appointed Admr.

Page 177: Will of Daniel THOMPSON (colored). All to daughter, Annie E. THOMPSON and she to be executor without security. 13 Aug 1889. Wit: Wm. M. ATKINSON, James M. FRYE. Proved Sept 19, 1889.

Pages 178-179: Appraisal of Estate of G. W. HARPER, dec'd. 18 Aug 1889. Among items: Parlor organ, coal stove, 2 sewing machines, apple butter kettle, blacksmith tools, grind stone, spring wagon & road wagon, Sleigh & Bells. Bonds & Notes of Jos. CLOWSER, A. J. CLOWSER, Ira S. CAPPER, E. J. HARPER. Appraisers: John H. CREBS, A. J. COPENHAVER, C. W. HOLLIS. Recorded Aug 21, 1889.

Pages 179-180: Jacob METZ, Guardian of Mertie & Fred GOSHERT, children of J. D. GOSHERT, dec'd. Accounting begins 1 July 1887. Among items: cash received of J. D. GOSHERT's Admr. Paid Attorneys fees & Clerk's fees; paid for wallpaper & painting office and for lumber, nails, hardware. Paid insurance, state and city taxes. Guardianship account settled Oct Term of Court 1889.

Pages 180-182: Will of Jacob LYDER, "of feeble body". Joseph H. LYDER, Trustee, to sell "a Lot of ground to be cut off of the western end of my Garden, fronting on German Street & adjoining Francis' Lot". Son, Joseph H. LYDER and Julie A. CLARK to have land next to Joseph, divided equally. To granddaughter, Virginia GRANT, small piece of land on Pall Mall Street. Rest of Lot where now living, including house & stable, to daughter, Cornelia E. LANGLEY, free from all control of husband. Three children to divide personal property which is small. 6 Dec 1889. Wit: Wm M. ATKINSON, Henry D. TODD. Proved 19 Dec 1889.

Pages 182-184: Will of Margaret TRIER, "now sick in bed". To step-daughter, known as Sissie TRIER, "the trunk in my room after the contents are taken out". To two nieces, Mary & Susie HOBSON, all furniture, bed & bedding "in my room". Also to them, all money & property of every kind left after paying debts and funeral expenses and buying stone. Brother, W. H. MAY, to be executor without security and no appraisal of property. 14 Oct 1889. Wit: H. M. BAKER, L. Dow HESS. Proved 22 Jan 1890. Inventory & Appraisal by Edward J. EVANS, Henry EVANS, H. M. BAKER, 23 Jan 1890. Total inventory: 2 Bonds, Cash, Rent & Interest Due, 2 Trunks, Chamber Furniture & Carpets, 2 stoves.

Pages 184-185: Will of Mrs. Sarah A. F. KERN. April 20, 1880. House in which now living to sisters, Susan E. & Lucenda G. B. LUPTON. Also money on hand and what is due on Notes from estate of husband, James KERN. Silver ware, Bed & Bedding to sisters. To niece, Sarah C. ROYSTON, silver spoons, pair of Blankets and Album Quilt. To nephew, Joseph Mcl. LUPTON, pair of blankets and red quilt. To Kate A. KERN, bed & bedstead "which she occupys". Sisters, Susan & Lucenda, to care for brother, Thomas D. LUPTON. Wit: W. T. GILBERT, H. R. LUPTON, A. J. HOUCK. Codicil, 9 Dec 1885: Lot on Market St. to two sisters and brother, Thomas D. LUPTON. Wit: B. GIBSON, P. H. WHISNER, Wm. S. WHITE. Proved Jany 22, 1890 by H. R. LUPTON, surviving witness. Wm. T. GILBERT and A. J. HOUCK are deceased and P. WHISNER is non-resident of this state.

Pages 186-187: Will of Sarah S. MAGILL. Requests Note of Judge T. T. FAUNTLEROY (now of Richmond, Va), dated Oct 1876 plus interest be used for the following bequests: Tombstones over "my father, mother, brother, Alfred and Sister, Virginia, in Mount Hebron Cemetery; money to Revd James GRAHAM to be used for gravestones over her grandparents, Charles MAGILL and wife, Mary; money to Revd James GRAHAM, to Mary Magill LONG, daughter of Revd Geo. A. LONG, and Balance to niece, Mary Young SOMMERS. Prayer book to cousin, Mrs. J. N. SWARTZWELDER. One silver cup to Charles Magill SMITH, son of A. Magill SMITH. One silver cup to Sallie LONG together "with my Breast Pin and Earrings with my Mother's hair in them". Bequest to sister, Mary A. NASON. Cousin, A. Magill SMITH to be executor. 12 Dec 1889. Wit: Augusta C. BROWN, Lizzie M. SMITH. Proved 23 Jany 1890. Appraisers appointed: John STEPHENSON, W. C. MARSHALL, R. M. WOOD, Wm. P. McGUIRE, W. Roy STEPHENSON.

Pages 187-188: Will of Ellen LILLIS, "being in sickness & extreme illness". 16 Jany 1890. All to "dear husband, John LILLIS". Wit: P. H. REARDEN, Dennis COLLINS. Proved Feby 17, 1890. John LILLIS appointed Admin.

Pages 188-189: Will of Fred NULTON. To sister, Annie SLOAT, wife of Alexander SLOAT, books, pictures, small "Ladys Gold Watch" and Set of Walnut Furniture. To Frederick NULTON, infant son of brother, John M. NULTON, "the Gold Watch I am in the habit of wearing". To children of brother, John M. NULTON, houses on Water Street & all contents in brick house. Should brother, John M. NULTON, desire to continue "the business I now carry on", he may have the Shop & Contents at appraised value. Any interest in house in which "my father is now living" goes to sister, Annie SLOAT and children of brother, John M. NULTON. Sister to be executrix. 10 Apr 1889. Wit: W. McP. FULLER, L. N. HUCK. Codicil, 13 Apr 1889. Sister to accumulate rents from frame building on Water Street and use to finish Hall & 2nd Story of Brick House. Sister to be trustee of funds in estate for benefit of brother, John M. NULTON's children. Proved 18 Feb 1890. Appraisers: R. T. BARTON, Tilden

REED, Jr., T. A. LATHAM, Wm. I. SLAGLE, T. C. WINDLE.

Pages 190-192: Will of Henrietta ROBINS. To Mrs. Merrifield, Etta, Ella, and Fannie, furniture now in the private apartment in The Taylor Hotel occupied "by my daughters and myself". Among items: to daughter, Mrs. MERRIFIELD, one embroidered chair, candlelabra set, breast pin, tea set; to daughter, Etta, furniture, silver tea set, six napkin rings, heavy curtains. Between Etta and Ella, one embroidered chair, parlour carpet, silver castor, wax flowers. Among many things to Ella: silver cake basket, furniture, dishes, one sewing machine for the unmarried girls, egg nog bowl, pair Easels. Part of bequest to daughter, Fannie: furniture, ottomans, piano, vases, fruit dishes, hall furniture, lace curtains, two pictures of Martha & George. To son, Gus, the secretary; to son, John, Armchair. Books to all children. Son, John, is on a bond to son, Gus. If not paid by John, it should be paid out of proceeds of furniture and other personality belonging to the Taylor Hotel Equipment. After her death, Taylor Hotel property, west side of Loudoun Street, including Livery Stable, to be sold. Holmes CONRAD, to be executor. 11 June 1888. Wit: James B. RUSSELL, Isaac W. RUSSELL. Proved 25 Apr 1880. Appraisers appointed: Geo. W. KURTZ, John RAY, Hugh GREEN.

Page 192: Will of Thomas CLAYTON, (colored), Oct 29, 1888. "I desire the Love & Charity bury my body at my death, I desire for the Loving Fisherman to place a tombstone at my and my dear wife's head or so much thereof as the money will allow". Mentions Brothers Isaac JACKSON, Edward HOLMES, Dennis COATS. Real Estate to niece, Kate LAWS, and niece Ellen LAYTON, "to have a home in it her lifetime". Wit: John H. QUIETT, Edward HOLMES. Proved 21 Apr 1890. John JONES to Administer. Appraisers appointed: John H. QUIETT, Edmund HOLMES, Thos. MOSS, Zach ADDISON, Samuel DERRICK.

Page 193: Will of Edwin L. RUSSELL, 3 March 1888. All to wife, Susan S. RUSSELL, and she to be executrix. Wit: Edward A. TALBOTT, John F. M. MULLEN. Proved 17 June 1890, "at the hour of 9 o'clock". Will proved by the oath of M. H. G. WILLIS, that he was acquainted with the testator's handwriting. Witnesses now non-residents of the state "and distant". Appraisers appt'd: L. N. BARTON, L. R. GRIM, Isaac W. RUSSELL, H. K. GREEN.

Pages 193-194: Appraisement of Estate of Mary V. TRIER, adjudged insane. Appraisers: P. H. REARDON, Scott A. AFFLICK, H. Clay KREBS. 28 Jan 1890. House & Lot on Kent Street and amound due on Bond by Lewis F. TRIER. Appraisal returned by Lewis F. TRIER for his sister, Mary V. TRIER.

Pages 194-195: Estate Account of Margaret TRIER, dec'd., with Wm. H. MAY, her exec. Begins May 1890 with cash received from Bonds, rent of Louis TRIER, and cash from Susie HOPSON and from sale of 2 Trunks & Chamber Furniture. Paid fees for settling and recording this account. Balance due estate: $1.97. If a commission is allowed the executor, the estate will owe $14.12. Executor declined fee. Recorded 21 Apr 1890.

Page 195: Appraisal of Personal Estate of Thomas CLAYTON, dec'd., returned by John JONES, his Admr. Some items: Dishes, Glasses, Side Board, Safe, Bedding, Rain Barrell, Wheelbarrow. Total estate: $19.04. Appraisers: Zack (later called Zachariah) ADDISON, Thomas MOSS, Samuel DERRICK. 23 Apr 1890. Recorded 13 May 1890.

Page 196: Sale of Personal Estate of Thomas CLAYTON (col'd.), dec'd.
Total proceeds: $22.42. Recorded May 13, 1890.

Pages 196-197: Estate Account of G. W. HARPER, dec'd., in Account with
Mary E. HARPER, his Admr. Begins June 1889, paying such debts as to
Undertakers, Funk & Rea; to Bushnell Apothecary; W. J. WHITLOCK for
coal; L. A. MILLER, Apothecary. Paid F. J. McDONALD's claim for Bed
Springs and Hampshire County fee to C. S. WHITE, Clerk. Paid G. W.
HAWKENS for Blacksmithing and C. E. HUNTSBERRY for funeral. Received
cash from Chas. McFARLAND for horse and Chas. FLETCHER for wagon;
received rents on Store House, Meat Shop and Upstairs Room. June 1, 1890.
Estate Account recorded July 12, 1890.

Pages 198-202: William B. BAKER's Estate Account with Albert, A. M. &
Wm. H. BAKER, his executors. Among items: cash received from Bank Stock;
from Bonds of A. M. SMITH & Godwin H. WILLIAMS; from R. R. & Gas Company
Stock; from Decatur, Alabama "Land 60s Stock" and interest on Wytheville
Bonds; Paid T. W. DOSH per will and Shoe Factory bill; Paid express
charges on Air Cushion and paid Balance as Trustee for Mrs. SHIELDS;
Paid copy of will to send to Cleveland, Ohio and for recording it there.
Also paid Delahunty for monument ($1,079.00) and paid Loans in Kansas City
and Waco, Texas. Balance due estate: $60,166.26. To Legatees: Trustees
of Lutheran Church, Mrs. W. B. BAKER, Miss Sophia BAKER, Albert BAKER,
W. H. BAKER, Mrs. C. R. PAGE, Mrs. H. H. POWEL. Account approved and
recorded Sept 17, 1890.

Page 203: Will of Rebecca Ann LATHAM. To brother, Daniel J. HUNSICKER,
all interest in House & Lot now occupied by testator, corner Cameron &
Clifford Streets. 3 April 1890. Wit: James M. HAYMAKER, C. W. HOLLIS.
Proved 20 Oct 1890.

Pages 204-205: W. W.BAKER, Ward, in Account with H. H. BAKER, his Guardian.
Begins Feb 1889 with such payments as to W. G. McCABE for tuition, and
J. C. VAN FOSSEN for rent. Paid for bycicle and money to ward. Paid Miss
A. E. STRIBLING for board. L. N. HUCK, Commr., re Guardianship Accounts:
"Some of the charges for payments to and on account of the ward, do not seem
to be entirely legal but the ward is now of age and has approved them."
Recorded 22 Oct 1890.

Pages 205-211: Estate of Henry S. BAKER, in Account with his Executors,
H. H. & R. W. BAKER. Begins Feb 1889 with cash receipts from SVN Bank &
Union Bank Stock, Winchester Gas Co. Dividends, Baker & Co. Liquidation,
Interest from many notes as those of Thos. COVER, G. W. KELLER, H. Wise
SOWERS, L. C. JANNEY, Bev. RANDOLPH, J. E. KERFOOT, Daniel JANNEY and on
"$100.00 Registered Reddlebergers". Some payments for: cablegram to
G. W. BAKER and on accounts of Oscar BARR, Geo. E. BUSHNELL, Geo. K. HEIST
and Ellis MALOY; Paid Safe Dep. & Trust Co.; expenses collecting Clowser
interest; Paid Mrs. E. H. BAKER Legacy. Among long list of Bonds & Notes
were those of H. S. BAKER, W. W. JONES, T. D. GOLD, C. M. PERRY, A. M. RUST.
Among Stocks owned were A. T. & O. Railroad, local banks, State of Georgia,
City of Mobile, Riddleberger Bonds, Front Royal Bank Stock, W. P. Railroad
Bonds & Stock. Made distribution to widow and 2 daughters and then to his
five children: R. W. BAKER, H. H. BAKER, Guardian of W. W. BAKER, H. H.
BAKER, Miss Gertrude W. BAKER and Miss Lily H. BAKER. Recorded 19 Sept 1890.

Pages 211-213: Will of John CARNELL, City of Philadelphia, Penn. To daughter, Eliz. F. CUSHING, one-half part and other half to child of deceased daughter, Esther R. COOK. Grandson, John C. COOK, to be executor. 29 Oct 1888. Wit: John NIXON, Clifford P. ALLEN, Clifford P. ALLEN, Jr. Testator died Sept 13, 1890 and will proved Sept 22, 1890, Philadelphis. Authentic copy to Winchester received by Rich'd. L. GRAY, Clerk.

Pages 213-214: Will of Alexander T. SLOAT. After payment of debts, all to wife, Anna Elizabeth SLOAT and she to be executrix. 10 May 1872. Wit: T. H. B. DAWSON, J. H. BUZZARD. In Winchester Court, Dec 15, 1890: Witnesses now residing out of state in Morgan County, WVa. J. Rufus SMITH, Notary Public, Morgan County, WVa, took depositions of witnesses, in Berkeley Springs. Will proved Jany 20, 1891. Wife bonded to execute will. Appraisers appointed: T. C. WINDLE, Wm. J. SLAGLE, L. Dow HESS, H. R. LUPTON, M. T. REED.

Page 216: Inventory & Appraisal of Estate of Sarah SCHULTZ, dec'd., 12 Dec 1888. Dwelling & Lot, Lots, Household Furniture. Appraisal recorded Jany 19, 1891.

Page 217: Appraisement, Estate of Sarah S. MAGILL, dec'd. Appraisers: W. Roy STEPHENSON, Wm. C. MARSHALL, John STEPHENSON. Total inventory: Bond of Judge T. T. FAUNTLEROY, 2 silver Cups, Clothing & Furniture. Total $343.00. 15 Nov 1890. Recorded 17 Nov 1890.

Pages 217-218: Bernard REILLEY in Account with M. M. LYNCH, his Committee. Begins 9 July 1890 to Aug 1890: Cash received from R. T. BARTON. Cash of R. E. TRENARY Judgment to T. M. BAUTZ, Mrs. ANDERSON, Eben TAYLOR, John T. FORD, T. A. LATHAM. Some payments: Railroad fare for B. REILLEY; Mrs. Bridget REILLEY for use of family; W. R. STEPHENSON, Legal Services in Hagerstown; Wm. PANNETT for cultivating corn. Balance of Account: $2.06. Recorded 17 Nov 1890.

Pages 219-220: Will of William G. RUSSELL, Sr. Executor to pay all just debts but not to sell House & Lot where testator now lives. Such sale to be made with consent of wife, Catherine RUSSELL. All property to wife and she to receive "interest, rents and profits thereto". After wife's death, to daughter, Hattie T. RUSSELL, the Stone House & Lot where "I now reside, on East side Loudoun Street". After wife's death, proceeds of estate as follows: To son in law, Bruce GIBSON, and to children other than Hattie T.: Dr. David S. RUSSELL, W. G. RUSSELL, Jr., Edwin L. RUSSELL, Mary E. GIBSON, wife of Bruce GIBSON, Sidney W. DORSEY, wife of U. L. DORSEY. Shares of Mary GIBSON and Sidney DORSEY to be free from control of husbands. No inventory and appraisal required. Dwelling & Furniture to be possessed and used by wife. 6 Oct 1885. Wit: Jas. B. RUSSELL, H. K. GREEN. Codicil, Oct 6, 1885. Hattie T. RUSSELL to have present dwelling on Main Street, all household & personal property and that to be her only interest in the estate. Proved 18 Feb 1891.

Pages 221-222: Appraisement of Estate of Samuel EVANS, dec'd., 20 Jany 1891. Appraisers: Chas. W. HENSELL, Sam'l. B. BAKER, C. M. GIBBENS. Some items: One Alderney Heifer, 1 incubater, several Rocking Chairs, articles in his Shop including lot Leather, 4 pairs Shoes, Lasts & Boot Trees, Tools, Household & Kitchen Furniture, 23 Chickens. E. J. EVANS, Admr. Recorded Feb 21, 1891.

Page 222: Will of Henry V. WILLIS. Property "I now own" situated on East side of Kent Street to remain as it is so long as my daughters, Hannah J. & Agnes & Mary remain single. If all marry or die, property to be sold and divided equally among my children or their heirs. If and when property is sold, wishes one of his sons to buy it "so it will remain in the Willis name". Any two of his sons, William R., John M., Henry R., and Frank E. to be execs.

9 April 1886. Wit: C. M. GIBBENS, Bentley KERN. Proved 16 Mar 1891.

Pages 223-225: Will of Alfred HITE. Real & Personal Property "to be disbursed of after my death: viz - pay debts; then one-third each to wife, Ann M. HITE, to son, Willie C. HITE and to daughter, Mary C. DENNY (free from all control of husband)". Son, Willie C. HITE, to be executor. 12 July 1884. Wit: H. M. BAKER, S. B. BAKER. Codicil, 5 Aug 1884. None of estate to be divided or sold during lifetime of wife, Annie M. HITE, without her full and free consent in writing and witnessed. Second codicil, 28 July 1886. Friend Henry M. BAKER to be executor in place of Wm. C. HITE. Wit: H. M. BAKER, Wm. R. ALEXANDER. Proved 16 March 1891. Henry M. BAKER, Executor. Appraisers appointed: L. Dow HESS, Wm. I. SLAGLE, Saml B. BAKER, Geo. Ed. JENKINS, Nathan BRENT. Inventory and Appraisal, 18 March 1891. Among items: 3 bedsteads & bedding, Wash Stand, Bureau, 3 Stoves, Tables, Lamp Stand, 14 Chairs, 2 Clocks. Recorded Mar 18, 1891.

Page 226: Appraisement of Estate of Miss Virginia M. BURNS, dec'd., 7 March 1891, with Appraisers: H. K. GREEN, John G. MILLER, Henry BAETJER. Total inventory: Cash in hands of Jas. B. RUSSELL, Exer., $2,450.59 and cash from sale of one half interest in Lot & House, Higginsville, Mo., $532.35. Recorded 16 March 1891.

Pages 226-227: Appraisement of Personal Estate of Alexander T. SLOAT. 28 Jany 1891, with Appraisers: M. T. REED, Wm. I SLAGLE, T. C. WINDLE. Among items: lot of Carpenter's Tools, Tinners, Tin Ware & Trimmings, 1 Showcase, 1 Safe, pair Scales, parlour & bedroom Furniture, 1 Refrigerator. Appraisal returned by Anna E. SLOAT, his Exec. Recorded Mar 11, 1891.

Pages 227-228: Will of William SWIFT. See that "my body, after death, is decently and properly buried". Executor to sell all personal property and real estate including House & Lot on North Market Street and give to "my widow, Sidney Ann SWIFT, a ratable dower or alottment in lieu of dower". Rest to nephews, Charles COOK, John COOK, Albert COOK and niece Eliza COOK and to brother, Warner SWIFT and to Mary Ellen HARRIS, now wife of William ROBINSON, and to the building comm. of the Odd Fellows, that is The Morning Star of the West, No. 1461, the sum of $100 to be equally divided amongst them. Balance of proceeds to estate of niece, Sarah E. WARD, who was Sarah E. WELLS before marriage, who is now a resident of Fair Haven, Conn. Friend, John T. MARKER, to be executor. 3 April 1891. Wit: Joseph A. NULTON, Joseph E. KIGER, A. H. H. BOYD. Proved 23 Apr 1891. John T. MARKER, exec. Appraisers appointed: J. C. RIELY, John H. CREBS, L. H. McKINSTER, B. M. KNIGHT, H. B. STRIKER.

Pages 229-230: Sale of Personalty of John PIRKEY, dec'd., Jas. P. WHITACRE, Trustee, 27 June 1887. Among sales of mostly household goods: To Mrs. TIMBERLAKE, Mrs. SHAULL, Henry BAILEY, T. J. COOPER. Paid for printing hand bills and for crier at sale. Balance due Trust, $145.72, paid Cooper & Bros on debt secured in Deed of Trust, dated May 13, 1887. T. J. COOPER, Exec. Account settled & recorded 20 Apr 1891.

Page 231: Inventory & Appraisement of Estate of Wm. G. RUSSELL, dec'd., Apr 21, 1891, Bruce GIBSON, executor. Appraisers: Geo. W. HILLYARD, Thos. K. CARTMELL, Samuel M. CHILDS. Total Inventory: Tract of Land in Frederick County, Shawnee District, about 305 acres; Tract of Land in Frederick County, Opequon District, about 343 acres; House & Lot, west side of Main Street, Winchester. Recorded Apr 25, 1891.

Pages 232-233: It appeared to Court that last will & testament of Michael COPENHAVER, dec'd., was, on 28 Nov 1823, probated and recorded and then destroyed. Original will was found in Clerk's office and produced to Court. Will is reproduced here. Will dated 28 Aug 1823. To wife, Margaret, all real estate and black man, William, who is to be free at wife's death. To wife, Margaret also all Household & kitchen furniture and "the first and last Notes due from Jacob COPENHAVER". To son, Michael COPENHAVER, "all my Lott wherein I live and one-half out Lott," also horse and cart. Rest of out Lott to be sold and divide between son, George COPENHAVER's five children when boys reach 21 and girls reach 18. Also to daughters, Catherine BRANNIN and Elizabeth CONRAD. Wife and son, Michael, to be execs. Wit: Jacob KIGER, Wm. LANGLEY, John NULTON. Proved 28 Nov 1823, with Margaret and Michael to execute will. Mentions Conrad, Michael, Margaret, Lucinda and George COPENHAVER, infant children of George COPENHAVER, dec'd., who was son of said Michael, dec'd., represented by Robert BRANNIN, their next friend, appeared to contest the will. A true copy, May 1891.

Pages 233-234: Inventory and Appraisal of Estate of William SWIFT, dec'd. Apr 23, 1891, John T. MARKER, exec. Appraisers: J. Chas. RIELY, J. H. CREBS, L. H. McKINSTER. Small inventory: House & Lot, Carpenters bench, Grindstone, Carpenters Tools, Iron Kettle & Anvil, Vacant Lot on Martinsburg Pike, Pistol, few pieces of household goods. Recorded May 4, 1891.

Pages 234-236: Estate of Margaret BYRD in Account with George W. WARD, Admr. Begins Aug 1878 with receipts on Sower's Bond and on Timberlake Bond, & from O. R. FUNSTER Est. Paid C. F. EICHELBERGER's Account and Clerk's and Commr. fees. Distribution: one-half to each Geo. W. WARD and Miss Emily FUNSTEN. Payments continued to 1891. Account recorded May 18, 1891.

Page 237: Will of Margaret Ann WINDLE. Devises Lot owned in Winchester to daughters, Rebecca J. DOUTHAT and Eliza C. SIX. Also to them what rent due from dower interest in husband's land. Appoints Nephew, Theadore WINDLE, executor. 16 May 1889. Wit: Chas. FELTER, J. R. NOEL. Proved in Pulaski County, Va, 7 Aug 1889 by Chas. FELTER, and on 8 Aug 1889, by J. R. NOEL. Sept 9, 1891, recorded in Winchester.

Page 238: Will of Mrs. Mary M. SNAPP, who makes her will "in the Words and Figures following". House, Lot and all real estate "to my own children" -- Mary, Sally, Margaret, Emma, Laura and Oliver, Dedrick and Benjamin SNAPP, "all of whom are my children and are now single and unmarried and to remain with the single until all are married". Personal property to go to children as may remain single. If all marry, divide equally to all children including son, Joseph. Son, Benjamin, to execute will. ____ day, April 1882. Wit: John H. CREBS, L. T. MOORE. Proved Oct 1, 1891.

Pages 239-243: Inventory and Appraisal of Personal Estate of Ezra ROUTZONG, of Clarke County. 16 Sept 1890, with Appraisers: in Winchester/Frederick County, James FUNK, John KAUFMAN, Vance BELL; in Clarke County, Doras JONES, Jesse RUSSELL, William F. DATTERER. Part of Inventory in Clarke County: 8 Horses, Wagons, Buggy, Sulky, Farm Equipment, Buck Boards, Sleigh Bells, Dinner Bell. Some of items in Winchester: Household furniture, including Knitting Machine, 3 Washing Machines & Ringers, Cherry Seeder, Apple Peeler, ½ ton coal. Silas ROUTZONG, Admr. Recorded Nov 16, 1891. At Sale of Personal Property, 24 Feby 1891, some purchasers: C. L. WOOD, J. K. RUBY, C. EVERHART, J. M. MORRISON, Wm. DUBROW, C. M. PHELNEY, E. L. FISHPAW, Wm. SWIMLEY, Evan THATCHER. Sale Account recorded Nov 16, 1891.

Pages 243-244: Will of Ellen GORSUCH, March 11, 1889. To brother, Charles T. GORSUCH, all property for his lifetime, then to cousins, Dr. Henry M. WILSON and Ellen M. WILSON, of Baltimore, Md. The family clock to Dr. Henry M. WILSON. To Ellen M. WILSON, personal property as clothing, fancy chair, cake basket and mahogany table. Brother, Charles T. GORSUCH, to be executor. Wit: W. S. MILLER, G. L. MILLER. Proved 21 Dec 1891. Appraisers appointed: Thomas PAGET, George HOOVER, John HOOVER, Bushrod CARPENTER, Daniel CLINE.

Pages 244-246: Estate of John PIRKEY, dec'd., in Account with T. J. COOPER, his exec. Begins Oct 1 (no year given) with proceeds of Sale of Personal Estate, cash received from R. A. SAUM, J. MILLER, P. W. JARRETT, John BAKER, E. H. BOYD. Cash received from Books sold. Among expenses: paid for funeral, for medicine, freight on books, fees & commissions. Mentions bonds of Clarissa ZEILER, Abraham STICKLEY; accounts of Jacob LEMLEY; bonds of William H. COPP and Zea, Crawford & Co. Recorded 21 Dec 1891.

Pages 246-247: Jacob METZ, Guardian of Mertie & Fred GOSHERT. Begins July 1889 with paying accounts of wards: insurance, medical bills, hydrant, painting, wallpaper, legal services, fees, taxes. Paid Emma C. GOSHERT for "necessaties for wards and for boarding wards". Income from Interest on investment and Rent on House. Account recorded Dec 21, 1891.

Pages 248-249: Will of Eliza BETZALL or Eliza DAVIS (formerly BETZALL). All property to William EVANS, son in law, and to son Frederick BETZALL, of Parkersburg, Wood Co., WVa. At death of son, that part goes to son in law. At death of son in law, to granddaughter, Annie Eliza ATHEY, wife of James ATHEY. At death of son in law and son, son's part to granddaughter, Florence Ida MASON, wife of John W. MASON, Berkley Co., WVa. Wishes son in law, William EVANS, "to have good support in his declining years". He to be executor. _____ July 1888. Signed Eliza (her mark) BETZALL. Wit: John H. CREBS, L. T. MOORE. Codicil: Margaret Elizabeth ATHEY, formerly EVANS, and a granddaughter, to share with other two granddaughters, Florence Ida MASON and Annie Elizabeth ATHEY. 2 March 1889. Signed Eliza (her mark) DAVIS. Wit: R. E. TRENARY, Richd. L. GRAY. 18 Jan 1892 proving date.

Pages 249-250: Will of Adam WINDLE. To wife, Martha E. WINDLE, all property "without reserve". She to execute will. 17 June 1890. Wit: Sam'l. B. BAKER, L. Dow HESS. Proved April 18, 1892.

Pages 250-252: Will of Juliet B. ABBOTT, of Frederick County. To niece, Amanda Moore WILEY, now CLINE, all household & kitchen furniture "save what I otherwise dispose of". To niece, Elmira Oldham CLINE, quilts & bedding items and full share of money coming from "my father's undivided estate", to be used for her necessities, particularly her education. This niece to have "my full wardrobe". It this niece dies before reaching 21, all to her mother, Amanda Moore CLINE, who is requested to administer. 10 Apr 1868. Codicil, 18 May 1871: Gives to niece, Elmira Oldham CLINE, many more household items. If this niece dies before 21, her portion to her mother, Amanda Moore WINKFIELD (formerly CLINE). Free of control of her husband, John H. WINKFIELD. Wit: Wm. L. BENT, R. B. HOLLIDAY. "Having lost my friend, C. A. B. COFFROTH and Elmira O. CLINE having arrived of age, she is appointed to administer will. Proved will of Juliet Beaty ABBOTT, Apr 18, 1892. Witness Wm. L. BENT now deceased and witness R. B. HOLLIDAY not a resident of Virginia. Signatures proved by oaths of Col. Joseph A. NULTON & Thos. K. CARTMELL.

Mrs. Elmira O. RENNER (nee CLINE) qualifies as executrix. Her husband, Geo. E. RENNER, joins in bond.

Pages 252-254: (No title) Joseph STINE in Account with J. L. REDMON, his committee. Begins Jan 14, 1891, with cash collected from D. HESS, from Cleveland for rent, for wood sold. Expenses paid: A. J. CLEM for repairing cellar door, himself for having house cleaned; paid Joseph STINE for washer woman; paid 2 days to self for looking after farm; paid self for dinner; paid Jas. R. GROVE for 2 nites lodging. Received cash from John THWAIT on rent and paid board bill to Mrs. CLEVELAND for Stine. The account of Jas. L. REDMON, Sergt. Committee of Joseph STINE, (an adjudged lunatic) recorded Apr 19, 1892. Joseph STINE "having been adjudged compos mentis and discharged" from the Western Lunatic Asylum, Aug 6, 1891, Jas. L. REDMON is discharged from his duty.

Pages 254-255: Will of William JENKINS. "Under authority and direction given me by the will of my deceased wife, Julia JENKINS," gives to his children: to son, William M. JENKINS, "one half dozen cane seated chairs". Rest of personal property to daughter, Kate K. JENKINS. To her, also, "all funds & benefits coming to me from the Legion of Honor", to be used for the benefit of her daughter, Julia. 2 May 1892. Wit: George E. JENKINS, Chas. B. WOODWARD. Proved 17 May 1892. Members of family of the deceased request James B. RUSSELL to administer. Appraisers appointed: Ed. J. EVANS, T. M. BAUTZ, Sam'l. B. BAKER, John ROY, Geo. McCORMICK.

Pages 255-258: Estate of Ezra ROUTZONG, dec'd., in Account with S. H. ROUT-ZONG, his Admr. Begins Sept 1890 with payments to auctioneer and repairing drill & buggy. Paid appraisers, W. F. DALTON & A. N. PIERCE; paid G. C. RHODICK 2 years subscription paper; paid W. T. MELTON fire insurance policy; paid Baker & Co. fertilizer bill; paid S. H. ROUTZONG, Admr., 5 percent commission. Received income of sales of wheat & corn, personal property sale, cash in bank. Paid Jas. W. LEEKE for collecting sale notes. Distribution: Sarah ROUTZONG, widow; Lottie & Jennie MORRISON, Mollie BLESSING, Ella WHITHINGTON, S. H. ROUTZONG. Recorded July 18, 1892.

Pages 258-259: Will of Daniel O'LEARY. To 3 children, Thomas, Daniel and Lizzie, who "have remained with me and contributed to my comfort & support in my old age", all property. He divides lots. Front portion of House in which 2 now live (4 rooms) to Lizzie and half interest in common with her brother, Daniel, of garden & yard. Daniel gets back portion of house. Thomas gets land northside Shawnee Bridge. 25 July 1892. Wit: M. M. LYNCH, Henry ARDERN. Proved Sept 19, 1892.

Pages 259-260: Inventory and Appraisement of Estate of Ellen GORSUCH, dec'd. Frederick County. Appraisers appointed: Thomas PADGETT, John HOOVER, George HOOVER, Bushrod CARPENTER, Daniel CLINE. 15 Oct 1892. Part of inventory: Freezer, Riding Saddle, Passage Lamp, Stove, Clock, mahogany Tables, Cooking Stove, Sewing Machine. Chas. T. GORSUCH qualifies as executor, 21 Dec 1891. Inventory recorded Oct 20, 1892.

Pages 261-263: Will of James H. BARNHART. Executor to sell all real estate. To John & Samuel SMALL, of York, Pa., Bonds of Columbia Water Works, of United States, and of Northern Central R. R. Company. "These bonds came to me through my wife, Annie Mary SMALL, sister of said John and Samuel." To Mrs. Julia CHILDS, of Jackson, Michigan, "my tall eight day clock". To niece, Catherine BUSH, all household & kitchen furniture except clock. Silver and Books to be

divided by Catherine with her sister, Sallie BARLEY. Bequeath $1,000 to
each: sister, Sarah STEINER, of Alexandria, Va, to nieces, Sally BARLEY
and Catherine BUSH, of Winchester; $500 to Miss Mary CHILDS, of Jackson,
Michigan, niece of deceased wife; $100 to friend, Dr. Godfrey L. MILLER.
Also gives to Methodist Episcopal Church congregation and to Revd. Harry
BOGGS. E. Holmes BOYD, exec. 5 Apr 1890. Wit: John G. & J. A. MILLER.
Proved 22 Nov 1892. Appraisers appointed: John G. MILLER, Geo. E. BUSHNELL,
S. H. HANSBROUGH, T. M. BAUTZ, Oscar BARR.

Pages 263-264: Inventory & Appraisement of Estate of James H. BARNHART,
dec'd. 23 Nov 1892, E. Holmes BOYD, exec. Inventory is mostly of bonds &
Notes, as mentioned in will. Some are those of Sam'l. L. & Lewis PIDGEON,
Isabelle NOONAN, J. Fred STROTHER, Chas. A. LUPTON, Jas. H. CLOWSER, Mrs. E.
MULVEHILL. Other items: House & Lot on Braddock Street, eight-day Clock,
Household & Kitchen Furniture, Books. Recorded 26 Nov 1892.

Pages 264-266: Inventory & Appraisement of Estate of John TOYE, dec'd.
26 Sept 1892. Mrs. Kate DEHAVEN, daughter of deceased, to administer.
Appraisers appointed: Oscar BARR, John STEPHENSON, R. A. HIETT, J. Ralph
GRIGSBY, L. Dow HESS. Appraisers in Harrisonburg, Rockingham County:
C. A. SPRINKEL, J. C. SLEIGEL, Wm. LOEB, Eugene WEST, Abram BYRD. 10 Oct
1892, signed by C.H. CHANDLER, Notary Public. Some of small inventory:
agricultural furnace, rendering kettle, Press & Boards, Carboy oil vitrol,
Tubs, Scrapers, Screens, Scales, 2,544 lbs. hair at Yancey SNELL. "The
amount of Fleshings on hand from 7,800 hides received from J. P. HOUCK's
Tanning Company"--supposed "to be about 33,500 lbs. (curred)". Winchester
appraisal, 30 Sept 1892: cash in bank, Note due by Edwin TOYE, and amount
of Armour Glue Works. Recorded Oct 25, 1892.

Pages 266-274: Serena P. DANDRIDGE, Helen N. DANDRIDGE, & Edmund P. DAN-
DRIDGE in account with A. R. PENDLETON, their guardian. Dates: Oct. 29,
1884 - Nov 1892. Cash and interest from A. R. PENDLETON, Admr. of E. P.
DANDRIDGE, dec'd. Paid Board of wards & servants hire; also Mrs. DANDRI-
DGE, Sr. for clothing for wards; paid church subscription and servants at
church; paid Telegraph Boy and expressage on Dandridge's papers. Paid
A. R. P.'s expenses twice to Charlestown and expressage on papers for Settlement of Kennedy heirs and Kate D. purchase matter. Paid Mrs. J. A. ANDERSON
for Garvin Children; paid Rebecca TAYLOR, widow of Stephen TAYLOR. Paid
"Spirit of Jefferson". "There may be a loss of $250 on act of an overpayment
by A. R. PENDLETON to Shepherds." Estate account settled Nov 18, 1892.

Pages 274-278: Estate of Sarah SCHULTZ, dec'd., in account with A. R. PENDLE-
TON, her Admr. Begins Oct 9, 1888 with cash from Miss BURGESS, rent. Paid
Jacob SMITH, cleaning cistern; paid servant, services as to R. R. damages;
paid E. H. DIEFFENDERFER & Fred NULTON for repairs; paid E. H. BOYD, agent
for Mary M. TIDBALL; paid for Deeds to John S. MILLER. Received cash of
Mrs. J. V. BELL, rent, and sent cash to Union Bank "to be credited on debt".
Made advance to Dr. & Mrs. P. W. BOYD. Account recorded Nov 18, 1892.

Page 279: A. R. PENDLETON, Guardian, in Account with E. M. & P. M. HOOVER.
Begins Mar 20, 1890 with cash from C. M. GIBBENS, Spl. Comr. in Trenary vs
Hoover. Other items: Mar 1877, paid, Motion to appoint E. P. DANDRIDGE
Guardian and paid services, Enquiry as to Hoover Tavern property. P. M.
HOOVER will be of age, Jany 21, 1891. Account of A. R. PENDLETON, Guardian,
recorded 19 Dec 1892.

Pages 280-282: Estate Account of Virginia M. BURNS, with James B. RUSSELL, her exec. Begins May 19, 1884 with cash received of H. CONRAD. Paid P. W. BOYD for cemetery lot; paid expenses of executor to Higginsville, Blackstone, & Lexington, Mo. Received "principal of J. C. HITE's bond". Paid legacy to: G. W. BURNS, Miss Fanny K. EVANS, Gertrude CAMERON, O. K. BURNS. Received rent of Isaac NEALE, of G. O. WASHBURN, of J. H. BROWN. Cash to Mrs. Fannie A. CASTLEM. Account recorded 19 Dec 1892.

Pages 282-284: Estate of Thomas J. RITT, dec'd., in Account with Daniel THOMPSON, exec. Begins June 1, 1883, by Balance due estate per last statement, plus interest. Total $298.08, less commr.'s fees, clerical services, recording & settling fees. For distribution to three legatees, $89.18 each: (1) Walter THOMPSON, his share less expenses as taxes, fees, and 3 payments for shoes. Annie THOMPSON produced receipt of Thos. W. THOMPSON (who is Walter THOMPSON) in full of amount due to him; (2) Elmer J. THOMPSON, her share less amounts paid for taxes, fees and 2 pairs of shoes; (3) Sarah THOMPSON, less expenses same as other two plus purchase of umbrella from W. V. HODGES. To be paid to her when she arrives at age 21. First two legatees have reached age of 21. Recorded 19 Dec 1892.

Pages 284-285: Will of Roberta E. MOREHEAD, "being impressed with the uncertainty of life". To daughter, Ella S. MOREHEAD, "whatsoever I own or have or may be entitled to and wheresoever". She is sole legatee. Mentions a sum of money due for certain dower interest in WVa. 12 July 1890. Wit: S. T. HOLLIDAY, Jas. W. STOTTLEMYER. Proved Feby 1, 1893.

Pages 285-286: Will of Rebecca M. CAPP. Dwelling House & Lots undivided in the County of Rockingham, Va, at Dayton, on High Street, to two grandchildren, Edmonia Belle CAPP & Winona Pauline CAPP. Gives permission for son, N. F. A. CAPP, to build house on lot adjoining. To daughter in law, Mollie B. CAPP, all household goods and personal property after special articles of Bedding given to two daughters. Son to have all money and to be guardian for the children and executor. Son to pay all expenses of last illness. 18 Dec 1891. Wit: C. H. CROWELL, Jas. M. BROWN. Proved 21 Feb 1893. On motion of Revd. N. F. A. CAPP, son, guardian of Edmonia Bell CAPP, aged 8, and Winona Pauline, aged 4, children of Revd. N. F. A. CAPP.

Pages 286-287: Will of Mary SHERER, of Frederick County. Remainder of "my worldly estate" after payment of debts: to daughter, Sidney A. STEPHENSON, household goods & personal property, Bonds & money. She to be sole executor. Also to her all real estate & other property to do with as she wishes. ___ day of May 1887. Wit: Millicent L. CATHER, James P. WHITACRE. Proved 21 Feb 1893.

Pages 287-289: Inventory & Appraisement of Estate of W. W. BAKER, dec'd., and Settlement thereof. H. H. BAKER, his Admr. 20 Feby 1893. Among inventory: Bank Shares & dividends, Bonds, Notes of J. G. H. MILLER, G. W. HADDOX, Thos. M. NELSON, Deeds of Trust of H. Wise SOWERS & Jno. W. RICE. Shares in Land Companies. Appraisers: Albert BAKER, Wm. H. BAKER, C. S. BAKER, Wm. S. WHITE. Among income & expenses: received from estate of H. S. BAKER, dec'd.; paid Mrs. B. NOONAN, Dr. Wm. P. McGUIRE, & Joseph GARBER, Undertaker. Distribution, 1/5th to each: Mrs. H. S. BAKER, R. W. BAKER, Gertrude W. BARTON, Lily H. BAKER, H. H. BAKER. Recorded 14 Mar 1893.

Pages 289-290: Will of Wm. FRIES. Notes & Bonds to pay debts and funeral expenses and divide rest among my children: Eliza J. SPENCE, Rachel A. HODGES, William O. FRIES, Mary E. BROWN, Geo. A. YEAKLEY's two boys (as one heir). New house, "adjoining my residence", to be sold & divide among my children. Same

for house & lot "where I now live". To Mary E. BROWN, organ in parlor.
18 Sept 1892. Wit: T. W. CAPPER, G. Casper FRIES. Proved 20 Mar 1893.
John J. BROWN, exec. Appraisers appointed: T. W. CAPPER, G. Casper FRIES,
R. R. BROWN, Edgar L. FRIES, D. W. BROWN.

Pages 291-293: Will of Miss Emily FUNSTEN. To two nieces, Margaret F. &
Emily R. WARD, brick house & lot, Washington Street, "in which we now reside".
All household goods, everything inside house except niece, Emily R. FUNSTEN,
"who is under my special charge", $8,000 plus what is coming from "my dear
deceased sister, Margaret BYRD". Also stock in railroad. Also to two nieces
250 acre farm in Clarke Co. Mentions "my dear brother, David (now deceased)
who owed a portion of price of a farm"-"the war coming on prevented the payment". Mentions share belonging to the estate of the father of Emily R. FUN-
STEN. Wishes Emily "to continue to live here with her cousins as she has
done with me". Gives to niece, Louise N. FLETCHER. Leaves money toward purchase of a silver cup to Margaret, daughter of Col. Wm. BYRD, with her name
handsomely engraved on it. Her part of property that belonged to her sister,
Margaret BYRD, now to nephews, Julian F., Robert M., David F., & George F.
WARD. Julian F. and Robert M. WARD, executors. 29 Oct 1884. Codicil,
Feby 1, 1886. In event of death of either brother, Robert M. or D. Funsten
WARD, without will or disposing of property left to them, it goes to sisters,
M. F. & E. F. WARD & surviving brother. Codicil, May 25, 1888. Additional
bequests to nieces. Will proved Mar 24, 1893. No witnesses so proved by oaths
of Wm. BYRD and L. N. HUCK. Julian F. WARD declined executorship. Robert M.
WARD qualified. Appraisers appointed: Wm. & R. E. BYRD, L. N. HUCK, T. W.
HARRISON, T. K. CARTMELL.

Pages 294-295: Will of Dr. Wm. A. McCORMICK. All estate to 3 daughters,
Margaret P., Elizabeth and Charlotte C. Present dwelling & lot, corner of
Washington & Amherst, to remain as it is and be home for them, in no way
subject to anyone's debts. Should daughter, Margaret P. SLODDERT, come into
possession of an income or property from her late husband's estate, or marry,
then estate to unmarried daughters. Son, Foxhall P. McCORMICK, executor.
19 Sept 1891. Wit: H. Douglas FULLER, Jno. W. PRICE. Proved Mar 27, 1893.
Appraisers appointed: Shirley CARTER, Clarence MILLER, Capt. Geo. KURTZ,
Fred O. MILLER, Luther HODGSON. Appraisal made room by room: Parlor, Hall,
Bedrooms Nos. 1-4, Upper Hall, Dining Room, Kitchen. Items other than usual
household goods: Domestic Machine, Refrigerator, Presses, Wot Not. (no date)

Pages 296-297: Will of George F. MILLER. To daughter, Minnie, office next to
Bank "and between Bank & my Store & Dwelling". Store House & Dwelling and all
furniture and fixtures to daughter during her natural life and then to 3 sons,
Charles, Godfrey and Clarence. Stock of drugs to Minnie, Godfrey and Clarence.
Rest of estate to all four children. Gives money to Julia CHASE and for miss-
ionary work. 29 Feby 1892. Wit: W. S. MILLER, J. A. MILLER. Proved Apr 24,
1893. George Clarence Miller, exec. Appraisers appointed: John Abe. MILLER,
John G. MILLER, Wm. S. MILLER, Hugh GREEN. Inventory & Appraisal, 1 May 1893.
Some items: City, County & R. R. Bonds; Stock of Drugs; Cash in Bank;
Stock in Union Bank, Gas Company & Winch. & Pot. R.R. Notes of Ira S. CAPPER,
Henry BEUTZEL, Dr. Samuel JANNEY, Jacob LOY. Farming animals & equipment.

Page 298: Will of Robert M. LUPTON. To niece, Nellie B. LUPTON, all property
after funeral expenses and doctor bills. H. R. LUPTON, exec. 8 Apr 1893.
Wit: John S. LUPTON, T. N. LUPTON, P. C. GORE. Proved 18 Apr 1893. Appraisers appointed: T. N. LUPTON, J. S. LUPTON, P. C. GORE, T.K. CARTMELL, R. M.
CARTMELL.

Pages 298-299: Will of Anna E. GRIM. Executor to sell all estate, pay debts and funeral expenses. Place suitable head & foot stones at the graves of her and her deceased husband, Jno. W. GRIM. Any remaining "to my children or their heirs, my grandchildren, taking their parents' share, there being ten shares". Pay for head & foot stone for deceased son, Charles, out of his share. 27 May 1889. Wit: C. M. GIBBENS, Robert T. GOSS. Proved Apr 25, 1893. No executor named so son, George W. GRIM, to administer. Appraisers: James FUNK, W. A. CARPER, Lyle GRIM, Charles CLARK, R. W. HAYMAKER.

Page 299: Will of Sarah BROWN. Sell Lot adjoining her residence to pay for writing will, doctor bills, funeral expenses & tombstone. Rest of property to "my afflicted son, George W. MOORE," except furniture & other like property equally to son, George, and daughter, Harriet. Alexander DAVIS to be exec. 12 Aug 1889. Wit: Jno. J. WILLIAMS, Elizabeth MACKEY. Proved May 3, 1893. Alexander DAVIS declined to be executor, so R. E. TRENARY, late Sergeant of this city, to administer.

Pages 299-301: Will of William P. LAUCK. Money to Isac GLENN & Mrs. Daniel ELI "for her kindness". One-half property to sister, Harriet GROSS; other half: 2/5th to Brother, Jacob LAUCK, 2/5th to Brother, Cornelius LAUCK, and 1/5th to nephew, Chas. Edwd LAUCK. Put headstones at graves of father, mother, sister and self. Sister, Harriet E. GROSS to be exec. Apr 17, 1893. Wit: G. L. MILLER, J. H. BARNETT. Proved 15 May 1893. Appraisers: J. H. BARNETT, Thos. E. SLOAT, Sam'l. MULLEN, Patrick CONNER, Joseph BELL.

Pages 301-303: Inventory & Appraisal of Estate of Miss Emily FUNSTEN, dec'd. Among bonds: of Sam McCUNE & wife, Justus E. SOWERS, Jacob F. EBERSOLE & Geo. V. OYLER, J. E. & S. F. BRYARLY, Jos. A. & Dudley S. MILLER, W. M. JEFFERSON & wife, Jos. F. & Sallie B. McKAY. Stock in Banks and in Episcopal Female Institute. This estate entitled to one-half share in estate of Margaret BYRD, dec'd. Appraisers: T. K. CARTMELL, Wm. BYRD, T. W. HARRISON. 19 May 1893.

Pages 303-305: Inventory and Appraisal of estate of William FRIES, dec'd. Appraisers: Richard R. BROWN, Walter CAPPER, G. Casper FRIES. Usual household furniture & fixtures including clothes chests, extension table, woven wire bed springs, 153 gal. vinegar, 1 set fly straps, alarm clock. Recorded May 1893. Sale bill, personal Estate of William FRIES, dec'd. Among items & purchasers: Axe, Andy HOUCK; rope, Joe ROE; Wood Horse, Wm. WRIGHT; 140 gals. vinegar, Oscar BARR; Jar & Jug, James LEWIS; Bee Hive, Joe BULLER.

Page 306: Will of A. H. LAWRENCE. Aug 14, 1893. Complete will: "This is to certify that when I am dead and all my expenses is paid, Aaron BOXWELL & wife is to have all that I have left for there kindness to me". Proved 18 Sept 1893 by oath of Wm. R. ALEXANDER, who testified he was acquainted with handwriting of deceased. R. E. BYRD to administer. Appraisers: C. F. GROVE, Geo. E. JENKINS, Sam'l. B. BAKER, Jas. L. REDMON.

Pages 306-307: Inventory & Appraisal of Estate of Daniel L. BROWN. Appraisers: Wm. Rob't. JONES, C. W. HOLLIS, Geo. Ed. JENKINS. 1 Oct 1892. Small inventory: Cash in bank and from sale of one-half dozen chairs, wash bowl, cooking jars, coffee mill, 2 stove pans, cake mold. Returned to court by Jas. L. REDMON & recorded 20 Oct 1892.

Pages 307-308: Inventory & Appraisal of Estate of Edward A. ROBINS, dec'd. Appraisers: R. M. CARTMELL, Geo. E. BUSHNELL, A. Lewis SHEARER. 19 Sept 1892. Part of inventory: Certf. # 5 of Indiana Central Savings & Loan, Bond of Consumer Gas Trust Co. of Indianopolis, Cash in Union Bank of Winchester, 3

Notes of John L. & Henrietta ROBINS. Recorded Nov. 26, 1892.

Pages 308-309: Inventory & Appraisal of Personal Estate of Fannie I.
ROBINS, dec'd. Same appraisers as for Edward A. ROBINS. Among inventory:
Household items as Bedstead, Spring Mattress, Embossed China, 2 pieces
Statuary & Table, Egg Castor. Dividend of Manhattan Life Insurance Co;
1/3rd interest in assets of Estate of Edward A. ROBINS. Chas. E. MERRI-
FIELD, Admr. Recorded Nov 26, 1892.

Pages 309-310: Geo. Ed. JENKINS, Guardian of Julia E. ROSENBERGER. Account
paid July 2, 1892, cash in full of legacy devised by will of William JENKINS,
dec'd., plus interest. From Bond of Kate K. WOODWARD, in Trust on Real Estate
to E. Holmes BOYD, Trustee, less payments for ward's board and Clerks and
Commr's fees. Account settled & recorded July 19, 1893.

Pages 310-311: Inventory & Appraisal of Estate of Charles H. POPE, dec'd.
28 Oct 1893. Appraisers: S. H. HANSBROUGH, J. Henry MOLING, G. Goodwin
BAKER. Among small inventory: Wardrobe, Dressing Case, Cherry Stand, Trunk,
Policy in Maryland Life Ins. Co, Shares in Winchester Bldg. & Loan Assn.
and Winchester Co-operative Bldg. Assn. Recorded 28 Oct 1893.

Pages 311-312: Estate of C. M. HIBBARD, dec'd., with James P. WHITACRE, her
Admn. Begins Sept 23, 1884 with cash from Sale and from Wm. M. ROBINSON,
James SLOLLEMYER (STOTTLEMYER?). Cash paid Clerk at Sale, Bell Ringer,
Appraisers, Attorneys, taxes and fees. Paid Dr. W. S. Love account and
balance of George KURTZ bill. Received from Mrs. P. LEE estate. Account
goes to Apr 19, 1887 with balance due Admr., $80.17. Recorded Oct 19, 1893.

Pages 313-316: Will of Hon. Judge Richard PARKER. Wishes to be buried in
own lot in Mt. Hebron Cemetery, "alongside my wife", with monuments over both
graves. Gold watch & chain to Parker CRENSHAW, son of sister, Elizabeth A.
CRENSHAW. Money & Bedroom Furnishings to Mary MASON, colored, for her "long
& faithful service & tender & affectionate attendance upon my wife and myself".
Large Bible, red Prayer Book and Hymnal which was used by wife, to wife's
sister, Mrs. Nancy B. McGUIRE or her daughter, Nanny W. McGUIRE. Gives to
niece, Mrs. Maggie STODDART; to wife's niece, Mrs. Annie R. BROWN and her
daughter, Mossie, wife of Dawson McCORMICK. Rest of estate of such "small
worth that it would be little help to any, if divided among all my & my
wife's kindred", so gives to those he thinks most need assistance. Gives
half of residence to sister, Mrs. Elizabeth A. CRENSHAW or her two daughters,
Nanny & Libby CRENSHAW. Also to the 3 daughters of deceased sister,
Charlotte, wife of Dr. Wm. A. McCORMICK, namely: Mrs. Mag STODDART, Elizabeth
and Charlotte McCORMICK. Share of Maggie STODDART, if she dies, to daughter,
Bessy. Other half of residence to wife's sister, Mrs. Nancy B. McGUIRE, of
Clarke County, or if she dies, to her 3 daughters: Mrs. Gettie WHITE, now
living Sioux City (no state given), Nanny W. & Evy McGUIRE. Also to daughters
of wife's sister, Rebecca JOHNSON, and to Annie Tucker McGUIRE, daughter of
Mrs. Ann Eliza McGUIRE, dec'd., & to Belle M. STEPHENSON, daughter of
Gertrude STEPHENSON, dec'd. Rest of personal estate, including Shares of
Stock and Books to be sold. Also household furnishings except pictures and
photographs, as specified, to Mrs. Maggie STODDART & Nanny W. McGUIRE.
Dr. Wm. P. McGUIRE to be executor. 24 July 1888. Codicil, Mar. 29, 1893,
re bequests to Mary MASON. Proved Nov 20, 1893. No witnesses so proved by
oaths of E. Holmes BOYD & L. T. MOORE, who knew handwriting. Appraisers:
James B. RUSSELL, John RAY, Hugh GREEN, Frank G. WALTER.

Pages 316-317: Will of L. Dow HESS, Dec 19, 1889. All property, in Trust, to wife, Annie R. HESS, to be used as she deems "wisest and best" until our youngest child is 21. Then estate to be divided: wife, 1/3rd and rest to surviving children or their heirs. If wife dies or marries again, estate to be divided at once among children/heirs. Wit: H. Clay KREBS, W. S. LOVE. Proved Novr 20, 1893. Annie R. HESS, executrix. Appraisers: Sam'l. B. BAKER, Edward DIFFENDERFER, Dr. Wm. F. HUTCHINSON, Wm. H. HARDY, Capt. Bruce GIBSON.

Page 317: Inventory of Estate of Mrs. Charlotte R. PENDLETON, dec'd. Two items only: Shares of Stock in Nat'l. Bank of Baltimore, Md. & in Merchants Nat'l. Bank of Baltimore, Md. 5 Apr 1893. Alexr. R. PENDLETON, Admr. Recorded Octr 19, 1893.

Pages 317-318: Settlement of Guardian's Account, W. O. HORSEY, Guardian, in Account with Sam'l. R. ATWELL, ward. Dec. 1892 to Aug 1893, with cash paid for items as Straw Hat, 2 Shirts & Ties, Rink Buttons, Suit Clothes. 1 Sept 1893, paid to S. R. ATWELL, $5,006.71. Account settled & recorded 21 Nov 1893.

Page 319: Sale Account, Personalty of Ross ROBINSON, dec'd. Among articles sold and purchasers: Window Sash, Geo. H. HAINS; Lot of Iron Pots, N. KOHN and Joseph WISECARVER; 6 Flatirons, Wm. ATKINSON; Snuffer Case, John VILWIG; Fireboard, Warner BELL; Pitcher and Dishes, Lizzie JOHNSON. Recorded Oct 19, 1893. R. E. TRENARY, Committee Admr.

Pages 320-326: Estate Account of Benj. SNAPP, dec'd., Report of Debt & Settlement of Estate Account. July 17, 1893. Account of J. L. REDMON, Sergt. Comm. Admr. of Benj. SNAPP, dec'd. Proceedings delayed from 23 July 1892 to 17 July 1893. Settling of Account of D. W. SNAPP, surviving partner of firm of Benj. SNAPP & Bro. Machinery sold to John FITZ. Paid expenses to Martinsburg, attorneys, clerks & appraisers fees. Paid for tombstones for Mrs. Mary SNAPP, dec'd. Full brothers and sisters: D. W., G. O. & C. J. SNAPP, Maggie BRYANT, Laura W. HODGSON, Emma SNAPP, Sallie MOLING, Mary V. CROW. Half brothers and sisters: H. H., M. J. & T. M. SNAPP, Mrs. Jane GRAY, Francis R. SNAPP. Rob't. L. GRAY, sole heir of Mrs. A. Jane GRAY. Bertie EDDY, Edgar F. & Rushton SNAPP, heirs of F. R. SNAPP. Mentions distributable share of estate to Mrs. Mary SNAPP, mother of Benjamin SNAPP, dec'd., who was living at time of his death but who has died since. Long and complicated settlement of income & expenses of firm shared with surviving partner. Appraisal of personal estate by H. B. HANCOCK, Scott A. AFFLECK, Samuel B. BAKER included such as Lathes & Attachments, Drill Press, Grindstone, Pulleys, Tools, Office Furniture. Recorded 18 July 1893.

Pages 327-329: Inventory & Appraisal of Estate of John T. MARKER, dec'd., with Appraisers: John G. MILLER, H. K. GREEN, P. H. REARDON, J. Henry MOLING. Nov 3, 1893. Some items: 6 Lanterns, Hanging Lamps, Cattle Powder, Barrels & Spigots, Box of Crackers, Cedar Buckets, 3 doz. Goblets, 5 doz. Laundry Blue, lot of Cocoa Nuts, 112 cakes Soap, 30 lbs. Candy, Lot Cassia, Axle Grease. Nancy E. MARKER, Admr. returns to Court the Inventory of items concerned "but I do not adopt the values fixed to the articles". Recorded Nov 9, 1893.

Pages 329-330: Will of Fanny B. EWELL. After paying debts & funeral expenses, rest to sister, Mildred E. EWELL, and she to execute will. 13 May 1892. Wit: William BYRD, L. N. HUCK. Proved 21 Dec 1893.

Pages 330-331: Appraisal of Estate of Samuel R. ATWELL, dec'd. Jany 15, 1894. Appraisers: Wm. R. SMITH, A. R. PENDLETON, Geo. K. KEIST, Bentley KERN. Some of inventory: US & Winchester City Bonds; Notes of M. CONWAY, Sam'l. GENN, L. J. CALDWELL, Alexander DEHAVEN, D. J. L. BOEHM; Cow, Horses, Carriages, Piano and Sewing Machine. W. O. HORSEY and S. R. ATWELL, Admrs. Recorded Jany 16, 1894.

Pages 331-333: Will of Jacob H. BRISTOR, of Martinsburg, Berkeley County, WVa. To wife, Jennie S. BRISTOR, for life or "as long as she remains my widow", All property, House & lot on west side of Raleigh Street, where they now reside. Also 4 houses, west side of South College Street & double frame house on East side of North Charles Street, all in Martinsburg. Executrix to sell House & Carriage or other property, if needed, to pay debts. Any funds left, to two sons, Charles M. BRISTOR and William M. BRISTOR, No. 31, North High Street, Baltimore, Md. Make annual payments to Methodist Episcopal Church of Martinsburg. 14 June 1892. Wit: W. O. NICKLES, A. B. FAHNESTOCK. Proved Apr 17, 1893, Berkeley County, WVa. In Winchester Corporation Court, 19 Jany 1894, received authenticated copy of will. Jennie S. BRISTOR renounces her right to qualify as executrix and requests I. L. BENDER be qualified and it was so done.

Pages 333-337: Inventory and Appraisal of estate of L. Dow HESS. Appraisers: Samuel B. BAKER, Dr. Wm. F. HUTCHINSON, Bruce GIBSON. 28 Nov 1893. Some items in long list of inventory: many yards of cottonade, cambric & calico; sheets & sheeting, overalls, jeans, bed ticking; 15 lbs. Hominy, 32 bottles catchsup, 6 bottles Godfrey's Cordial, 20 lbs washing soda, many pairs hose & stockings. Among many Accounts due: Wm. STINSON, Scott BROWN, James MARSH, J. R. CRABLE, Festus HAHN, Mrs. Dr. Julian WARD, R. W. SCHMIDT, Jos. CAD-WALLADER (dec'd.). Annie R. HESS, Exec. Recorded Nov 29, 1893.

Pages 337-338: Will of John W. SMITH, of Frederick County, Va, "residing in Opequon Distr." To wife, Sarah J. SMITH, $700 or "enjoy the rents & profits on my house and lot in Winchester, on Main Street, on what is called Potato Hill". To son, George W. SMITH, $400 (later changed to $500); to daughter, Minnie E. SMITH, $35 plus share in residue of estate. Mentions four children: sons, James F. SMITH, Samuel R. SMITH, and daughters, Annie Sophia CRAIG and Minnie E. SMITH. Friend, T. K. CARTMELL, to execute. 19 Feby 1892. Wit: J. R. TREPLETT, Perry C. GORE. Proved Feby 19, 1894. T. K. CARTMELL declined executorship. Mrs. Sarah J. SMITH, widow, waived her right; son, James F. SMITH, to administer. Appraisers appointed: Jessie BAILEY, Kenzie SMITH, John CLINGER, Wm. PARKINS.

Pages 339-343: Inventory and Appraisal of Estate of Hon. Richard PARKER, dec'd., with Appraisers: John RAY, E. Holmes BOYD, James B. RUSSELL. 24 Nov 1893. Large inventory made in the 9 rooms of the three-story house. Other items included Bonds, Stock, Cash in Banks, Parker Lot Company. Sale total was $12,511.40. Distribution made as stated in will: Mrs. Dawson McCORMICK, Misses L. & C. McCORMICK, Mrs. Marshall McCORMICK, Miss Annie McGUIRE, Mrs. Wm. P. & Mrs. N. B. McGUIRE, Mrs. Edward JOHNSON, Mrs. CRENSHAW, Mrs. MILSON, Julia HUNTER, Maggie STODDARD, Mary MASON, Mrs. A. R. BROWN, Chas. BROWN. Recorded 15 Feby 1894.

Pages 343-344: Appraisal of Estate of John W. SMITH, with James F. SMITH, his Admr. Appraisiers: Jesse K. BAILEY, Kenzie SMITH (later Kinsay SMITH), J. W. PARKINS. 23 Feby 1894. Among inventory: 35 sheep, 1 colt, 7 tons hay, 8 bbls. Corn, Grain Cradles, Sand Seive, 100 gals Vinegar, 240 bu. Wheat. Recorded 7 Mar 1894.

Pages 344-345: Will of Patrick TRACY. To son, James TRACY, $1.00. To wife, Catherine TRACY, all rest of estate, including 58 acres, "3 miles south of White Hall, in Frederick County". At wife's death, all except the $1.00 bequeathed to son, James TRACY, goes to daughter, Mary Isabel TRACY, and she to execute will. 12 Apr 1888. Wit: Maurice M. LYNCH, J. COOPER, B. B. PARKER. Will proven March 19, 1894. Appraisers appointed: John STEPHENSON, R. M. WARD, T. K. CARTMELL, T. M. BAUTZ, Jas. L. REDMON.

Pages 345-347: Appraisal of Estate of Mrs. Sarah S. LAREW, dec'd. Apprs: Jas. F. FAULKNER, D. H. BRAGONIER, Ed. J. CORRELL (CONNELL?). 29 Apr 1893. Among small estate: Lot of flowers in Pots, Carpeting, Matting, Joints & Elbow Pipes, Coal Skuttle, Diavan, Lard Can; rent due from Wm. M. DESHON; Claim of Dr. G. L. MILLER against estate of Sam'l. L. LAREW, dec'd. Appraisal recorded Mar 5, 1894. Estate Sale held May 15, 1893. Among items: 4 Plates, Hatten LOVETT; Tea Pot, Robert BROWN; Pitcher, Conrad KREMER; Cupboard, Caroline RAGLAN; Picture, Cyrus HOWARD; Matting, Major FORD. Also same day, Sale of Personalty of Estate of Samuel L. LAREW, dec'd. Total: 4 chairs, 1 Share Well Town T.P. Stock, to GIBBENS; Office Desk, to STOTTLEMYER; Bonds & Stocks to G. O. MILLER, J. K. McCOWN & Thos. KEATING, T. M. BAUTZ. C. M. GIBBENS, executor of Sam'l. L. LAREW. Settled and recorded March 5, 1894.

Pages 348-349: Will of John F. GRAY. To wife, Jane GRAY, all property of every kind and she to execute will. 13 June 1893. Wit: M. M. LYNCH, Jno. H. QUIET, Robert (his mark) SMITH. Proved 29 March 1894. Appraisers appt'd: R. Wm. WALTER, W. Ray STEPHENSON, Thos. W. HARRISON, Jas. B. RUSSELL, Julian F. WARD.

Pages 349-350: Estate of Mertie & Frederick GOSHERT, Jacob METZ, Guardian. Begins Jan 1, 1891 with cash received, rent of Stable and House and Interest on Funds. Among payments: for children's clothing, for wallpaper and painting, for insurance & taxes, for boarding children. Similar accounts for 1892 and 1893. Recorded 22 March 1894.

Page 351: Will of John H. NULTON. To daughter, Mrs. Annie E. SLOAT, all property "to be used, occupied and enjoyed by her, for and during her life". After her death, to children as may then be living of son, John M. NULTON. To John NULTON, son of son, John M. NULTON, silver watch. L. N. HUCK, exec. 16 Jany 1893. Wit: Wm. BYRD, C. BALDWIN. Proved 19 June 1894, by oath of Doct. C. BALDWIN. Other witness too ill to be present in court, 22 June 1894. Appraisers appt'd: T. C. WINDLE, M. T. REED, John C. BENTLEY, L. T. MOORE, John Godfrey MILLER.

Pages 352-355: Will of Frederick W. KOHLHOUSEN. To wife, Sally E. KOHLHOUSEN, all household and personal property "as may be in our residence or about the same, at the date of my death, belonging to me for her own absolutely". To daughter, Emma A. KOHLHOUSEN, $1,000 above her share of estate. Executor to invest $400 "in some safe way with interest to educate my child or children". Mentions advancements made to sons, W. A. KOHLHOUSEN, Luther Waldo KOHLHOUSEN, Theophilus F. KOHLHOUSEN, C. B. KOHLHOUSEN and daughter, Emma A. KOHLHOUSEN. Wife appointed guardian of children that are minors at his death. Part of estate for son, W. A. KOHLHOUSEN, to be in Trust for his maintenance and support all his life. Mentions W. A. KOHLHOUSEN, Jr., son of W. A. KOHLHOUSEN. Mentions sums paid by W. A. & Theophilus "for said Luther at Wheeling". At Luther's death, if he has no issue, his share to daughter, Emma and son, B. Frank KOHLHOUSEN. Writes at length about investing estate for children and paying them interest. W. Roy STEPHENSON, executor. 24 Dec 1887. Wit: Jno. W. RICE, Clark CATHER, W. Roy STEPHENSON. Codicil, same day, re deed of land to wife and other directions for children's shares. Wit: W. S. LOVE, Rich'd. L. GRAY. Proved 18 July 1894. Appraisers appt'd: J. W. RICE, R. M. WARD, Wm. L. EVANS,

Shirley CARTER, Dr. W. M. A. BELL.

Page 356: Will of Henry E. BARTLETT. Real estate, including House and 2 Lots north of residence and all personal estate to wife, Sarah Jane BARTLETT, At her death, divide equally between 3 children, to wit: Henry Wesley BART-LETT, Sarah F. BARTLETT, Clementine BARTLETT. Wife to be executrix. 8 Aug 1894. Wit: Clementine N. BARTLETT, Samuel MASH. Proved 18 Sept 1894. Appraisers appt'd: J. E. CORRELL, Albert BROWN, George McGRUDER, C. M. GIBBENS, James PRESTON.

Page 357: Will of James FULLER. (very short will) All property to wife, Ellen A. FULLER. 4 Sept 1888. Wit: Wm. S. LOVE, W. A. CARPER. Proved 15 Oct 1894.

Pages 357-358: Will of Julia A. CLARK. To husband, Charles H. CLARK, all her right and title to certain lot of ground, now occupied by Mrs. Cornelia E. LANGLEY, which was devised to Mrs. LANGLEY for her life and at her death, to testator and Joseph H. LYDER, by the will of Jacob LYDER, "my father". Wearing apparel to niece, Annie SPURR. Rest of personal property to husband and he to execute will. 8 Sept 1894. Wit: Wm. A. BELL, Geo. W. KURTZ. Proved 15 Oct 1894.

Pages 358-361: Estate of Sarah L.(S?) LAREW, dec'd., in Account with C. M. GIBBENS, her Admr. Account beginning Apr 1893, in part: Funds rec'd. from Sale, Share Feby Wheat from Town lot & Lenn Place, and from rent. Expenses: paid moving effects to courthouse, paid appraisers, paid E. L. HODGSON for walling grave, paid Wm. DESHON grave bill. NOTE: Mrs. Sarah L. LAREW died intestate and left one child surviving her by Samuel L. LAREW. Said Samuel L. LAREW is a minor and sole heir. C. M. GIBBENS to be guardian. Dr. G. L. MILLER has claim vs estate of Sam'l. L. LAREW, dec'd. Settlement of Estate of Sarah L. LAREW recorded 4 May 1894. Guardianship Account of S. L. LAREW with C. M. GIBBENS begins April 7, 1893 with income as: rents, cash from wheat and hay and from Abram CRIM for potatoes. Among expenses: cash paid ward, paid E. L. HODGSON for repairing chimney, paid insurance on farm buildings, paid for repairing shoes. Account settled and recorded 28 May 1894.

Pages 361-363: Estate Account of John TOYE, with Jas. L. REDMON, Comm. Admr. Begins Sept 20, 1892 with cash in bank and cash from sale "of hair" and of Glue Stock. Among expenses: paid appraisers at Harrisonburg; paid B&O RR freight; paid E. E. DEHAVEN's expenses to Harrisonburg; paid Edward D. SULLIVAN rent; paid for "loading flesh". On 22 Apr 1892, Edwin TOY, one of distributees, made Note Payable to John TOY. Distribution made to: Edwin TOY, Walter TOY, Kate D. DEHAVEN, only children and heirs at law of John TOY, dec'd. Recorded May 4, 1894.

Page 364: Inventory and Appraisal of Estate of J. Albert HARMER, dec'd. Apprs: H. K. PRITCHARD, J. N. W. FUNK, James SIBERT. Part of the inventory: Money in Bank, Note of C. S. W. BARNES, two 8-day wooden clocks, many kinds of clocks, watches and watch cases; watch maker's tools. Few household items. 13 April 1893 (later dated 12 April 1894) Appraisal recorded June 16, 1894.

Page 365: Inventory and Appraisal of Estate of John W. SUMPTION, dec'd. Apprs: Oscar BARR, Robt. T. McVICAR, C. E. HUNTSBERRY. 9 Apr 1894. Among items: Top Wagon & Horse; lot of Garden Tools, Crocks, Jars, Dishes, Keg & Pan, Spirit Level & Hatchet, Bedding; Bonds of James A. GRIMES and Jos. H. RITTER. Recorded May 4, 1894.

Page 366: George E. JENKINS, Guardian of Julia E. ROSENBERGER, His ward. Income and expenses beginning July 2, 1893: "By amount of Legacy by will of William JENKINS, dec'd"; by Bond of Kate K. WOODWARD. Paid Kate K. WOODWARD one year's support of ward, $57.50. Paid clerk's and commr's fees. Recorded 15 Oct 1894.

Pages 366-369: Inventory and Appraisal of Estate of Charles H. STINE, dec'd. Appraisers: J. Stewart YEAKLEY, Clark H. PURCELL, James L. ROBINSON, July 18, 1894. One-half interest in all items, some of which were: Wagons, Horses, Cattle, Sheep, Hogs, Farming Equipment, 50 acres growing corn, hay ricks, Poultry. Notes & Accounts of Jno. OMPS, B. F. STINE, Jacob LOY & J.P. SHADE, C. P. JACK, W. HOLLAR. Sale Account of E. S. STINE returned by W. E. BARR, Admr. of Chas. H. STINE, dec'd., July 31, 1894. Sales included: Keg of Iron, Farm Equipment, Cattle, Mowing Knives, Single Trees, Blacksmith Tools. Some purchasers: S. F. FAHNESTOCK, S. M. CHILES, J. H. ZELL, J. W. BAGEANT, C. H. BOXWELL, T. S. JOLLEFFE. Recorded in court Dec 11, 1894.

Pages 369-370: Will of Pauline F. RIELY. Letter of Mrs. Pauline F. RIELY, dec'd., mailed at Pass Robles, California, in April 1894, to her daughter, Mrs. Gavin D. HIGH (Lillian RIELY), who was residing in Philadelphia, Penn. Letter used as will. Long, personal letter telling of her illness and wishes. Begins: "Ranch, April/94. My darling dearest, I received your dear sweet letter of the 11th in due corse of mail. I was so glad to get for it is the only solace I have here on my sick bed and my poor dear child absent and cant get to me." She is sorry to hear how poorly off her daughter is for clothes. Mentions "Alf will pay me if he ever gets any money" and "Irene thinks it is dreadful that Henry used up my money". "Your sister is the one who kept my dollar." Signature of letter proved by oaths of M. H. G. WILLIS & H. Douglas FULLER. Gavin D. HIGH to administer will.

Pages 371-372: Will and Codicil of Esther A. RICHARDSON, "this 10th month 25 1884". To daughter, Priscilla A. RICHARDSON, 600 dollars of the lien on the Harris Property. "The balance of said Trust to Mary C. HARRIS for her share of her father's estate." Codicil, "9th month 24th 1893". Priscilla having departed this life, requests the six hundred dols divided equally with the other five of "my children". To Martha S. HARDESTY, "my gold watch and fine Tedy and chair covers". To Blanch, silver knives and picture of Golden Wedding. Also gives to Lizzie GOVER, Mary C. HARRIS, Minnie A. HARRIS, Esther HARRIS, Anna KREAMER; to Webster and to Josiah A. RICHARDSON. Mentions picture of Golden Wedding of George ATKINSON, "my first cousin". Gives Edith, picture of four generations and to Hugh's son, Charles, family Bible. Webster and Josiah A. RICHARDSON, executors. Codicil of 3-18-94: "there shall be no disturbance about the disposition of what is left as Mary has poor health and needs it more than the others". Will proved 21 Jany 1895. Appraisers appointed: Richard R. BROWN, E. Luther HODGSON, James L. REDMON.

Pages 372-376: Estate of Catherine GRAICHEN, dec'd., with F. August GRAICHEN, Admr. Begins June 1st, 1885, with paying taxes, painting roof & house; received rent on house for 1 year and interest on Bonds. Accounting continues to June 1, 1894. Each year amounts are credited to 3 children: Anna C., Caroline (Carrie D.), and Frederick A. GRAICHEN. Recorded in court: Aug 30, 1894.

Page 376: Will of William L. EVANS, May 10, 1893. To sister, Sarah BRACKEN-RIDGE, Shen. Valley Nat'l. Bank Stock. To sister, Mary E. KUHN, So. Branch Valley Nat. Bank Stock. Rest of estate to Mollie and Lillie EVANS, daughters of H. EVANS. Leaves to H. EVANS stock of goods now owned by H. EVANS & Bros.

and money in Shen. Valley Bank. Proved 23 Feby 1895 by oath of Edward J. EVANS. Mollie C. EVANS, executrix.

Page 377: Will of Mrs. Amanda E. HUFF. James R. RUSSELL to execute. Exec. to bury her in Mt. Hebron with marble slab. To Jessie SHIPE, nephew, $200. Rest of estate to niece, Miss Emma V. SHIPE; Executor to purchase for her a little home if sufficient funds. Wit: Mrs. J. V. BELL, Mrs. M. E. MESMER. Proved 26 Feby 1895. Appraisers: J. Vance BELL, I. W. RUSSELL, Hugh K. GREEN. (Date of will 21 Feby 1895.)

Pages 377-378: Inventory and Appraisal of Estate of Mrs. Amanda E. HUFF, dec'd. 26 Feby 1895. Among items: Gold Watch, Chain, Box Jewelry, H.H. Goods, Clock & Mantel Ornaments, Double Mourning Shawl, Foot Tub; Bonds of Josiah L. BAKER, G. G. BAKER, Wm. B. CALMES, John W. RICE, Jas. B. RUSSELL. Recorded Mar 4, 1895.

Page 379: Appraisal of Estate of F. W. KOHLHOUSEN, dec'd., with appraisers: W. L. EVANS, Robert M. WARD, Shirley CARTER. 4 Sept 1894. Total inventory: Two of each, Tables, Clocks, Stoves, Bureaus; three each of Mattresses and Washstands; Bedstead, Wardrobe, Secretary, 7 Chairs, 2 Stands; two-story brick Storehouse, corner Market & Piccadilly Streets. Recorded Sep 1894.

Pages 379-382: Estate of Emily FUNSTON, dec'd., in Account with R. M. WARD, her Exec. Begins March 1893, with such cash payments as for Burial Permit, Telegram, Hacks. Paid Geo. E. BUSHNELL for medicines. Long list of other payments, including to Mrs. Louisa N. FLETCHER under direction of will. Paid Emily R. FUNSTON in full of Bequest of $8,500. Many receipts for dividends, interest and rent on Sommerville Farm. Recorded 17 Sept 1894.

Pages 382-383: Estate Account of L. Dow HESS, in Account with Mrs. A. R. HESS, his executrix. Begins 2 Oct 1893, with cash on hand and proceeds of Sale, cash from J. H. A.COOPER "part pay for stock in Store". Paid W. A. HESS "case of goods till sale". Paid doctor, taxes, fees, attorneys. Balance in Account of $195.40 not sufficient to pay claims in full, so paid 15% on each. Recorded 23 Jany 1895.

Pages 383-384: Estate of Anna B. DENNY, dec'd., in Account with Robert A. DENNY, her Admr. Balance to distribute: $236.00. "The decedent died intestate, unmarried and childless." Heirs: sister, 3 children of deceased brother, James DENNY and four children of deceased sister, Mrs. Hollis. Maria M. DENNY, the sister, entitled to one-third share. Three children of James DENNY: Richard, Nilla and Effie. Four children of Mrs. HOLLIS: Carson, Willis, Marian (only 3 named). Recorded 15 Oct 1894.

Pages 384-385: Appraisal of Estate of Benjamin JACOBS, dec'd. Appraisers: Jacob F. EBERSOLE, Noah W. SOLENBERGER, Levi T. F. GRIM, John M. WEICHT. 22 March 1895. Part of appraisal items: Wagons, Carts, Farm Equipment, Mowers, Rollers, Milk Wagon, Harness, Crowbars, Spades. Appraisal accepted by Selinda JACOBS, Admr.

Pages 385-387: Estate of George F. MILLER, dec'd., with George Clarence MILLER, his Exec. Begins May 1, 1893 with items as "cash in box", rent and income of City & R. R. Bonds, personal Notes, Bank Stock, household furniture, "contents of stable", Horses, Cattle. Paid such expenses as funeral, insurance, recording will, Homer CREBS Services, Ran PIFER taxes, M. D. ALBIN headstone, John W. NAIL, work, Jacob WOMER, work. Paid C. C. MILLER, devisee of will. Gave furniture to Minnie A. MILLER and "Drugs to value of $666.66-2/3", Stocks & Bonds, and 1/3rd stock on farm and equipment. Godfrey O. & George Clarence MILLER received other 2/3rd of Drugs, Stocks & Bonds and farm stock & equipment. Recorded 16 Oct 1894.

Pages 387-393: Will of Mrs. Ann R. H. POWELL, 5 March 1887. Wishes tomb-stone similar to one on husband's grave. Gives $20 to Pastor of Loudoun Street Church "whoever he may be at time of my death, as it is my wish he should attend my funeral". Money will be in small purse in her Morocco pocketbook. Balance of property equally to all children, to wit: Gertrude, Laura, Louisa, Levin, Kate, Marietta, Millicent, Hunter, Pendleton and Raleigh, Julia FORD and Anna PAYNE, the daughters of deceased daughter, Sallie. Everything given to daughter to be free from debts and contracts of husbands. Daughter, Marietta, had sent money to Pendleton when he was in Denver, Colorado. Son, Levin, had borrowed money when he went to Costa Rico. Gives to grandson, Levin POWELL. Sons, Levin and Hunter, to execute will. If son, Levin, living in Washington Territory, son-in-law, John Randolph TUCKER, to execute in Levin's place. Mentions she is president and treasurer of "the Mite Society". Secretary is Miss Tillie RUSSELL. Undated codicil: to arrange for paying note of son, W. L. POWELL, and debt on son, Pendleton. Codicil: heard that grandson, Powell HARRISON, is very poor, so deducts from bequest to Annie Holmes PAYNE and gives to him, "as Annie is well off". Codicil dated June 1st, 1888 re funds borrowed by son, Pent. Memorandum of 20 Oct. 1894 and meant to be part of will gives specific division of personal estate. To daughter, Gertrude, and her 2 daughters, Bettie GILDERSLEEVE and Annie CAMM; to daughter, Laura TUCKER and her daughter, Nannie, and Nannie's daughter, Evy. Gertrude has son, Harry TUCKER. To son, Levin, portrait of his great-grandfather, Col. Levin POWELL. Son, Pent, is in Army. Other names: Jennie CARMICHAEL, Nannie CLARK, Bettie DANDRIDGE, Lizzie McGRUDER, Evy POWELL, Judge TYLER, Richard HOLLIDAY, C. H. GIBSON, Meta SAMPLE, Ellen BOYD, Gertrude COLSTON, Ran SHIELDS, Leila McGUIRE, Janie HOWARD. Proved 17 Apr 1895. Hon. J. Ran TUCKER and H. H. POWELL, executors named in will, declined, so Dr. W. P. McGUIRE to administer will. Appraisers: Albert BAKER, E. Holmes BOYD, James B. RUSSELL, Dr. R. W. STONE. Part of Inventory: cash, bank stock, personal notes. Admr. added what appraisers declined to include: stock in Bank of Buenna Vista and notes to L. POWELL, P. W. BOYD, and P. P. POWELL. All considered worthless. 22 April 1895.

Pages 393-395: Settlement of Estate Account of James H. BARNHART, dec'd., E. Holmes BOYD, executor. Begins 22 Nov 1892 with paying motion to prove will. Among long list of income and expenses: Bank deposits, Cash of George W. BUSH; paid D. WALTER for examining books of Barton & Williams for proof of paying of purchase money by George BARNHART of House & Lot. Paid for telegram to Horace KEESY. Paid legacies to Dr. G. L. MILLER, Mrs. Sarah STEINER, Mary CHILDS, Sallie BARLEY. Paid Mrs. Catherine BUSH her interest in estate. Bonds turned over to Samuel G. & John SMALL. Settlement recorded July 28, 1894.

Pages 395-396: Settlement of Guardianship Account, Samuel L. LAREW, Ward of C. M. GIBBENS. Begins May 1894 with Cash by rent of T. D. D. CLARK & Jos. A. McCARTY and Cash from Sarah LAREW's estate. Paid Sol. HABLE for Clothes for ward, Abram GRIM for clover seed & phosphate, Geo. E. COPENHAVER for plastering. Paid Dean & Snyder for fixing bird box at Clark & Larew House. Recorded Apr 18, 1895.

Pages 397-399: Estate of Richard PARKER, dec'd., in Account with W. P. McGUIRE, his exec. Begins Nov 1893, by value of Watch for Parker CRENSHAW. Among many receipts of cash: for rent of Stable, for furniture, for Books sold, property sold, dividends, Among expenses: cash paid H. Bentley SMITH for portrait ordered by Judge PARKER prior to his death. In Dec 1893, paid devisees under will: Miss Annie McGUIRE, Misses Charlotte & Lizzie McCORMICK, Mrs. N. B. Mc-GUIRE, Miss Maggie STODDARD, Mary MASON, Mary & Gertrude JOHNSON, Mrs. Robt.

JAMESON, Belle M. JOHNSON, Mrs. A. P. CRENSHAW. Paid Robert SMITH for taking care of property. Recorded Feby 25, 1895.

Pages 400-402: Will of Mrs. Millicent B. CATHER. "Know all men by these presents that I, Millicent B. CATHER, being in ill health -- " To nieces, Mary Ann LUPTON and Francis CATHER, wife of Jonah CATHER. To Susan HOWARD who has "nursed me so faithfully". To nieces: Adaline CATHER, Sarah LEATHERMAN, Margaret LARRICK, Elizabeth WHETZELL, Sarah R. JENNINGS, Emily S. SIMPSON, Blanch SIMPSON, Margaret E. LUPTON, Mary H. CANNON, Lucy SIMPSON, Alice May WOODS, Millicent LUPTON. Brother, Thos. N. LUPTON, exec. Wit: W. S. LOVE, John S. LUPTON. Proved 20 May 1895. Appraisers: W. W. GLASS, Samuel L. CHILDS (later CHILES), Oscar BARR, T. K. CARTMELL, John RAY. Inventory & Appraisal, 21 May 1895, included 314½ acres land on Back Creek; 73 acres Mountain land; Bond of Thos H. STODDER; Notes of Joshua S. & Chas. A. LUPTON, J. W. CLEVENGER & J. S. CARTER; Bank Stock, HH Goods incl. Piano, walnut, cherry and mahogany furniture. Recorded, no date.

Page 403: Will of Chas. F. EICHELBERGER, Merchant. Will made 16 March 1861. "Boath" witnesses now dead. Now renews and reaffirms the same. To wife, Charlotte E. EICHELBERGER, all real and personal property in Winchester and Frederick County. 14 Jany 1886. Will proved by oaths of Dr. Wm. A. BELL and Dr. C. W. REED. Widow is executrix.

Pages 404-405: Authenticated copy of will of Mary A. CAMPBELL, of Roanoke County, Va., widow of Thos B. CAMPBELL. Wishes to be buried in family plot, Mt. Hebron. One-half each to two daughters, Anna Virginia, wife of Harvey E. JONES, and Laura M., wife of Rev. Lewis G. M. MILLER. Two sons in law to be execs. 7 June 1882. Wit: Wm. McCAULEY, L. G. M. MILLER. Codicil, 8 June 1882, requests tombstones for self and husband. Will proved in Roanoke County, Feby term, 1886. Copy to Winchester City Court, 31 Aug 1895.

Pages 405-407: Chas. P. HARDY's Estate in Account with Wm. H. HARDY, Admr. Begins June 1888, paying land tax, Dr. Love's bill, Clifton WHEAT's bill, Hunter GRIM for repair chimney, Ran TAYLOR for paper hanging. Received cash from dividends, sale of pinewood, house rent. R. R. dividends credited to Miss M. R. HARDY. Shows income and expenses for years thru 1894, with balance due Admr. Acct. recorded Apr 18, 1895.

Pages 407-408: Estate Account of John H. NULTON with L. N. HUCK, his Exec. Executor stated he had made diligent search since June 1894 for personal property of deceased but found none, except amount due on salary as Supt. of Water for city of Winchester. Son, J. H. NULTON, and daughter, Mrs. SLOAT, said he had nothing else. Recorded Apr 18, 1895.

Pages 408-410: P. A. CLARK, Guardian of Ambrose, Elmer and Herbert HINER. Account begins Nov 1888 with paid for shoes for Ambrose and Herbert. Other items: rec'd cash from sale of House & Lot and from estate of Mrs. Louisa T. HINER, dec'd. In March 1889, paid for medicine, grave and burial of Ambrose. Jany 1891, paid for clothing, Hat & Shoes, RR ticket and cash for Elmer. In 1894, paid Elmer HINER "his share in fund in Guardian Account". Mar 4, 1895, Herbert sends affidavit to court requesting his share of funds, saying he will be 20 years old in Sept 1895, is married, had job but due to severe winter, is unemployed and has debts so needs balance in funds. Court ordered guardian to pay $50.

Pages 410-411: Inventory and Appraisal of Estate of Mrs. Elizabeth E. STONE, dec'd. Appraisers: M. H. G. WILLIS, Lewis N. BARTON, Dr. Wm. P. McGUIRE. 28 May 1895. Bank Shares, Va. Coupon Bonds, Bonds of J. C. WHEAT, Jr. and J. A. MILBURN & Co., interest in Bank Balance "to the credit of Stone & Wisslers". Recorded 4 June 1895.

Pages 411-412: Inventory & Appraisal of Estate of Douglas LOCKWOOD, with John S. SOLENBERGER, Admr. Appraisers: S. M. CHILES, R. E. GRIFFITH, J. S. HALDERMAN. 20 July 1895. Half interest in 2 Colts; Cattle, Pigs, black Horse Dick; Tools, Rope, wirefencing, axle grease, gallons oil, Buggy, Wagon, farm equipment; many accounts and notes due estate, some of which: of Jacob CRYSMAN, Chas. ENSWELLER, Wm. HAYSLETTE, A. B. ROTHGET, Mat EBERZOLE, Chas. KITCHEN. Recorded Nov 29, 1895.

Page 413: Julia E. ROSENBERGER, Ward of Geo. Ed. JENKINS, Guardian. Begins July 1893 by paying amount of Legacy by will of Wm. JENKINS, dec'd., plus Bond of Kate R. WOODWARD. Paid expenses as fees and support of ward. Account recorded 2 Aug. 1895.

Pages 414-415: Settlement of Estate of John TOYE, dec'd., in Account with James L. REDMON, Sergeant Commee. Admr. Begins May 1894 paying fees and commissions. Jany 1895 paid expenses to Philadelphia and Harrisonburg. Paid Edmon SULLIVAN witness fee. Balance for distribution: $18.75 or $6.25 to each of three heirs. Edwin TOYE, one of heirs, is indebted to estate for $15.58. Other heirs: Walter TOYE, Kate DEHAVEN. Recorded 31 Oct 1895.

Pages 415-417: Inventory and Appraisal of Estate of John VILWIG, dec'd. Oct 26, 1895. Appraisers: P. H. REARDON, John L. GRANT, Robert L. GRAY. Some of bonds and notes due estate: of F. H. KREBS, Jas. P. SILER, Ralph & Jos. SAVAGE, Chas. F. NELSON. Much household furnishings as Pictures, Mirrors, Lace Curtains, Organ, Brussell Carpet, inlaid Table, Howe Sewing Machine, onix-top Table. M. M. LYNCH, Admr. Recorded 29 Oct 1895.

Pages 417-418: Estate of Hector H. BELL in Account with James B. RUSSELL, Admr. Begins July 1894 by amount received of Maryland Insurance Company policy. Paid Seth BRIDGMAN, Washington; paid Josephine T. BELL, widow; paid attorneys fees and other bills. Decedent left surviving widow, Josephine T. BELL and one child now under age of 14. Balance of estate, 1/3rd to widow and 2/3rd to child or guardian. Recorded 23 Nov 1895.

Pages 419-420: Estate of Emily FUNSTON in account with Rob't. M. WARD, exec. Begins July 1894 with many receipts of payments on Bonds and interest and Sale of Bank Stock. Paid taxes and legacies to M. F. WARD and L. F. WARD. Recorded 23 Nov 1895.

Pages 420-422: Settlement of Account of A. R. PENDLETON, Admr. of Sarah SCHULTZ, dec'd. Begins Jany 1893 with paying court costs for settling & recording accounts and paid attorneys of Mary TIDBALL on balance of Trust. Paid Mrs. L. A. MILLER on her lien. Received rent of J. B. LOVETT on Mansion House. Settlement recorded 31 Oct 1895.

Pages 422-423: Will of Mingo WALKER. To life long friend, T. K. CARTMELL, entire estate, to hold in Trust for: Burying in the old Graveyard, on Old Greenwood Farm, in Frederick County, erect tombstone and build fence. Rest of estate for benefit of wife, Cordelia WALKER, "while she remains my widow". Trustee to hold estate, after wife's death, for 12 months for any next of kin to claim. If none comply with terms, funds for use of Mrs. Annie G. CARTMELL and daughter. 3 Sept 1895. Wit: Sam'l. BAKER, Clementine HARRIS. Proved 17 Dec 1895.

Pages 423-424: J. S. HALDERMAN, Guardianship Account with J. D. GOSHERT's infants, Frederick and Mertie. Begins May 1894 with paying official fees, taxes and for boarding. Received cash for payment of bills and "rent from Green". Settlement of Guardianship account held up due to death of Lewis N. HUCK, late Commr. of Accounts of Court. Settled and recorded 31 Oct 1895.

Page 425: Will of Frank R. PETERSON. Leaves watch and 1 Blanket and money to Clara HARRIS. Two comforts and money to Matilda ROBINSON. Trunk and clothes to "Brother John". Rest, after expenses, to Jennie WILLIAMSON Annie HOGAN & Brother John. Contents of trunk in Providence to legatees. Hunter McGUIRE, exec. 21 Dec 1895. Wit: Wm. P. McGUIRE, T. B. PATTON. Proved 24 Dec 1895. Appraisers: T. B. PATTON, Hugh GREEN.

Pages 425-426: Appraisal of Personal Estate of Fredericka A. ROSENBERGER. Appraisers: Jos. E. KIGER, John R. A. ROSENBERGER, S. H. HANSBROUGH. 26 Nov 1895. Total: Bond and 6 Notes of Charles R. CAMPBELL, Cash in Bank. Mary J. ROSENBERGER, Admr. Recorded 26 Nov 1895.

Pages 426-430: Will of Atwell SHELL. Body to be buried in "respectable manner but without unnecessary expense". Had already given money to son, William Harrison SHALL, "and having lost to him as his surety", now wills nothing more. Lot on Valley Turnpike, west side, adjoining Haddox, Windle & Others, to son, Strother SHELL, and Winfourd, his wife. Gives to daughter, Mary Ann SPURR, wife of Andrew L. SPURR. Also to wife, Nancy "as long as she remains my widow". At death of wife, estate to Strother SHALL and wife, Missouri. House where George GRIM now lives to daughter, Mary Ann SPURR. Strother SHELL & A. L. SPURR, executors. 27 May 1889. Wit: D. H. BRAGONIER, Perry C. GORE, E. T. HANCOCK. Codicil, 18 Jany 1893, changes bequests because wife has died. Now bequeaths to Bertha MILLER, wife of Charles MILLER, and daughter of Samuel Strother and Missouri SHELL. Mentions Arthur SHELL, son of Strother. Wit: Jos. A. NULTON, Hunter Boyd GOLD, Clayton HOLLIS. Will proved 17 Feby 1896. One of witnesses, Joseph A. NULTON, has died. Edward G. HOLLIS, father of Clayton HOLLIS, says son not now a resident of state. Strother SHELL, exec. Appraisers: D. H. BRAGONIER, Hunter B. GOLD, C. H. PURCELL, Edward M. BARR, J. Wm. TAYLOR. Inventory, Feby 17, 1896, in total: Bonds of M. H. G. WILLIS, Wm. D. RITTER, Geo. W. MURNAN; Gas Co. stock; few household goods as black cushion sofas, bed/bedding, burea, rocker, chair, cook stove; farming equipment; amount due from Edward CONNER for curbing.

Page 430: Will of Louisa M. HOLTZMAN. To sister, Sallie M. CLARK, money left by will of Wm. F. CHEECK, of Danville, Va. Brother, Aylett T. HOLTZMAN, exec. 29 May 1895. Wit: Margaret & Mary HANSBROUGH. Proved 25 Feby 1896, by Margaret HANSBROUGH (Mary HANSBROUGH is now distant from the city.) Appraisers: S. H. HANSBROUGH, Shirley CARTER, W. R. ALEXANDER, V. R. GRIGSBY, P. C. GORE.

Pages 431-432: Will of Mrs. Maria Louisa TOTTY. To sister, Soloma E. TOTTY and her children undivided one-half interest in House and Lot on Braddock Street where testator now lives. Other one-half to niece, Mary E. DOWNING. Also to them whatever coming from suits pending or from any legacies. To Louisa H. TOTTY "my little walnut suit of furniture, bedding and cherry table:. Wardrobe to Willie TOTTY. Also gives to Mary E. TOTTY. 29 Dec 1894. Wit: L. N. HUCK, John H. MYERS. Proved 16 March 1896. L. N. HUCK, witness, now deceased. Mary E. DOWNING, exec. Appraisers: Wm. E. MATHEWS, James C. TOTTY, Wm. E. GRIM, Wm. H. BAKER of George, Wm. H. HARDY.

Pages 432-433: Will of Chas. W. ANDERSON. All to wife, Elizabeth, and she empowered to dispose of same among my children. Wife to execute. 8 Feby 1894. Wit: C. M. GIBBENS, D. H. BRAGONIER. Added: Insurance policies to wife, Elizabeth B. ANDERSON. Will proved March 17, 1896. Wife to execute with sureties: Chas. E. ANDERSON, F. H. & Edwd. ANDERSON, George E. BUSHNELL. Appraisers: Geo. E. BUSHNELL, Wm. B. BAKER, Jr., Dr. J. E. JANNEY, Edwd. STONE.

Pages 433-435: Will of James McNIDER, of City, County and State of New York. Authenticated copy. Will to New York Probate 23 Jany 1896. To wife, Jennie S. and son, James Stanley McNIDER, all effects and property. Wife Jennie Simons McNIDER, executrix. 26 March 1880. Wit: John H. BELL, M. ROSENSHINE. NOTE: for family reasons my name has been spelled with the abbreviated Mc in full since 1890". Signed: Jas. Mac NIDER. In Winchester Court, 28 March 1896, Jennie S. Mac NIDER presented copy of will. 31 March 1896 she is appointed executrix. James MacNIDER died 23 Jany 1896. Appraisers: E. Holmes BOYD, Maurice M. LYNCH, W. Roy STEPHENSON, Holmes BOYD, Jr., C. M. GIBBENS. Inventory of property in Virginia: Bond and Stock of Stanley Furnace & Land Co. and Interest on same; Open Account against same; Stock in Company. Recorded 6 April 1896.

Pages 435-437: Will of Caroline NEVILLE. Gives "enough money to purchase Kitty, or Catherine NEVILLE, my sister, a plain comfortable house, not to cost above six or seven hundred dollars". At sister's death, house to Edward NEVILLE. To Harry C. A. FUNK, Lydia A. FUNK. Remainder to Willie RAY "in rememberance of her mother's kindness to me". John RAY, exec. Apr 6, 1896. Wit: Jackson D. GRIM, Stewart GRIM, Philip T. GRIM. Proved 20 Apr 1896. Appraisers: Oscar BARR, Wm. G. CONWAY, Jackson D. & STEWART GRIM, James N. W. FUNK. Inventory & Appraisal, 28 Apr 1896. Total: Cash in Bank; Shares Winchester Home Bldg. Assn & Coop. Bldg.; Notes of Harry C. A. FUNK, John RAY, A. L. & Mary A. SPURR, Wm. A. CARPER, Jas. A. & Ellen E. FULLER's estate; Furniture.

Pages 437-438: Will of Ellen A. FULLER. Requests Tombstones at graves of herself, her husband and her mother in law. House, corner of Market & Monmouth Sts to son, John Scott FULLER. The slate roof house to dau., Annie E. ALDERMAN. "It was will of my husband that John Scott FULLER have 8 ft. more ground to his Lot". 23 Oct 1894. Wit: J. N. W. FUNK, John RAY. Proved 20 Apr 1896. John RAY to admin. Appraisers: Oscar BARR, Wm. G. CONWAY, Jackson D. & Stewart GRIM, James N. W. FUNK. Inventory & Appraisal, 28 Apr 1896. Only property is 2 dwelling houses and out buildings upon lots on South Market Street. Will says John RAY to rent out these buildings. Appraisers estimate annual rent at $180. Recorded Apr 29, 1896.

Pages 439-442: Will of Joseph FRYE. "I, Joseph FRYE, of the city of Baltimore, in the state of Maryland". To daughter, Cornelia FRYE, 5 trunks and 3 boxes of wearing apparel of her mother. Trunks and Boxes now in the Eutaw Parsonage. Also to daughter, gold watch and silver plate of her mother. To children, Joseph FRYE and his sister, Cornelia FRYE, all real estate. Other property to be converted to funds to support children "in their respective minority". If both children die without issue, estate to children of deceased sister, Mary MARTEN, late of Frederick County, Va. Lists where his various estate may be found by executor/appraisers. Items in Winchester: Note on Trustees of Methodist Episcopal Church, House & Lott in Winchester, Bonds of David FRIES & Wm. CLARK, Bond on Isaac PIGEON for land in Frederick County, Va. Three friends to execute, Robert G. ARMSTRONG, John PLASKETT, Philip HESS. 6 May 1841. Wit: Alexr. YEARLEY, John RANSDELL, Thos. C. YEARLEY. Will proved 9 June 1845. Executors named refused, 16 June 1845. Nephew, Aquila D. STINCHCOMB, and niece, Rebecca STINCHCOMB refused to administer but requested letters be granted to Fielder & J. Robert ISRAEL. 21 May 1894, Thos. W. MOORE, Register of Wills, Baltimore, certified to true copy of will, received in Winchester Court, 22 Apr 1896.

Pages 442-443: Estate of Catherine GRAICHEN, dec'd., in Account with F. August GRAICHEN, her Admr. Begins Augt 8, 1894 with paying taxes and bills. June 1st 1895, received rent, interest on Bonds and dividends. Mentions suit "Graichen vs Graichen". Estate account recorded 24 Jan 1896.

Page 443: Will of Rebecca A. KURTZ. 25 Jan 1887. Gives without restrictions to sisters Mary & Julia KURTZ. Wit: G. L. MILLER, H. K. PRITCHARD. Will proved 21 May 1896. Mary E. KURTZ to administer.

Pages 444-446: Inventory & Appraisal of Estate of Lewis BARLEY. 21 May 1895. Appraisers: John RAY, Oscar BARR, R. H. LEWIS. Among items: Tall Clock, Refrigerator, Turkey Dishes, Demijohns, Coffee Mill, Stock in Winchester Gas & Martinsburg Turnpike. George W. BUSH, Admr., received cash from Sale of Personalty and paid debts. Balance due estate: $62.73. Recorded 21 May, 1896.

Page 446: Inventory and Appraisal of Estate of Frank P. PETERSON, dec'd. Appraisers: T. B. PATTON, H. K. RUSSELL, Hugh K. GREEN. Gold Watch & Chain, silk Hat, Gloves, 2 Canes, Overcoat, Slippers, Shoes, Vest, Box Handkerchieves, Pins, Rings, Watch Chain, Umbrella, 2 Bibles, Life Insurance (if collected), Blankets, Shaving Mtls, Suit of Clothes, Underwear, Cash in Bank. Hunter McGUIRE, executor. May 11, 1896.

Pages 446-448: Estate of Chas. H. STINE in Account with W. E. BARR, his Admr. Begins July 1894 with cash received from chickens & hay sold and sale of land. Rec'd on Notes, Sale of Personalty, and interest in property of Henry STINE, dec'd. Paid funeral expenses, appraisers, E. L. STINE for running farm, and for baling hay, shucking corn and boarding hands. Estate distribution: E. L. STINE, Henrietta B. STINE, Laura ALSDORFF, J. Gertrude HAUCK, Alice E. GLAIZE, Susie C. BARR. Recorded Apr 30, 1896.

Pages 448-449: Inventory and Appraisal of Estate of Maria L. TOTTY, dec'd. Appraisers: J. C. TOTTY, Wm. H. BAKER, W. E. GRIM. 18 Mar 1896. Mostly household items already bequeathed to M. E. TOTTY, M. E. DOWNING, S. E. TOTTY, W. L. TOTTY & L. H. TOTTY. Also 2 Notes of M. J. & M. E. DOWNING. Mary Evelyn DOWNING, exec. Recorded 30 March 1896.

Pages 449-450: J. D. GOSHERT's Children & Estate of J. S. HALDERMAN, Guardian of Mertie and Frederick GOSHERT. Begins Jan 1895 to Jan 1896. Received rent on Stable. Paid insurance on Stable and for board and clothing children. Paid E. S. MARSHALL for music lessons. Recorded 30 April 1896.

Pages 450-451: Inventory and Appraisal of Estate of Mrs. Anna G. NOAKES, dec'd. Appraisers: John R. A. ROSENBERGER, Geo. W. KURTZ, Robert D. DODD. Among items: Capital Stock of Nat'l. Valley Bank of Staunton, parlor furniture including "Fancy Articles" on Sideboard and Tables, Mohair Chairs, hanging Lamp, Hassocks, 2 cooking stoves, gasoline lamp. Contents of Parlor, 3 Bedrooms, Kitchen, Back Room. Approved May 16, 1896. Hermon E. NOAKES, Admr.

Pages 451-452: Estate of Wm. MILLER, dec'd., in Account with J. Few BROWN, exec. Begins July 1890 with funds received of Williams & Williams on Claim vs J. C. BAKER; received on R. F. MASSEY Claim and on Lucy BRIGGS Claim. Received dividend on Berryville Turnpike Co. Paid attorneys on Claim of Benj. MILLER vs J. C. BAKER and Benj. MILLER on McDonald's Claim. Paid J. Few BROWN, Trustee for F. A. SHIELDS. Recorded 30 Apr 1896.

Page 452-454: Estate of Madame M. SWANDEMAN in Account with Wm. P. McGUIRE, her Committee. Feby 1895 to Feby 1896. Received by draft on several Richmond Banks. Received check on Annuity, Provident Life & Trust Co. and on Bond of H. W. TYLER; Collected on Note of L. H. TELIT and sent to John F. GODDIN who has always invested Madam's money. Paid cash in going to and from Lake Minnecordia (later Minnecostia) for self in railroad fare, hotel bills, telegrams; paid for Parlor Car Service for Madame SWANDEMAN and fees for porters requiring lifting frame part of the way; paid meals for nurse, for transfer of baggage, carriages, etc. Paid Church Home & Infirmary of Baltimore and board; paid Dr. A. H. KEMPTER, Philadelphia, professional services. Paid RR and Carriage fares, Baltimore & Winchester; paid Maria TRIPLETT, Nurse, and Miss Gertrude MASON from Philadelphia to Lake Winnawaska to aid Madam "who was unconscious at that point, June 30 to July 8). Settlement of estate Account recorded 21 May 1896.

Pages 454-457: Will of F. August GRAICHEN. Divide whole estate among wife, Elizabeth GRAICHEN, and children, Anna, Carolina, Frederick, Revd John George, Ann Elizabeth, Carolina Dorthea, Frederick August GRAICHEN (some names repeated?). If child by Elizabeth after his death, give equal share. Special devises: House on Water Street, The Old Shop, to daughter, Caroline Dorthea GRAICHEN. House on Water Street, the Thompson Purchase, to son Frederick August GRAICHEN. Storehouse on Water Street to daughter, Ann Elizabeth. Small brick building on Market Street to wife. Requests inventory of Stock in Trade, "the skins on hand". Wife to execute will and be guardian of infant children. To son, William C. GRAICHEN, $500. Son, William, had called father "a Thief, Liar and Scoundrel and destroyed my business by using my Trade Mark against my wish and orders". He to have no further share in estate. Requests "the Court and all good citizens to protect my family from the said William C. GRAICHEN". 4 May 1894. Proved 18 June 1896 by son and daughter, John George GRAICHEN and Anna Elizabeth BOOZER. Appraisers: Henry BAETZER, Geo. E. BUSHNELL, Geo. R. BLAKE, Thos. Cooper, Hugh K. GREEN.

Page 457: Will of Miss Kate M. SCHULTZ. July 2, 1895. Leaves her Bonds & Notes held by Philip BOYD, also his life insurance for her benefit, to Frederica. She to have use of any property from Mother's estate. After Fredericka gets a home of her own, what comes to Kate M. SCHULTZ divide between sisters, Mary E. MILLER and Fredericka S. BOYD and their children. If any money from Barton estate, her share to Fred Schultz BOYD. Proved 19 June 1896. Frederick S. BOYD, Admr., Mrs. Fredericka Schultz BOYD, surety. Appraisers: Henry MOLING, John MILLER, W. S. WHITE.

Pages 458-459: Inventory & Appraisal of Personal Estate of F. August GRAICHEN. 18 June 1896. Some items: Morning Glory Stove; wash stand & bureau in Servants Room; Sofa in Spare Room, Stock & Machinery in Houses Nos. 16, 18, 20, and in Log House, Tan House & Bark Mill. Cash in Office & Bank; life insurance policy; many book accounts. Recorded 29 June 1896.

Pages 459-460: Will of Bernard REILLEY. Sell lots without buildings to pay lawful debts. Keep lots with buildings for support of wife, Bridgett, and son, Farrell. Whatever remains after death of wife and son, to children of brothers, John & Farrell REILLEY. Maurice M. LYNCH, exec. 19 June 1896. Wit: Geo. V. OYLER, Jeannie O'LEARY. Proved July 25, 1896. Apprs: Geo. OYLER, Jno. H. KAUFFMAN, Wm. M. BOWEN, Andrew J. MILLER, Michael LILLIS.

Pages 460-461: Estate of Wm. MILLER, dec'd., in Acct. with J. Few BROWN, exec. July 1890-June 1895. Amounts rec'd on Claims vs J. C. BAKER and paid on Claim of Benjamin MILLER vs J. C. BAKER. Rec'd on A. W. McDONALD's Claim & on Lucy BRIGG's Claim. Account settled and recorded on Pages 451-452.

Page 461: Inventory and Appraisal of Estate of John William LILLIS, dec'd.
Appraisers: L. T. MOORE, P. H. REARDON, John STEPHENSON. 11 June 1896.
Total: Money in Shen. Valley Nat'l. Bank of Winchester. Recorded June 18,
1896.

Pages 462-463: Estate Account of Ann R.H. POWELL in Account with Wm. P.
McGUIRE, Admr. Begins Apr 1895 with cash found in Pocket Book, Apr 22,
1895, and cash in Bank. Received by purchase of Bank Shares by Mrs. J. R.
TUCKER and by John W. BRYARLY. Also by surrender of Endowment Certificates.
Paid legatees: Mrs. Kate H. POWELL, R. C. POWELL, Lizzie McGRUDER, P. P. &
H. H. POWELL, Mr. & Mrs M. P. GIBSON. Paid cash to many others. Account
settled and recorded 21 May 1896.

Pages 463-464: Estate Account of C. E. MERRIFIELD, Admr., of Estate of
Fannie I. ROBINS, dec'd. Among "assetts": Piano, Paintings, set Hall
Furniture, Chinaware, Horse Dolly, Pheaton Buggy, Amount due from Estate of
Edwd. A. ROBINS. Paid M. FAHAY, undertaker; paid Ella & Etta ROBINS for
money advanced to Fannie I. ROBINS during her last illness. Paid 4 heirs:
Mrs. MERRIFIELD, Etta B., Ella C. and John L. ROBINS. Account settled &
recorded 27 June 1896.

Pages 465-466: Estate account of Edward A. ROBINS with C. E. MERRIFIELD,
Admr. "Assetts" of Estate: Certificate of Indiana Central Savings & Loan,
Bond of Consumers Gas Trust Co. of Indianapolis, and Notes of John L. ROBINS
& Henrietta ROBINS. Division of Estate: Mrs. Sallie R. MERRIFIELD, John L.,
Etta B., Ella C., and Fannie I. ROBINS. Account recorded 27 June 1896.

Pages 466-467: Inventory and Appraisal of Estate of George Frederick GLAIZE,
dec'd., with Appraisers: George W. KURTZ, Geo. E. JENKINS, James W. BARR.
24 Sept 1896. Part of Inventory: Parlour Suit, 10 pieces; Knabe Piano;
Center Table in Back Parlor; Stocks in Bank & Bldg. Assn.; Interest in
Stock of firm of Glaize & Bro. Inventory recorded 5 Oct 1896.

Pages 467-469: F. A. GRAICHEN, Guardian, in Account with Annie E. GRAICHEN,
his Ward. Begins June 1885, with payments for Shoes, Gingham, Silk Dress &
Trimmings, Nun's Veiling Dress, Dress Maker's Wages & Board, Hats & Trimmings,
Dentist's Bill, Lace & Corset, Music & Sheets, School Books, Board, Gold
Fillings. Account to June 1896. Settled and recorded Aug 1, 1896.

Pages 470-471: Caroline D. GRAICHEN, Ward of F. A. GRAICHEN, Guardian,
Settlement of Account. From June 1884 to June 1896 with payments as:
for Bonnet, Music Lessons, Silk Dress, Sash, Parasol, Corset, 8 yards
Sattean, Stockings/Leggins, Dentist's Bill, 2 Gold Fillings, Ribbons,
Rubber Shoes. Received dividends. Account recorded Aug 1, 1896.

Pages 471-473: Frederick A. GRAICHEN, Ward of F. August GRAICHEN, Guardian-
ship Account beginning June 1884 with such payments as: for 2 pairs Shoes,
Suit of Clothes, Overcoat, 52 weeks Board, 3 yds Casimeer, Buttons, making
Pants & Coat; Dictionary, Music Lessons, pair Gum Shoes, Hose & Collars.
Paid Public School bill. Received Dividends , Rent & Interest. Account
settled and recorded 1 Aug 1896.

Page 474: Will of Miss Gettie McGUIRE, "Richmond, March 11th". All to sister,
Annie T. McGUIRE and at her death, $800 to each niece, Annie M. TAYLOR,
Laura & Gettie McGUIRE. Wit: Edward & Mary S. McGUIRE, Annie Moss TAYLOR.
Proved 24 Oct 1896. Annie T. McGUIRE, sister, to admin. Appraisers: Lewis
N. BARTON, Jas. B. RUSSELL, Dr. Rob't. W. STONE, Holmes BOYD, Jr.

Pages 474-476: Will of Miss Josephine W. CARSON. Pay funeral expenses, including erection of a cross, like as possible to the one which marks resting place of brother, John. "I desire no epitaph - In Memoriam - Josephine Warren, only daughter of Joseph S. & Eliza J. CARSON, died ---" Leaves funds to apply to maintenance of cemetery lot. To brother, Theodore M. CARSON, all Bonds, Notes, Monies due except $2,200 to nephew, J. Preston CARSON. To him also many household items. Also gives to Maud Lee CARSON and to faithful, devoted friend, Allie CHRISMORE. Jan 16, 1888. Codicil, 5 Jan 1895, to add to bequest to Allie Vaughn CHRISMORE that "it must in no degree benefit her father's family". Mentions Maud Carson LILE and daughter, Eleanor LILE, who are to have dishes "used by her great grandmother, Sarah MYERS." Codicil of 26 Oct 1896, re Bonds of Hutton LOVETT and C. M. PERRY. Wit: R. T. BARTON, Zide C. HUCK, C. J. JACOBS. Proved 29 Oct 1896. Theodore M. CARSON, exec.

Page 477: Geo. Ed. JENKINS, Guardian of Julia E. ROSENBERGER. Shows amount of legacy as of July 2, 1896 plus interest. Paid Kate V. WOODWARD on Support of Ward. Guardian declined "usual commission". Account settled for 1895 & 1896 and recorded 22 Sept 1896.

Pages 477-478: Inventory & Appraisal of Estate of Bernard REILLEY, dec'd. Appraisers: J. H. KAUFFMAN, Michael LILLIS, A. J. MILLER. Several houses and lots with total value of $2,920. 12 Sept 1896. Recorded Oct 26, 1896.

Pages 478-480: Appraisal of Estate of Madame M. SWENDEMAN (sometimes SWANDEMAN). Notes of Thomas H. WINSTON, Cora D. WALTER, W. J. GILLUSAR, H. D. GODDIN, P. H. DUNNING, plus Bonds, City of Richmond and Lehigh R. R. and Annuities. Appraisal entered 29 Oct 1896. Default made on Notes of H. D. GODDIN & Horace D. TYLER. Appraisers: Jas. B. RUSSELL, Lewis N. BARTON, R. W. STONE. Appraisers noted that none of the interest Notes referred to in their Inventory ever came into their possession as they had been deposited by Madam SWENDEMAN into First Nat'l. Bank of Richmond. Recorded 3 Sept 1896.

Pages 481-482: Will of Nathan KOHN. To wife, Emma, House on Main Street "in which I live and where my Store is". Also vacant lot and "rest & residue of my property". Included two Baltimore City Bonds. Wishes wife to keep up "my business". Partner is Leopold FRANKLE. Wife to execute. 11 May 1891. Wit: E. Holmes BOYD, R. T. BARTON. Proved 19 Feby 1897. Widow qualifies.

Pages 482-484: Sam'l. L. LAREW, Jr., Ward, in Account with C. M. GIBBENS, his Guardian. Begins Feb 1895, with receiving rent income of Revd. T. D. CLARK, Marshall McDONALD, Jos. S. McCARTY, Wm. DESHON. Received cash from Abram CRIM for corn & wheat. Some payments: for repairs to McDonald House & Fence, to James C. TODDY for Clothes for Ward, paid taxes and for papering dining room. Paid Wm. DESHON board for Ward for 12 months. Summary: overpaid Ward, $24.34. Second Account begins Feb 1896 with income and expenses much as previous year. Also paid Mrs. Green for making quilts for ward and J. W. SUMPTION for laundry for ward. Samuel L. LAREW, Jr. reached the age of 21 years on the 8th day of January 1897. Account settled and recorded March 3, 1897.

Pages 484-485: Dorsey WALTER, Trustee in Deed of Trust from Bernard REILLEY, dec'd. Begins July 1894 with receiving cash of J. D. THOMPSON, purchaser at Sale, and rent of Henry WOOD. Paid for Deed to purchaser, taxes, fees. Paid "B. REILLEY & His Committee". Recorded Settlement 3 March 1897.

Pages 485-486: Settlement of Estate Account of P. A. CLARK, Guardian of Ambrose, Elmer & Herbert HINER, Wards. Begins Apr 1895 with paid fees to clerk & committee for recording and settling accounts. Paid Alberta RITTER on board bill and John J. WILLIAMS, Atty. Balance in Guardian's hands,

$17.91. Paid more comor.'s & clerk's fees and "Amount due by Guardian $11.00". Recorded 3 March 1897.

Pages 486-487: Will of Malinda CAPPER. Nov 17, 1896. To Irene Virginia and Hannah Letitia CAPPER, "my two daughters". all estate on condition they support and take good care of their father, Meredith CAPPER. At death or marriage of daughters, all estate to "my five sons except Ira's CAPPER and if he gets all the proceeds of the Mountain Land", he gets nothing of Town property. Daughters to get all rents...if not enough, sell lot "over the railroad". If Walter CAPPER wants part of Barn & Lot, he gets it at fair value. Michael L. CAPPER to execute. Attest: James E. & Vance YEAKLEY. Proved 19 Apr 1897. 20 Apr 1897 M. Lohr CAPPER, son, made bond to execute.

Pages 487-489: Will of German SMITH. "As to the worldly estate I shall have at my death": Pay debts; to wife, Hannah D. SMITH, all estate, "also all debts" to be her absolute property. He has two life insurance policies to benefit wife. He has a Sumac & Bark Mill. Gives instructions on receiving, curing & selling stock of this mill. Wife to execute will with brother, John SMITH, Junior, of Camden, New Jersey. 7 July 1874. Wit: Wm. BYRD, Richard PARKER. Codicil, 18 Jany 1889. Has increased life insurance, to wife. Now has son, German SMITH, Jr. Leaves out brother as executor. Wit: Wm. R. WILLIS, Jno. W. RICE. Codicil on Letter Sheet Heading: Sumac & Quercitron Bark, Winchester, Sept 2nd, 1889. "Fearing my former will & codicil may not be sufficient to avoid any controversy or litigation" repeats that wife is to have all estate. Will proved 22 Apr 1897 by Wm. BYRD, one of surviving witnesses. Richard PARKER now deceased. Codicils proved by S. H. HANSBROUGH who was well acquainted with handwriting.

Pages 489-491: Will of Mary A. SHAULL. Requests executor to pay all bills and cost of a suitable Gravestone. Also to safely invest remaining funds, collect interest annually and pay to husband, David SHAULL. To daughter, Fanny R. HEISTON, $100 as "a slight reminder of my affection for her". She had already received more than her share of estate. After death of husband, divide estate into 4 equal shares: to daughter, Emma G. CATHER; to David CATHER, son of dec'd. daughter, Annie Cordelia CATHER; to daughter, Sally E. KOHLHOUSEN; to children of dec'd daughter, Mary N. WARE, viz: Charles S. & Homer S. WARE. Bequests to these depend on their conveying to daughter, Catherine SHAULL, named properties in Winchester. Sally E. KOHLHOUSEN & Clark CATHER to exec. 9 Apr 1894. Wit: Rich'd L. GRAY, Wm. H. M. MAHANEY, John STEPHENSON. Proved 23 Apr 1897. Sallie E. KOHLHOUSEN declined, so Clark CATHER qualified as exec.

Page 491: Will of Miss Susan E. LUPTON. 29 Oct 1896. "Calling to mind the frail tenor of life -- " To Lucinda B. G. LUPTON, all property. Wit: John W. CAPPER, Daniel R. JANNEY, Jas. M. LUPTON. Proved May 17, 1897 (no mention of exec. or admr.)

Page 492: Estate of Christopher FUNK, dec'd., in Account with J. N. W. FUNK, Admr. Begins with amount received from Insurance Co. on Loss of Store House on Main Street, burned Apr 1, 1894. Among expenses paid: for casket, case & hearse; for embalming body; for burial permit & monuments. Paid Mary E. RAY, daughter and heir of decedent, $4.68. Amount reinvested in new Store Room on Main Street, $2,085.00. Settled and recorded 3 March 1897.

Page 493: Estate of Mary E. LAUCK, dec'd., in Account with Richard E. BYRD, Admr. Sold Stock in Winchester & Potomac RR; paid fees & comms. Cash balance: $16.90. Re Shares of Stock bequeathed to daughter, Mrs. Emily Caroline BENTLEY. Letter from Annie E. BENTLEY says her mother, Emily Caroline BENTLEY, died 10 Feby 1895, leaving 5 heirs: Annie E., George A., Mary V., Chas. P. K., and Kate D. BENTLEY, residents of Washington, D. C. Settled and recorded 3 Mar 1897.

Page 494: Estate of Ellen GORSUCH in Account with Chas. GORSUCH, executor. Shows income from Ground Rents in Baltimore, 1892-1896. Paid doctor bill, casket, embalming, hacks, digging grave. Account records "from death of decedent, Oct 11, 1891" to Oct 1896. Recorded in Court, 3 March 1897.

Page 495: Estate of Henry E. (later G) BARTLETT, dec'd., in Account with Sarah J. BARTLETT, exec. Received rent, Sept 1894-1896. Paid funeral expenses, probating will, city & state taxes. Amount due estate: $40.48. Recorded March 3, 1897.

Pages 495-496: Inventory and Appraisal of Estate of Mrs. Caroline PARKER. Appraisers: J. C. TOTTY, John F. KREMER, J. P. SANTELLE. 26 Feby 1897. Bedroom furniture and carpeting at Mrs. L. BARR; Side Board, Stove, Chairs, Beds, etc. taken by Mr. A. S. PARKER before Appraisal. Recorded Apr 25, 1897.

Pages 496-498: Settlement of Estate of Madame M. SWANDEMAN with W. P. McGUIRE, her Comm. Begins Feb 1896 with income from Dividends & Annuities and Collections on Notes. Made payments to: Nannie TRIPLETT, maid; Miss E. L. PAGE, board; Thos. KEATING, whiskey; Miss Gertrude MASON, travelling companion; Mrs. B. T. HOLLIDAY, board. Account settled and recorded May 22, 1897.

Pages 498-500: Estate of Wm. G. RUSSELL, dec'd., in Account with Bruce GIBSON, exec. From Apr 1891 to Mar 1894. Received cash of real estate sold, of bonds, of sale of house & lot, of John VOILETT & A. GARDINER. Made payments as of Wm. G. RUSSELL Notes; Winchester Times for ads; refunded B. GIBSON for cash loaned estate; for redemption of land sold for non-payment of taxes. Paid legacy due B. GIBSON and distribution to M. E. GIBSON, S. W. DORSEY, Wm. G. RUSSELL, M.D. Amount not distributed: $402.79. Executor brought bill for $516.35 for goods furnished the decedent in his lifetime. It can be considered debt against the estate unless legatees plead Statute of Limitations. Account recorded May 22, 1897.

END OF WILL BOOK NO. 4

ABBOTT, Juliet B., 72
  Juliet Beaty, 72
AD(D)AMS,
  Catherine Maria, 39
  George M., 11
  Peter, 10
  Richard, 9
ADDISON, Z., 42
  Zach, 67
AFFLECK, Scott A., 79
AFFLICK, Mrs. A. E., 39
  Janet, 32
  Manan H., 32
  P., 39
  S. A., 39
  Scott A., 67
AKIN, Wm., 22
ALBERT, Adrain, 5
  Catherine 20
ALBIN, M. D., 56, 57, 84
ALDERMAN, Annie E., 89
ALEXANDER, Gemima, 20
  Jemima, 20
  John, 20
  Nancy, 20, 56
  Peggy, 4
  W. R., 88
  Wm. R., 55, 64, 70
ALLEN, Clifford P., 69
  Clifford P., Jr., 69
ALSDORFF, Laura, 90
AMBLER, Dr. R. C., 39
AMIK, John, 16
ANDERSON, C. W., 34, 45, 61
  Catherine, 3, 18
  Chas. E., 88
  Chas. W., 88
  Edwd., 88
  Elizabeth B., 88
  Evan, 60
  Evan P., 56, 64
  F. H., 88
  G. W., 17, 23
  George, 22
  George M., 61, 63
  Geo. W., 18, 25, 31, 42, 59
  Geo. Wash., 58
  Hannah, 4
  Henry, 18
  Isaac K., 56

Mrs. J. A., 74
Jacob, 18
James, 5, 18
James W., 63
John C., 18, 24, 61, 62
John J., 50, 55
Lewis H., 61
Mary E., 24, 62
Mary Ellen, 62
Mary M., 63
Marenda, 18
Nancy, 58
Nathan, 2, 3, 4, 5, 6
Robert E. Lee, 62
Virginia, 58
Wm., 18
ANNAN, Heriot R., 58
  James R. 58
  William L., 58
ARDERN, Henry, 73
ARMSTRONG, Robt G., 89
ARNOLD, John W., 16
ASHBY, Benjamin, 2
ATHEY, Annie Eliza, 72
  Annie Elizabeth, 72
  James, 72
  Margaret E., 72
ATKINSON, Betty J., 23
  George, 83
  Juliet, 23
  Rev. Dr., 54
  W. M., 16
  Wm., 79
  William M., 23, 27, 29, 41, 46, 48, 58, 59, 63, 64, 65
ATTRICK?, Fredk., 9
ATWELL, S. R., 79, 80
  Sam'l. R., 36, 43, 44, 79, 80
AULICK, Alberta, 26
  Ann Maria, 5
  Ann Mary, 4
  Charles, 1, 2, 4, 5, 7
  Chas. Andrew, 4
  Eliza Margt., 4
  Fredk. Albert, 4

George, 4
Henryetta, 4
John H., 4, 25
J. Wiley, 25
J. Wyley, 26
Ralph O., 25
Richmond, 25
Rich. Ogston, 25
Susanna C., 4
William, 4
AVIRETT, Mary. T. D., 37

BAETJER, H., 24, 46, 59
  Henry, 31, 45, 61, 62, 65, 70, 91
BAGEANT, J. W., 83
BAGG, Wm. G., 39
BAGLEY, Mary, 9
BAILEY, Abraham, 1
  Catherine, 1
  Elizabeth, 1
  Henry, 70
  James, 1
  Jessie, 80
  Jesse K., 80
  John, 1
  Peggy, 1
  Sally, 1
BAILY,
  Elizabeth Baker, 33
  Hezekiah B., 33
BAKER, A. M., 63, 68
  Abraham, 2, 10
  Albert, 63, 64, 68, 75, 85
  Aletta, 63
  Andrew, 7, 11, 12
  C. S., 38, 55, 58, 75
  Camillus, 5, 35
  Charles W., 33
  Christian S., 62
  Mrs. E. H., 68
  Elizabeth, 2, 62
  Emma C., 58
  Emma V., 41
  Emily C., 28, 34
  F., 35
  G. G., 59, 84
  G. W., 68
  George, 91
  Geo. P., 55, 62
  Gertrude, 63, 68
  G. Goodwin, 78

BAKER, cont'd.
  H. H., 64, 68, 75
  H. M., 40, 47, 60, 66,
    70
  H. S., 28, 35, 68, 75
  Mrs. H. S., 75
  Harry H., 63
  Henry, 2, 3, 10, 11,
    12, 13
  Henry M., 59, 70
  Henry S., 63, 64, 68
  Henry Wm., 2, 8, 10,
    12, 13
  Isaac, 2, 10, 13, 33,
    36, 61
  Isaac T., 18
  J. C., 90, 91
  J. I. H., 45,46
  Jacob, 2, 9, 10,13,
    28
  John, 2, 4, 5, 9, 10,
    12, 13, 72
  John I., 55
  John Ike, 22
  John J. H., 23
  Joseph, 2, 12
  Josiah, 56
  Josiah L., 84
  Lily, 63, 68, 75
  Mary, 11, 12
  Mary Ann, 11
  Mary C., 36
  Portia, 58
  Potia, 28
  Potra, 34
  R. W., 64, 68, 75
  Rob't L., 35
  Rob't W., 63
  Rosanna, 11
  S. B., 70
  Sam'l, 87
  Sam'l B., 69, 70, 72,
    73, 77, 79, 80
  Sam'l C., 11, 12
  Sophia, 68
  W. B., 48, 58
  Mrs. W. B., 68
  W. H., 62, 68
  W. W. 68, 75
  William B., 28, 30, 35,
    62, 63, 68, 88
  Wm. H., 41, 61, 63, 64,
    68, 75
  Wm. of George, 88

  Wm. Henry, 8
  Wm. W., 63
BALDWIN,
  Archibald S., 13
  C., 81
  Cornelius, 2
  D. W., 45
  Hite, 13
  Isaac Hite, 45
  John H., 54
  Margaret, 13
  Mary E., 45
  Mary Julia, 13
  Portia, 54
  Portia L., 54, 61
  R. T., 54
  Sally, 37
  William D., 13
  Wm. Ludwell, 54
BALL, Evelyn, 36
BANKS, Rob't T., 49
BANNISTER, T., 48
BARLEY, Lewis, 19,90
  Sallie, 74, 85
BARNES, C. S. W., 35,
    38, 43, 52, 61, 64,
    82
  John W., 21
BARNETT, David, 34
  J. H., 77
BARNHART, George, 12,
    16, 85
  Jacob, 60
  Jas. H., 30, 40, 41,
    59, 60, 73, 74, 85
BARR, E. M., 32. 53
  Edward M., 88
  Fanny, 38
  Hugh, 16, 17
  J. W., 32, 50,62
  James W., 32, 53, 55,
    61, 92
  Oscar, 21, 43, 47, 48,
    61, 62, 68, 74, 77,
    82, 86, 89, 90
  Susie C., 90
  W. E., 83, 90
BARRETT, David, 26
  Margaret J., 36
BARTLETT, Clementine &
  Clementine N., 82
  Henry E., 82,95
  Henry G., 95
  Henry Wesley, 82

  J. A., 62
  Mary, 9
  Sarah F., 82
  Sarah Jane, 82, 95
BARTON, B. T., 24
  D. W., 21, 31
  David, 27, 38
  David W., 14, 15
  Gertrude W., 75
  L. H., 60
  L. N., 67
  Lewis N., 86, 92, 93
  R. T., 26, 27, 31, 32,
    40, 45, 55, 60, 61,
    66, 69, 93
BAUTZ, T. M., 47, 69, 73,
    74, 81
BEAN, Kate V., 38
BEATTY, H., 3
  Henry, 9, 10
BECK, Dewees, 19
BEELER, F. L., 61
BEEMER, John W., 20
BELL, Ferguson, 21
  Hector, 21, 87
  Hubbard, 21
  J. V., 64
  Mrs. J. V., 74, 84
  James, 26
  John, 4, 8, 9, 11
  John H., 89
  John N., 13, 25, 28, 44,
    55, 58
  Jno. W., 51
  John U., 29
  John U., Jr., 29
  Joseph, 77
  Josephine T., 87
  J. Vance, 56, 84
  Kate, 36
  Lewis, 21
  Milly, 21
  Sawney, 21
  Susan, 21
  Vance, 71
  W. M. A., 82
  Warner, 79
  Wm. A., 29, 32, 57, 63,
    82, 86
BENDER, I. L., 80
BENT, Charles, 2
  Lemuel, 2, 4, 6, 8, 11
  Martha C., 58, 59
  N. A., 40

97

98

BROWN, cont'd.
Ellis A., 59
Emma, 28
Fannie, 28
Geo. A., 60
Henry B., 55
Isaac W., 31
J. F., 59
J. H., 75
J. P., 48
Jas. M., 75
Jesse, 6
J. Few, 90
John, 2, 49
John J., 76
Maria, 55
Margaret H., 49
Mary E., 75, 76
Nellie, 28
O. M., 15, 34, 48,58
Oliver M., 39
R. R., 48, 49, 75
Richard Jr., 49
Richard R., 15, 49,
   77, 83
Robert, 81
Samuel, 11, 12, 15,
   17
Sarah, 77
Sarah Ann, 49
Scott, 80
Susan, 28
Virginia, 23
Wm., 64
Wm. D., 21
Wilson L., 47
BRUCE, Sydney, 21
BRUMBACK, Joseph, 37
BRYANT, Maggie, 79
BRYARLY, J. E., 77
John W., 44, 92
S. F., 77
BULL, William, 7
BULLER, Joe, 77
BURGESS, James B., 38
Jas. H., 46
BURKE, Elizth. A., 59
Isaac, 6
Sarah, 6
BURNS, G. W., 75
G. Washington, 49
O. K., 75
Oliver M., 50
Virginia M., 49,
   70, 75

BURNSIDE, Miss, 48
BURWELL, Mrs. Ann R.,
   38
P. C. L., 38
BUSH, Catherine, 73,
   74, 85
Charles A., 22
Daniel, 19, 33, 52,
   56
Evy M., 22
George W., 85, 90
J. Andrew, 44
John A., 18, 20
M. B., 32
Phil, 2
Regina(h), 11, 12,
   14
William, 11
BUSHNELL, Geo. E.,
   23, 68, 74, 77,
   84, 88, 91
BUTTON, Jesse, 1
BUZZARD, J. H., 69
BYARLY, John W., 43
BYRD, Abram, 74
Geo. H., 27,
Jennie, 33
Margaret, 26, 27,
   30, 34, 71, 76
R. E., 21, 76, 77
Richard E., 20, 94
Wm., 26, 27, 29, 33,
   44, 76, 77, 79, 81,
   94

CADWALLADER, Jos., 80
CAIN, John, 42
CALDWELL, L. J., 80
CALMES, Wm., 56
Wm. B., 84
CALOHAN, Wm. S., 25
CALVERT, Mary, 3
Milly, 3
Sam'l., 3, 4, 11
Wm. H., 56
CAMERON,
Mary Gertrude, 49
Gertrude, 75
CAMM, Annie, 85
CAMPBELL,
Ara Anna, 18
Chas. R., 88
George Wm., 12
J. W., 22
Mrs. J. W., 23

James Victor, 12, 13,
   14
Mary A., 86
Thomas, 29
Thomas B., 12, 13, 14,
   86
Thomas R., 12
W. T., 29
Wm., 12, 13
William S., 12
CANAFORD, Henry, 8
CANNON, Mary H., 86
CAPP, Edmonia Belle, 75
Mollie B., 75
N. F. A., 75
Rebecca M., 75
Winona Pauline, 75
CAPPER,
Hannah Letitia, 94
Ira S., 65, 76, 94
Irene Virginia, 94
John W., 94
M., 42
Malinda, 94
Meredith, 38, 64, 94
Michael L., 94
M. Lohr, 94
T. W., 76
Walter, 77, 94
CAREY, Alex, 55
CARLIN, Bennett, 36
CARMICHAEL, Jennie, 85
CARNELL, John, 69
CARPENTER, Bushrod, 72,
   73
C. L., 56
CARPER, Annie Jane, 65
John D., 17
Margaret Elizth., 17
P. P., 65
W. A., 77, 82
Wm. A., 89
CARRIGAN,
Catherine C., 46
CARSON, Mrs. Ann, 35
Beaty, 3, 6,11, 13, 14
Eliza J., 37, 93
J. R., 44, 64
J. S., 18, 22
Jas. H., 15
John, 93
John R., 57
Jos. S., 93
J. Preston, 93
Josephine W., 37, 57, 93

CARSON, cont'd
  Maude Lee, 93
  Theodore, 93
CARTER, J. S., 86
  John, 13
  Shirley, 76, 82, 84,
    88
CARTMELL, Annie G., 87
  N. M., 44
  Nathan, 3
  R. M., 76, 77
  T. K., 76, 77, 80,
    81, 86, 87
  Thos. K., 70, 72
CARVER, James, 18
CASTLEAR, Bessie, 50
  Eloise, 50
  Fannie, 50
  Fannie A., 50
CASTLEM, Fannie A., 75
CASTLEMAN, David, 4
  Elizabeth, 1
CATHER, Adaline, 86
  Annie Cordelia, 94
  Clark, 81, 94
  David, 94
  Francis, 86
  Jonah, 86
  J. S., 86
  Millicent B., 86
  Millicent L., 75
  W., 22
CERFOOT, Wm., 4
CHAMBERLIN, Jno. W, 31
CHANDLER, Benjamin, 10
  Eunice, 10
  Goldsmith, 3, 4, 9,
    10
CHANDLER, C., 48
  C. H., 74
CHAPPEL, Martha, 40
CHASE, Charles, 21
CHEECK, Wm. F., 88
CHILDS, Julia, 73
  Mary, 74, 85
  Sam'l L., 86
  Samuel M., 70
CHILES, S. M., 83, 87
  Samuel, 56
  Sam'l L., 86
CHRISMAN, Jane, 8
CHRISMORE, Allie, 93
  Allie Vaughn, 93

CLARK(E),
  Alexander, 18
  Caroline, 18, 20
  Charles, 77
  Charles H., 15, 82
  Daniel, 2, 3
  Imogen, 54
  Julia A., 65, 82
  Lawrence, 54, 61
  Louisa M., 14
  Nannie, 85
  Nancy, 30
  Mrs. Nancy F., 30
  Peyton, 54
  P. A., 86, 93
  Robert L., 54
  Sallie M., 88
  T. D., 93
  T. D. D., 85
  W. L., Jr., 61, 64
  Wm., 89
  William C., 22
  Wm. L., 29, 37, 56,
    61, 64
  Wm. S., 52
CLAYTON,
  Sarah Ann, 58
  Thos., 67, 68
CLEM, A. J., 73
CLEVENGER, J. W., 86
CLINE, Amanda M., 72
  Daniel, 72, 73
  Elmira Oldham, 72
CLINGER, John, 80
CLOUSER, M. J., 64
CLOWSER, A. J., 65
  Jas. H., 74
  Jos., 65
COATS, Dennis, 67
COBB, J. M., 56
COCHRAN, James, 3
  Wm., 9
COE, John C., 27,
    34, 55
COFFROTH,
  C. A. B., 34, 46,
    72
  Edwin M., 52
  Elizabeth M., 52
COLLET, Catharine, 15
  Juliet, 15
COLLINS, Dennia, 66
COLSTON, A., 31

COLSTON, cont'd
  Gertrude, 85
COLVERT, Samuel, 1
CONNELL?, Ed J., 81
CONNER, Edward, 88
  J. Wm., 63
  Patrick, 77
CONRAD,
  Cath. Brooke, 27
  Chas. Fredk., 27, 28
  Chas. Michael, 63
  Chas. M., 24
  Conrad, 5
  Daniel, 22, 27
  Daniel Burr, 27, 28
  Elizabeth, 26
  Ellen, 63
  Frances Edwd., 27
  George, 32
  Geo. W., 26
  Geo. Cuthbert Powell,
    27
  Govenor, 27
  H., 41, 75
  Henry, 41
  Holmes, 43, 44, 50,
    62, 67
  James, 43,63
  John, 1, 4
  John R., 24
  Margaret R., 14
  Mary G., 63
  Robert Y., 27
CONROD, Michel, 43
CONVERSE,
  Eliza J. L., 44
  Thos. E., 28
CONWAY, M., 80
  N. T., 39
  Wm. G., 89
COOK, Albert, 70
  Charles, 70
  Eliza, 70
  Esther R., 69
  John, 5, 70
  John C., 69
  Julian, 5
COONTZ, C. A., 22
  C. W., 50
  Emma V., 50
  Jo. Esther, 50
  L. P., 16, 20
  Louisa M., 50

DERRICK, Samuel, 67
DESHANN, W., 25
De SHIELDS, Francis, 7
DESHON, Wm., 82, 93
  Wm. M., 54, 81
DEWS, D. H., 24
DICK, Henry, 56, 64
  John, 5, 6, 9, 11
  Mary Ann, 18
DIFFENDERF(F)ER,
  E. H., 74
  Edward, 79
  John, 27,
  Wm., 18
DINKLES, C., 39
DIXON, Wm., 12
DOCTER, Michael, 36
  Peter, 36
DODD, Rob't. D., 90
DOHANE, Louis, 49
DORSEY, S. W., 95
  Sidney, 69
  U. L., 69
  W. L., 27, 31, 35
DOSH, Rev. T. W., 62,
  68
DOSWELL, Jas. T., 22
  Thomas, 22
DOTSON, Jeremiah, 9
DOUTHAT, Rebecca J., 71
DOWDALL, James G., 3, 8,
  10
  Jane, 3
  John, 3
  Margaret, 3, 8, 10
  Maxwell, 3
  Rebecca, 3
DOWNING, M. E., 90
  M. J., 90
  Mary E., 88
  Mary Evelyn, 90
DUBROW, Wm., 71
DUFFIELD, John, 1
  Mary, 1
DUNGING, J. N., 3
DUNNING, P. H., 93

EAGER, Albert, 1
  Elizabeth, 1
EAGLE, George, 31
EARLE, A. M., 49
  Mrs. A. M., 49
  Mary E., 50
EBERSOLE,
  Jacob F., 77, 84

EBERZOLE, Mat, 87
EDDY, Bertie, 79
  Mary E., 61, 65
  Wm. N., 45, 61, 62,
  65
EGGLESTON,
  Rev. Wm. C., 22
EICHELBERGER,
  C. F., 58, 71
  Charlotte E., 86
  Charles F., 86
EICHELBORGER
  Lewis, 17
ELLIOTT, Peter, 2
ELSE, John, 11
ENDERS, James, 24
  John, 23, 24
  Mary Ann, 23
ENSWELLER, Chas. 87
EVANS, E. J., 69
  Ed. J., 73
  Edward J., 59, 66,
  84
  Elizabeth, 72
  Fannie M., 49
  Fanny K., 75
  H., 83
  Henry, 48, 66
  Lillie, 83
  Mollie, 83, 84
  Wm. L., 81, 83, 84
  Samuel, 27, 42, 69
  Wm., 33, 60, 72
EVERHART, C., 71
EWELL, Fanny B., 79
  Mildred E., 79

FAGAN, John 24
FAHAY, M., 92
FAHNESTOCK, A. B., 80
  S. F., 83
FAIRFAX, Wm. Henry,
  54, 55
FARQUHARSON, Rob't, 56
FAULKNER,
  Isaac H., 19, 28
  James F., 81
FAUNTLEROY, Kate, 27
  P. Williams, 37
  Sallie, 27
  T. T., Jr., 44, 69
  Thos. T., 20, 21,
  23, 44
FELTER, Chas., 71
FENESTER, Mrs. E., 27

FENESTER, cont'd
  Emily, 26, 30
FENTON, Belinda, 24
  Evelina, 22
  Eveline, 24
FESTUS, Gabe, 55
FIELDS, Aaron, 48
  Abraham, 48
  Charles, 48
  Felicia, 48
  Raph, 48
  Robert, 48
  Sally, 48
  Sarah, 48
  William, 48
FINLEY, Mathew, 61
FISHER, Rev. Chas., 36
  P. O., 32, 53
FISHPAW, E. L., 71
FITZ, John, 79
FITZSIMMONS, Chas., 9
  Nicholas, 12
FLANAGAN, Elizabeth, 14
  Speak(e), 6, 14
FLANNIGAIN, Nannie, 64
FLEET, Martha E., 20
FLETCHER, Chas., 68
  John, 14, 16
  Louise N., 76, 84
  Polk, 61
FLINN, Dr., 24
FOLK, Harriet, 18, 20
  Mrs. 19
FORD, John T., 69
  Julia, 85
  Major, 81
FORNEY, Adam, 55
  M., 64
  Nancy, 55
FOULK, George, 18
FOX, W. Tazewell, 40
FRANKLE, Leopold, 93
FRANK, A. J., 64
  Andrew J., 56
  Ashby, 64
  C. W., 56
  W. H., 64
  Wm. H., 56
FREDERICK, Cath., 15
  Elizabeth, 15
  Julyann, 15
FRENCH, Sarah, 44, 58
FRICK, J. Swan, 40
FRIES, David, 89
  Edgar L., 76

FRIES, cont'd
  G. Casper, 76, 77
  Wm., 75, 77
  Wm. O., 75
FROST, Patsey, 47
FRYE, Cornelia, 89
  George M., 3, 4
  James M., 38, 65
  John M., 61
  Joseph, 89
FUG?, Joseph H., 45
FULLER, Douglas, 48
  Ellen A., 82, 89
  Ellen E., 89
  H. Douglas, 76, 83
  James, 82
  Jas. A., 89
  John Scott, 89
  W. McP., 66
FULLERTON, James, 27
FUNK, C., 36, 45
  Christopher, 94
  Harry C. A., 89
  J. N. W., 82, 89, 94
  James, 71, 77
  Lydia A., 89
  Obed, 59
FUNSTEN, D., 34
  David, 76
  Emily, 34, 76, 77,
    84, 87
  Emily R., 76, 84
FUNSTER, Emily, 71
  Col. O. M., 37
  O. R., 71

GAENSLEN, Bessie, 49
  Frederick B., 49
  George R., 49
  John Jacob, 49
  Mary Cornelia, 49
  S. F., 49, 50
  Samuel F., 55, 65
GALLAGHER, Wm. G., 30
GAMBLE, Joseph, 2, 3,
    4, 7, 12
  Josh., 8, 9
GARBER, Joseph, 75
GARDINER, A., 95
GARNER, Elizabeth, 57
GENN, Sam'l, 80
GIBBENS, A. M., 25
  C. M., 49, 54, 56, 59,
    65, 69, 70, 74, 77,
    82, 85, 88, 89, 93

GIBBENS, cont'd
  C. W., 25, 48
  J. H., 48
  Mary, 48
GIBBONS, Cornelius, 4,
    7, 8
GIBSON, B., 66
  Bruce, 69, 70, 79,
    80, 95
  Mrs. Bruce, 45
  C. H., 85
  M. E., 95
  Mr. & Mrs. M. P.,
    92
  Mary E., 46, 69
  Mary Elizabeth, 21
  N. F., 36
GIFFIN, Jas., 64
GILBERT, Mrs. E. A.,
    60
  W. T., 27, 33, 66
  Wm. T., 33, 50, 60,
    66
GILDERSLEEVE,
  Bettie, 85
GILES, Edwin G., 34
GILKESON, J. Smith,
    57
GILLNER, Tevault, 3
GILLUSAR, W. J., 93
GLAIS, Geo., 38
GLAIZE, Alice E., 90
  Geo. F., 33, 50
  Geo., Fred'k., 92
  John, 60
GLASS, Robt P., 48
  Sarah S., 48, 52
  W. W., 86
GLAZIER, Christian, 1
  Dorothy, 1, 2
GLENHO(L)M(ES),
  Eliza, 29, 52
GODDIN, H. D., 93
  John F., 90
GOLD, Daniel, 7, 9,
    10, 11, 12, 13,
    14, 17
  Hunter B., 88
  Samuel, 61
  T. D., 68
GORDON, Betty, 36
  Wm., 36
GORE, P. C., 76
  Perry C., 80, 88
GORSUCH, Chas., 95

GORSUCH, cont'd
  Chas. T., 72, 73
  Ellen, 72,73, 95
GOSHERT, C. E., 53
  Emma C., 53, 61, 72
  Fred, 65, 72
  Frederick, 81, 87, 90
  J. D., 53, 65, 87, 90
  Jacob D., 61
  Mertie, 65, 72, 81,
    87, 90
GOSS, Robert T., 77
GOVER, Lizzie, 83
GRAHAM, J. R., 50, 52
  Revd James, 66
  Richard J., 35
  Wm. D., 35
GRAICHEN, Anna, 91
  Anna C., 83
  Ann Elizth., 91
  Anne, 59
  Annie E., 92
  August, 50
  Caroline, 83, 91, 92
  Carrie, 59
  Catharine, 51, 59,
    83, 90
  Elizabeth, 91
  F. A., 92
  F. August, 55, 59, 83,
    90, 91
  Fred. A., 59, 83, 92
  Fred. August, 91
  Frederick, 91
  J. A., 51
  Jno. George, 91
  Wm. C., 91
GRANT(T), Charles, 39
  Elizabeth A., 39
  Hannah, 31
  James Stewart, 39
  John L., 87
  S., 7
  Stewart, 6
  Virginia 65
GRAY, A. Jane, 79
  Gertrude, 58
  Ida, 58
  James, 36
  Jane, 79, 81
  Jno., 10, 58
  John F., 58, 81
  Mary, 58
  R. L., 64
  Richard L., 59, 69, 72,
    81, 94

GRAY, cont'd
  Robert, 2, 3, 4
  Robert L., 79, 87
GREEN, H. K., 67, 69,
    70, 79
  Hugh, 67, 76, 78, 88
  Hugh K., 84, 90, 91
  J. G., 60
  J. Gus, 56
  Sela S., 41
GRIFFITH, A. D., 37
  Aaron H., 33
  Ann Virginia, 37
  Henrietta, 37
  Isaac N., 33
  Mary P., 33
  R. E., 87
GRIGSBY, J. Ralph, 74
  V. R., 88
GRIM, Abram, 85
  Anna E., 77
  Ann Elizth., 45
  C. H., 50
  Cammillus, 38
  Catherine, 20
  Chas., 7, 20, 37, 37,
    38, 39, 45, 77
  Cornelia, 24, 62
  Elizabeth, 38
  Frank, 38
  George, 88
  Geo. W., 16, 20, 27,
    77
  Henry D., 38
  Hunter, 55, 86
  Hunter B., 38, 50
  J. R. T., 65
  Jackson D., 89
  Jacob, 24
  James W., 20
  John W., 24, 45, 77
  L. R., 67
  L. T. F., 24, 57
  Levi T. F., 24, 61, 84
  Lizzie, 38
  Lyle, 77
  Philip T., 89
  Stewart, 38, 89
  T. F., 53
  Washington, 38
  Wesley, 38
  Wm. E., 38
GRIMES, Jas. A., 82
GRIMSHAW, Thos., 9

GROSS, Harriet, 77
GROVE, Abraham, 16
  C. F., 77
  James H., 36
GRUPY, F. H., 39

HAAS, Catharine, 15
  16, 17
  John, 15
  Mildred, 15
HADDOX, G. W., 60, 77
HAINES, Evelina, 22
  Eveline, 23
  G. H., 42
  Georgianna, 22, 23
  George E., 24
  Harriet, 24
  John, 61
HAINS, Geo. H., 79
HALDERMAN, J. S., 90
HALL, Elizabeth, 21
HAM, Benj, T., 7
  Peter, 4, 7, 8
HAMILTON, David, 32
  42, 43, 46
  James, 32
  Rebecca, 32
  Robert, 21
  Sidney, 32
HAMMAKER, Michael, 11
HAMMOND, Geo. W., 47
  Harriet M., 47, 57
  Sarah A., 47
  Thos. B., 47, 57
HAM?, Catharine, 33
HANCOCK, C. B., 28, 31,
    32, 36, 53, 65
  Chas. B., 35, 60, 62
  E. T., 88
  H. B., 79
HANSBROUGH,
  Margaret, 88
  Mary, 88
  Presley, 6
  S. H., 51, 74, 78, 88,
    94
HANSUCKER, P., 22, 51
  Philip, 32
HARDER, Caroline, 39
HARDESTY, A., 36
  Cordenia, 7
  George, 7
  Martha S., 83
  R. D., 58

HARDY, Charles, 27, 29,
    57
  Charles P., 86
  Harriet, 27, 29
  Hattie, 57
  John, 30
  Lucy, 27, 57
  Miss M. R., 86
  Martha, 27, 29
  Rebecca, 53
  Wm. H., 27, 55, 79,
    86, 88
HARKNESS, Andrew, 30,
    38
HARMER, J. Albert, 82
HARMON, John, 31
HARPER, B. F., 55
  E. J., 65
  G. W., 65, 68
  Mary E., 68
  Nelly, 9, 12
HARRIS, Clara, 88
  Clementine, 87
  Esther, 83
  James, 6
  Mary C., 83
  Mary Ellen, 70
  Minnie A., 83
HARRISON, Powell, 85
  T. W., 43, 76, 77
  Thos. W., 81
  Wm. B., 20
HARRY, James, 5, 10,
    11, 15
  Jonathan, 10
  Joseph, 7
  Lydia N., 24
  Stephen, 23
HART, Camullus S., 50
  Joanna B., 50
HARTMAN, Daniel, 7, 8
  Lewis P., 29, 36
HAUCK, J. Gertrude, 90
HAUGHMAN, Geo. F., 2
HAVENNER,
  Mary Cornelia, 30
  T. H., 30
HAVILAND, Rebecca, 2
  Samuel, 2
HAWKENS, G. W., 68
HAYMAKER, Adam, 3
  Catharine, 3
  Christiana, 3
  Edward D., 34

HOLLIS, cont'd
  Carson, 84
  Chas. W., 32, 34, 42
  Clayton, 88
  Edward G., 88
  Hannah, 36, 43
  Marian, 84
  O. W., 57
  Sarah S., 16
  Wm., 43
  Willis, 84
HOLMES, E. H., 2
  Edward, 67
  E. T., 30
  Edmund, 67
  Wm., 2
HOLPHINS, Cornelia, 54
HOLT, J. H., 28
  J. R., 28
HOLTZMAN, Aylett, 88
  Louisa M., 88
HOOVER, E. M., 74
  George, 72, 73
  Jacob, 53
  John, 15, 18, 19,
    27, 72, 73
  P. M., 74
HOPEWELL,
  Catherine, 33
  John, 7
HOPKINS, John, 14
HOPSON, Susie, 67
HORN, Hannah, 59
  Perry, 59
  Solomon, 16, 59
HORNER, Richard B., 16,
  17
  Richard R., 18
HORNEY, Alfred, 55
HORSEY, W. O., 79, 80
HOTTEL, J., 53
  W., 53
HOUCK, A. J., 66
  Andrew J., 47, 49
  Andy, 77
  Chas. W., 49
  Harrison, 49
  J. P., 74
  James, 49
HOUSE, S. S., 57
HOUT, H. R. M., 64
  Urilla V., 64
HOWARD, Cyrus, 81
  Janie, 85

HOWARD, cont'd
  Maria, 58
  Susan, 86
HUBER, Henry, 53
  Jno., 53
HUCK, Byrd, 47
  L. M., 33
  L. N., 20, 25, 27, 28,
    36, 44, 53, 60, 65,
    66, 68, 76, 79, 81,
    86, 88
  Lewis N., 24, 26, 30,
    50, 55, 87
  S. N., 40, 47
  T. N., 29
  Zide C., 93
HUFF, Amanda E., 34, 84
HULETT, Chas., 13
HUNSCIKER, Dan'l J., 68
  Mary R., 43
  Thomas, 5
HUNTER, Julia, 80
HUNTSBERRY, C. E., 68,
  82
HUTCHERSON, Chas. 2
HUTCHINSON, Wm. F., 79,
  80
HYDE, Henry W., 58

IRWIN, John, 3, 7, 8,
  9, 11, 12, 14
ISRAEL, Fielder, 89
  J. Robert, 89

JACK, C. P., 83
JACKSON, Isaac, 67
  Lafayette, 53
  Nancy, 36
  Phillippa, 54, 61
  Wm. E., 54
JACOBS, Benj., 84
  C. J., 93
  Selinda, 84
JAMESON, Henry M., 53,
  54
  J. B., 53, 54
  Mary A., 53, 54
  Mrs. Robt., 86
  Rush, 53, 54
JANNEY, Daniel, 68
  Daniel R., 94
  J. E., 88
  L. C., 68
  Samuel, 76

JARRETT, P. E., 72
JEFF(S), James, 1
  Thomas, 1
JEFFERSON, John, 42
  W. M., 77
JENKINS, Chas. S., 59
  Edwin G., 34
  Geo. E., 25, 33, 45,
    46, 52, 55, 58, 60,
    73, 77, 83, 92
  Geo. Ed., 70, 77, 78,
    87, 93
  John, 2
  John B., 34
  John H., 38
  John Z., 20, 22, 34
  Julia A., 63, 73
  Kate K., 73
  Mary, 14
  Millie, 60
  Sarah, 34
  Stephen, 11
  W., 22
  William, 73, 78, 83,
    87
  Mrs. Wm., 46
JENNINGS, Sarah R., 86
JOHNSON, Belle M., 86
  Brutus, 23, 32
  Mrs. Brutus, 23
  Edward, 4
  Mrs. Edward, 80
  Gertrude, 85
  James T., 29
  Lizzie, 79
  Mary, 85
  Rebecca, 78
  "Shack", 23
  Shedrock, 23
  Wm., 9
JOLLEFFE, T. S., 83
JONES, Anna Va., 86
  Doras, 71
  Dunlavy, 33, 57
  Edward, 22, 26, 42, 43,
    48
  George, 42, 48
  Harvey E., 86
  James W., 16
  Jno. R., 47, 48, 67
  Julie E., 42, 48
  W. W., 68
  Wm. R., 55, 56, 64

NEILL, Catherine, 28
  Lydia, 28
  Dr. S. S., 28
  Widow, 2
NELSON, Chas. F., 87
  T. M., 64
  Thos. M., 75
NEVILLE, Caroline, 89
  Catherine, 89
  Edward, 89
  George C., 55
  Kitty, 89
NEWBRAUGH, Joshua, 11
NEWBY, Martha, 40
  Miles White, 40
NICKENS, George, 55
  George W., 49
NICKLES, W. O., 80
NILES, Sam'l V., 26
NIORDAN, Richard, 1
NIXON, John, 69
NOAK(E)S, Anna G., 90
  Annie E., 52
  Hermon E., 90
  Redman, 3
  Sam, 23
  Sam'l G., 52, 55
NOEL, J. R., 71
NOONAN, B., 27, 32,
  35, 40, 41, 47
  Mrs. B., 75
  B(Bartholemew), 53
  Casper, 30
  Isabella, 53, 74
NORRIS, Ann, 3
NOTT, W. T., 55
NOURSE, Anne, 3
  Gabriel, 3
NULTON,
  Abraham, 19, 20, 21,
  24
  Arthur, 35
  Christianna, 5
  Fred, 66, 74
  Frederick, 66
  George A., 24
  George Anna, 24
  J. A., 27
  John, 5
  John H., 31, 35, 81,
  86
  John M., 66, 81
  Joseph A., 44, 65,
  70, 72, 88

NULTON, cont'd
  Sarah, 24
  Susanna, 5

OFFUTT, Mary, 23
O'LEARY, Daniel, 73
  Jeannie, 91
  Lizzie, 73
  Thomas, 73
OMPS, Jno., 83
ORK, Constantine, 54
  Sarah, 54
O'ROKE, M., 56
ORORK, Milliard, 54
ORRICK, John, 27
  Margaret, 16
  Robert, 49, 55
  Wm., 54
ORWIN, Catharine, 16
OSBOURN(E), David, 6
  Margaret, 6
OVERAKER, Daniel, 3,
  4, 7
OVERSTAN?, Daniel, 2
OYLER, George V., 56,
  77, 91

PADGETT, Thos., 73
PAGE, C. R., 62
  Mrs. C. R., 68
  Miss E. L., 95
  Ella, 62
  Emily S., 21
  John E., 12
  Jno. W., 20
  R. P., 58
  Mrs. Tom, 21
PAGET, Thos., 72
PAINTER,
  John Rob't., 34
  Joseph, 34
  Wm. Henry, 34, 35
PANNETT, Wm., 69
PARKER, A. S., 95
  B. B., 81
  Caroline, 15, 95
  Judge, 25, 85
  Mary, 36
  Nichena, 21
  Philip, 23
  R. M., 55, 56,
  57, 64
  R. U., 64
  Rich'd., 78, 80,

PARKER, cont'd
  Rich'd., cont'd: 85,
  94
PARKES, Rich'd M., 56
PARKINS, J. W., 80
  N., 8
  William, 80
PATTON, T. B., 88, 90
PAYNE, Anna, 85
  Lucy, 46
PEERY, C. M., 64
PENDLETON, A. R., 37,
  38, 39, 41, 53, 64,
  74, 80, 87
  Alex R., 55, 79
  Charlotte R., 79
  E., 27
  Edmund, 8, 37
  Frank R., 88
PENN, George, 55
PEREGOY, Chas., 24
  Elizabeth, 24
  Joshua, 5, 24
  Julia Aker, 24
PERRY, C. M., 68, 93
PETERSON, Frank P., 88, 90
PETZOLD, Rob't T., 49
PEYTON,
  Elizabeth C., 14
  Mary Jane, 32
PFEIFFER, John C., 35
PHELNEY, C. M., 71
PHILLIPS, E. J., 41, 42
PIDGEON, Lewis, 74
  Sam'l L., 74
PIERCE, A. N., 73
  Amos, 43, 44
  Thomas, 4
PIFER, J. W., 45
  Ran, 84
PIGEON, Isaac, 89
PINE, Mary, 39
PIRKEY, Frank, 59
  John, 59, 70, 72
PLASKETT, John, 89
POPE, Chas. H., 78
POWELL, Ann R. H., 85,
  92
  Benezer, 4
  Emma, 62
  Evy, 85
  Gertrude, 85
  H. H., 62, 85, 92
  Mrs. H. H., 68

SHELL (SHALL) cont'd
  Winfourd, 88
SHEPARD, Clara K., 45
  George C., 45
  Mary A., 60
  Nathaniel, 7
SHEPHERD, Ann, 41
SHERER, Catharine, 15
  Mary, 75
  Philip, 18
SHERMAN, Ellen, 53, 54
SHERRARD,
  Elizabeth K., 64
  Joseph H., 64
  P., 22
  Virginia B., 64
SHERRER, Philip, 32
SHIELDS, F. A., 90
  Florence A., 35
  Ran, 85
  Mrs., 34
SHIPE, Emma V., 84
  Jessie, 84
SHIRER, N., 18
SHOCK, Mary, 9
SHULL, Atwell, 34
  Briscoe, 30
SHULTZ, Elizabeth, 22
  Lewis O., 22
  Matthias, 21, 22
  William, 22
SHUMATE,
  Eliza, 51, 52, 53
  Elizth., 47, 52, 53
  Martha, 47, 52
  Martha J., 53
  Rebecca, 52, 53
  Tilman, 33, 36, 39,
    43, 47, 48, 52
SIBERT, James, 82
SIDWELL, Ann M., 41, 42
  Hugh, 40
  Martha S., 41, 42
  Mary F., 41
  Mary T., 42
  Mrs. R. J. (Thomasen),
    37, 41, 42
  Rebecca Jane, 39
  Richard, 27, 37, 39,
    40, 41, 42
SIGAFOOSE, Catherine, 20
  Florinda, 19
  Georgianna, 19, 20
  John Montgomery, 19, 20

SIGAFOOSE, cont'd
  Martha Ellen, 19, 20
  Milly Ann, 20
  Robt Baldwin, 19, 20
  Susan, 19, 21
  Virginia, 19
  William, 19, 20. 21
SILER, J. P., 55
  James P., 87
SIMPSON, Emily S., 86
  Lucy, 86
SINGHASS, H. S., 59
  Margaret, 11
  Samuel, 11, 16
SINGLETON, Alex. C., 23
  Georganna, 23
  James, 5
  Josephine, 23
  Maria, 23, 25
  Obed W., 23
  W. G., 16, 18, 20
  Washington G., 23, 25
  William A., 23
  Wm. Marcus, 23
SIPS, George, 6
SISCOE, Adaline, 35
  Adeline, 34
SIX, Eliza C., 71
SLAGLE, Heirs, 43
  H. S., 63
  Henry S., 43
  John, 8
  Jos., 8, 9, 12,
    14, 16
  Mary Ann, 49
  W. I., 51
  Wm. I., 49, 55, 67,
    70
  Wm. J., 69
SLATER, Betsy, 13
  Edwd., 2, 7, 8, 11
  Exalina, 13
  Nancy K., 13
  Samuel, 3
  Susan, 13
SLEIGEL, J. C., 74
SLOAT, Alex T., 69, 70
  Alexander, 20
  Anna Elizth., 69, 70
  Ann C., 20
  Ann E., 20
  Annie, 66
  Charles D., 37
  Thos. E., 77

SLODDERT, Margt. P., 76
SMALL, Annie Mary, 73
  John, 73, 85
  Samuel, 73
  Sam'l G., 85
SMITH, A. M., 33, 57
  Alfreda, 21
  A. Magill, 66
  Chas. Magill, 66
  Edward, 4
  Elizabeth D., 21
  Elizabeth H., 52
  Emily, 56
  Emily A., 52
  Evalina, 61
  Frank, 61
  George, 19
  Geo. W., 80
  German, 60, 94
  German, Jr., 94
  Gustine, 7
  Hannah D., 94
  H. Bentley, 85
  Horace, 24
  Irving G., 22
  J. P., 21
  Jacob, 74
  Jas. F., 80
  James G., 29
  John, 24
  John Jr., 94
  John W., 80
  J. Philip, 17
  J. Rufus, 69
  Kenzie, 80
  Lizzie M., 66
  Mrs. M. A., 46
  Mahlon, 1
  Maria, 39
  Mary Ann, 18, 21, 46
  Minnie E., 80
  Patrick, 10
  Philip, 21
  R. G., 53
  Rob't., 18, 55, 81, 86
  Rose, 33
  Sam'l R., 80
  Wm. A., 52, 56
  Wm. R., 80
  Wm. Randolph, 33
SNAPP, Benj., 71, 79
  C. J., 79
  D. W., 79
  Dedrick, 71

SNAPP, cont'd
  Edgar F., 79
  Emma, 71, 79
  F. R., 79
  Francis R., 79
  G. O., 61, 79
  H. H., 79
  Joseph, 71
  Laura, 71
  M. J., 79
  Margaret, 71
  Mary, 71, 79
  Mary M., 71
  Oliver, 71
  Rushton, 79
  Sally, 71
  T. M., 79
SNYDER, Alysina, 23
  Daniel, 33
  David H., 33
  Elexina, 22, 23
  Elizabeth Ann, 33, 36
  Jacob, 22
  N. W., 22
  Newton W., 23
SOLENBERGER,
  Barbara A., 60
  N. W., 60
  Noah W., 84
SOMERVILLE, Geo., 3
SOMMERS, Mary Y., 66
SOWERS, D., 34
  H. Wise, 68, 75
  John C., 13
  Justus E., 77
SPENCE, Eliza J., 75
SPENCER, Chas., 58
  John, 58
  Sarah Ann, 44, 58
  Willie, 58
SPER(R)Y, Jacob, 1
  John, 8
  Wm. M., 13
SPOTTS, F. P., 58
  Frank P., 61
  M. H., 52
  Marcus, 22
  Sarah A., 22
SPRINKEL, C. A., 74
SPRINT, Thomas, 14
SPURR, A. L., 89
  Andrew L., 88
  Mary A., 89
  Mary Ann, 88

STACKHOUSE, J. S., 24
  Jas., 25
  S. P., 52,60
  Stephen, 27, 29
  Stephen P., 38
STANSBURY, Mary A., 61
STAUB, John, 56
STEELE, J. M., 63
  Robert, 22, 29, 37
STEINER, Jonathan, 20
  Sarah, 85
STENSON, James, 31
STEPHENS, Helen S., 52
  R. J., 58
STEPHENSON, Ann, 20
  Belle M., 78
  Gertrude, 78
  John, 66, 69, 74,
    81, 92, 94
  Sidney A., 75
  W. R., 69
  W. Ray, 81
STEWART, A. H., 22
  Alex. Hamilton, 22
STICKLEY, Abraham, 72
STINCHCOMB, Aquila, 89
  Rebecca, 89
STINE, B. F., 83
  Charles H., 83, 90
  E. L., 90
  E. S., 83
  Henrietta B., 90
  Henry, 90
  Joseph, 73
STINEBRIDGE, Philip, 14
  Regina, 14
STINSON, Wm., 80
STODART, Bessy, 78
  Maggie, 78
STODDARD, Maggie, 80,
    85
STODDER, Thos. H., 86
STONE, Edwd., 88
  Elizabeth E., 86
  Philip, 9
  R. W., 85, 93
  Robert W., 92
STOTTLEMYER,
  James, 53, 78
  James W., 75
STOUT, Julia M., 26
  Mary B., 26
STOVER, Elizabeth, 10
STRANGE, Sarah, 19, 55

STREIT, Amie, 28
  Anna, 58
  Anna V., 50, 55
  Miss Annie, 34
  Christian, 4
  Evalina, 58
  Evelina N., 34
  Evelina U., 28
  H. B., 13
  Jacob, 4
  James B., 50, 55
  Susanna, 4, 7
  Wm. H., 16, 22, 25,
    33, 34, 51, 55
STRIBLING,
  Miss A. E., 68
  Ann, 47
  B. Taylor, 47, 57
  Edward M., 47, 57
  John, 47
STRIDER, Henry, 23
  Thomas, 31
STRIKER,
  Eliza Jane, 46
  Elizabeth, 46
  H. B., 36, 70
  Harry, 32
  James, 32
  James, H., 32
  Susan Catherine, 32
  V. W., 43
  Vance W., 32, 46, 62
STRONG, William, 53
STROTHER, J. Fred, 74
  J. N., 36
SULLIVAN, A. S., 47
  Algenon, 47
  Edmon, 87
  George H., 47, 57
  Mrs. M. M., 57
  Mary, 47
SUMPTION, G. W., 45
  J. W., 93
  John W., 82
SWANDEMAN, Mme. M., 90,
    91, 95
SWENDEMAN, Mme. M., 93
SWARTZWELDER, A. C., 21
  Mrs. J. N., 66
  Josepha N., 21
  Leonard E., 21
  Mary Ann, 21
SWHIER, Geo. W., 37
  Jacob G., 37

115

SWIFT, Sidney Ann, 70
  Warner, 60, 70
  William, 70, 71
SWIMLEY, William, 71
TALBOT, Ann H., 39, 40,
    42
  Edward A., 67
  H. Marshall, 39
  Marshall, 39
TANQUARY, A. B., 20
TAYLOR, Albert, 58
  Annie Moss, 92
  Busrod, 47, 49
  E. S. W., 47, 49, 57
  Mrs. E., 36
  Eben, 42, 45, 69
  Elizabeth S. W., 47
  Hannah, 49
  J. William, 88
  Ran, 86
  Rebecca, 74
  Stephen, 74
  Thomas, 60
  William, 21, 47, 49
TELIT, L. H., 90
THATCHER, Evan, 71
THOMAS, Abijah, 29
  D. W., 3, 4, 7
  Daniel W., 3
  T. W., 8
  William, 5
THOMPSON, Annie E., 65,
    75
  Daniel, 44, 45, 50,
    65, 75
  Elma J., 44
  Elmer J., 75
  J. D., 93
  Mary,   42
  Sarah, 75
  Sarah F., 44
  Sarah Theresa, 44
  Thos. Walter, 44, 75
  Walter, 75
THORNBURY, Daniel, 6
  George, 6
  Jacob, 6
  James, 6
  John, 6
  Robert, 6
  William, 6
THWAIT, John, 73
TIDBALL, Alex. S., 13, 15
  Ed. M., 29

TIDBALL, cont'd
  Joseph, 18
  Mary, 60, 87
  Mary M., 37, 74
  Susan W., 37
  T. A., 18
  Thomas, 5
TILFORD, Bessie T., 47,
    57
  Florinda, 47, 57
  Frank V., 47, 57
TIMBERLAKE, Mrs., 70
TOCUS, Cornelia, 48
TODD, Henry D., 65
TODDY, J. C., 95
  James C., 93
TOLIVER, Mary, 45
TOTTY, J. C., 90
  James C., 88
  L. H., 90
  Louisa H., 88
  M. E., 90
  Maria Louisa, 88, 90
  Mary E., 88
  S. E., 90
  Soloma E., 88
  W. L., 90
  Willie, 88
TOY(E), Edwin, 74, 82,
    87
  John, 74, 82, 87
  Walter, 82, 87
TRACY, Catherine, 81
  Eliza L., 45
  James, 81
  Mary Isabel, 81
  Patrick, 81
TRENARY, R. E., 59, 69,
    72, 77, 79
TREPLETT, J. R., 80
TRESLER, George, 13
  Hannah, 13
  Jacob, 13
  James, 13
  Jane Eleanor, 13
  Joel, 13
  Mary Ann, 13
  William, 13
TRIER, Lewis F., 67
  Louis, 67
  Margaret, 66, 67
  Mary V., 67
  Sissie, 66

TRIPLETT, Maria, 91
  Nannie, 95
TRISLER, George, 14
TRUEBLOOD, Jason, 40
  Mary, 40
  Minarva, 40
TUCKER, Alfred E., 47
  Eliza, 47
  Mrs. J. R., 92
  John Randolph, 85
  Laura, 85
  Harry, 85
TURNBULL, A., 3
  R., 3
TURNER, Bettie, 55
  J. R., 18
  Jane, 27, 30
  Mary, 8
  Nancy, 55
TYLER, Elizabeth, 20
  H. W., 90
  Horace D., 93
  Judge, 85

VANCE, James D., 4
VAN FOSSEN, J. C., 61,
    68
VANHORN(E),
  Eliza Jane, 18
  William, 9
VILWIG, John, 53, 79, 87
  Jon., 30, 32
VIOLETT, John, 95
VON RIESEN, John L., 18
  John T., 18
VON REISING, John, 12
  John L., 18

WADE, Bettie A., 63
  Daniel, 63
  Virginia A., 63, 64
WAITE, Obed, 3, 11, 13,
    14, 23
WALKER, Cordelia, 87
  Rev. Cornelius, 21
  Cornelius H., 41, 42
  Elizabeth S., 28
  Frank G., 31
  J. Ed, 41, 42
  Mingo, 87
  Rachel, 3
WALL(S), Elizth., 32, 53
  J., 7
  James, 1, 3, 4, 6

WALL(S), cont'd
  Martha M., 32
  Mattie, 53
  T. T., 31, 32, 53, 55
  Thos. T., 31
  Virginia, 53
  Virginia A., 32
  W. W., 58
  William W., 32
WALLIN, Frank, 42
WALTER(S), Cora D., 93
  D., 36, 85
  Dorsey, 18, 23, 35,
    36, 44, 46, 48, 55
    60, 63, 93
  Frank G., 25, 40, 58
  R., 38
  R. Wm., 36, 48, 58,
  81
WARD, Mrs. Ann, 30
  David F., 76
  D. Funsten, 76
  E. F., 76
  Elizabeth Ann, 13
  George F., 76
  George W., 18, 30,
    34, 71
  Julian F., 76, 81
  L. F., 87
  M. F., 76, 87
  R. M., 81, 84
  Robert M., 76, 84, 87
  Sarah E., 70
WARDEN, Jacob, 45
  Mary, 9, 13
WARE, Chas. S., 94
  Homer S., 94
  Mary N., 94
WARREN, Luther, 15
WASHBURN, Geo. O., 49,
  75
WASHINGTON,
  Abraham, 32
  Felicia, 48
  Frank, 49
  Lucy, 49
WATERS, Jefferson, 65
WATROUS, C. S., 42
  Sophia G., 39
WATSON, A., 15
  James W., 58
WEAVER, Elizth., 34, 36
  James, 34
  James W., 62

WEAVER, cont'd
  Lewis, 35
  Masha, 62
  Nancy, 54
WEBB,
  Alfred Burwell, 17
  James, 16, 17
  Maria, 16
  Patsy, 60
  Robert, 46
WEDLOCK, J. John, 61
WEICHT, John M., 84
WEIR, Samuel, 59
WELCH, James S., 27
WELL(S), Alfred, 16
  Betsy, 16
  Emily, 16, 17
  Maria, 16
  Robert, 1
  Sarah E., 70
WELLINGTON, Jno. A., 49
WENDLE, Eve, 16
WEST, Eugene, 74
WHEAT, Clifton, 86
  J. C., 48
  J. C., Jr., 86
WHEELER, Xenophon, 39
WHETZELL, Elizth., 86
  James, 53
  Mr., 5
WHISNER, P., 66
WHITACRE, J. P., 52,
  53
  James P., 52, 56,
    70, 75, 78
WHITE, A. P., 23
  C. S., 68
  Frances, 40
  Francis A., 40
  Gettie, 78
  Juliet O., 23, 41
  Margaret H., 40
  Mary B., 41, 46
  Miles, 40
  Nancy H., 33
  R. B., 41, 46
  Rebecca, 40
  Richard J., 40
  Rob't B., 23
  Sarah Elizth., 40
  W. S., 91
  Wm. D., 41
  Wm. Donagle, 41
  Wm. S., 75

WHITHINGTON, Ella, 73
WHITLOCK, W. J., 68
WICHAM, Levi A., 6
WICKHAM, Levi A., 6
  Lewis A., 6
  L. H., 10
WILEY, Amanda Moore, 72
WILLIAMS, Benj., 65
  Godwin H., 68
  Harriet, A., 46
  Henry, 19
  Isham, 55
  James H., 22, 45
  James W., 65
  Jim, 19
  John J., 35, 44, 46,
    47, 49, 52, 55, 57,
    58, 77, 93
  John James, 37
  L. D., 55
  Lucy, 55
  Lucy Dunbar, 37
  Mark, 55
  Margaret A., 35
  Mary J. J., 55
  Mary L. L. (or S. S.),
    37, 38
  Nelson, 19
  P., 37, 55
  Philip B., 65
  S., 53
  Sallie, 55
  Sarah Ellen, 37
  T. C., 55
  T. Clayton, 37
WILLIAMSON, Jennie, 88
WILLIMS, Philip, 23
WILLIS, Agnes, 69
  Frank E., 69
  George, 1
  George E., 48
  Hannah J., 69
  H. Benton, 55
  Henry R., 69
  Henry V., 69
  M. H. G., 54, 60, 62,
    67, 83, 86, 88
  Mary, 69
  Mrs. Marshall, 45
  Mary E., 46
  W. R., 59
  Wm. R., 69, 94
WILLS, G., 42
  Joanna, 13

WILSON, Alpheus, W., 30
  Augusta Va., 30, 31
  C. W., 45, 47
  Celia, 21
  Cornelia L., 30
  Edmund H., 30
  Ellen M., 72
  Henry M., 72
  John B., 20
  Norval, 30, 31, 35
  Selia, 46
WINDLE, Adam, 42, 44,
    72
  Ann, 7, 9, 10
  Elizth. Ann, 10, 11
  Eve, 5, 12
  Evelina, 9, 10, 11
  F. C., 50
  John, 5, 7
  Margaret Ann, 71
  Margaret, 12
  Martha E., 72
  Richard, 7, 10, 11
  Sam'l, 5, 7, 8, 9,
    10, 11, 12
  Sam'l Washington, 7
  Sarah Matilda, 7,
    10, 11
  T. C., 42, 45, 67,
    69, 70, 81
  Theodore, 29, 71
WINKFIELD, Amanda M., 72
  John H., 72
WINSTON, Thos. H., 73
WISECARVER, Joseph, 79
WOLF(E),
  Catherine Otto, 25
  D., 22
  Elizabeth, 25
  Fannie R., 25
  Godfrey Miller, 25
  Kate, 46
  Lewis, 2
  Mary, 41,
  Mary C., 41
  Philip, 9
  R. B., 46
  Rob't B., 19, 20, 22,
    25, 41
WOMER, Jacob, 84
WOOD(S), Alice May, 86
  C. L., 71
  Henry, 93
  Mary, 1

WOOD(S), cont'd
  R. M., 66
WOODWARD, Chas. B., 73
  Kate K., 78, 83
  Kate R., 87
  Kate V., 93
WRIGHT, James, 14
  W. H., 60
  William, 77
WULFERT, Fredk., 47
  Gertrude, 47
  Henry, 47, 53
WYNN, John, 1

YEAKLEY, George A., 75
  J. H., 58
  James E., 94
  J. Stewart. 83
  R. B., 22, 30, 43
  Vance, 94
YEARLEY, Alexr., 89
  Thomas C., 89
YEATMAN, Lillie C., 62
YOUNG, Adam, 1, 2, 3
  Catharine, 2
  Catherine Elizth., 4

ZEILER, Clarissa, 72
ZELL, J. H., 83